A RIGHT TO THE LAND

A Right to the Land

ESSAYS ON THE FREEDMEN'S COMMUNITY

Edward Magdol

GREENWOOD PRESS

WESTPORT, CONNECTICUT ● LONDON, ENGLAND

*Contributions in
American History,
Number 61*

Library of Congress Cataloging in Publication Data

Magdol, Edward.
    A right to the land.

    (Contributions in American history; no. 61)
    Bibliography: p.
    Includes index.
    1. Freedmen. 2. Reconstruction. 3. United States.
Bureau of Refugees, Freedmen, and Abandoned Lands.
I. Title.
E185.2.M35   301.45'19'6073   76-39707
ISBN 0-8371-9409-1

Library of Congress Catalog Card Number: 76-39707
ISBN: 0-8371-9409-1
ISSN: 0084-9219

First published in 1977

Greenwood Press, Inc.
51 Riverside Avenue, Westport, Connecticut 06880

Printed in the United States of America

To Mim, Lynn, and Joe

Contents

Illustrations
and Tables

Preface

About midway through his monumental and pioneering book *Black Reconstruction in America,* W. E. B. Du Bois interjected one of his many rueful observations on the systematic neglect of the blacks in American historiography. It seems a long long time ago, although the book was published in 1935. Du Bois's most poignant regrets, in a work of more than 600 pages of narrative and analysis of the black people's role in Reconstruction, centered on the difficulty in finding material. He justly asserted that

> Little effort has been made to preserve the records of Negro effort and speeches, action, work and wages, homes and families. Nearly all of this has gone down beneath a mass of ridicule and caricature, deliberate omission and misstatement. No institution of learning has made any effort to explore or probe Reconstruction from the point of view of the laborer and most men have written to explain and excuse the former slaveholder, the planter, the landholder, and the capitalist.

Taking their cue from Du Bois, a succeeding generation of scholars has revised the earlier white supremacist version of Reconstruction. The ethnic balance generally has been redressed. Too few institutions, however, have seriously taken up the study of Reconstruction from the point of view of the laborer. There is much yet to be done, for this class approach remains Du Bois's most penetrating contribution to the study. He deplored the weakness of his work because it lacked "most essentials to a complete picture." Yet Du Bois was convinced that the story of Reconstruction was "the story of a normal working class movement, successful to an unusual degree, despite all disappointment and failure" (page 383). Even these qualifications do not diminish the stature of *Black Reconstruction.* They demonstrate Du Bois's high standards of scholarship and spur students of his to pursue the subject to a "complete picture."

This book attempts to respond to Du Bois's suggestions. It follows the path of recent scholars who pay closer attention to the Afro-American freed people in the Reconstruction era. But it departs from that road by emphasizing the working-class viewpoint. The following pages focus on the freedman's quest for land and self-definition in a community of his own. The essays dwell upon the freed people's active and self-determinative roles in reconstructing their lives and their communities.

Fortunately, this and other works benefit from the storage and opening up of the Freedmen's Bureau records and others in the National Archives. In this sense an advance in working conditions for scholars has been made over those faced by Du Bois in his generation. With careful use of those records we are now able to view the freedmen's quest through their eyes, through their experiences, and through their expressions.

This book consists of connected chapters on an American working class, a landless agrarian laboring class attempting but failing to gain lands and independence. It attempts to reveal vital cultural elements in the process of making community. It is largely confined to the Civil War and Reconstruction era, which I have extended back to 1861 and forward to 1880, as Du Bois did. That period has also been compared to the narrow neck of an hourglass for the Afro-American people. Another and possibly more apt metaphor is that of an isthmus between two continents: a narrow neck of uncertain terrain over which a people traveled from one imperfect world to another.

This work does not deal with every aspect of the freed people's experience. For example, the world of leisure and creativity on the positive side and the world of regressive behavior on the negative side have been left to the revisionist works of such scholars as Vernon L. Wharton and Joel Williamson. These two components of the freedmen's social life undoubtedly played roles in making the community, but they appear to have been secondary to the influences of kinship networks and their ethos of mutuality, which were the normative and decisive elements.

Nor is this a book about slavery as such. In this work that system is a point of departure. Rather, this book seeks to explain the slave and freedman in a deeper context than that of a derivative personality, as in the Elkins thesis, or in terms of planter paternalism, as in Genovese's. Above all, this work seeks to participate in the continuing study of the active roles that freedmen and other lower classes played in history.

Acknowledgments

Du Bois was our first great teacher about those once hidden streams of American history, the roles of Afro-Americans in the making of America. I am indebted to him and his works and to the scholars of the Reconstruction era who followed his path. James S. Allen, Herbert Aptheker, John Hope Franklin, Benjamin Quarles, and Alrutheus Ambush Taylor particularly stand out among the earliest revisionists.

Herbert G. Gutman, a most stimulating friend and colleague, generously shared much research data with me and offered rigorous guidance and exciting insights. Jon Wakelyn and Ira Berlin read the manuscript and offered helpful suggestions for improvement. Willie Lee Rose read Chapter 7 before it was enlarged and posed some thoughtful questions for me to ponder. Eugene D. Genovese heard a reading of Chapter 5 when it was a paper in a history department colloquium at the University of Rochester and encouraged its publication. If my work does not rise to the heights of their expectations, I accept responsibility but am also grateful for their interest and help.

Elaine Everly, James Walker, and Robert Clarke of the U.S. National Archives in Washington, D.C., gave me considerable help in finding materials. Also helpful were librarians Edith Frankel, Chris Gulick, and Eleanor Vorse; and Carol Wolstenholme, interlibrary loan clerk at the Frederick W. Crumb Memorial Library, State University of New York at Potsdam.

Friends and co-workers in the study of Reconstruction history who gave me the benefit of their thoughts and hints about sources are Barry A. Crouch, Leslie Rowland, John O'Brien, and Eric Perkins.

I wish to thank the State University of New York Research Foundation for a fellowship that enabled me to spend fruitful time in the National Archives and the Houghton and Widener libraries at Harvard University during the summer of 1972.

Joseph Starr and Werner Braatz, the editors of *Societas—A Review of Social History,* kindly gave me permission to reprint portions of Chapter

5 that originally appeared as an article in the Spring 1974 issue under the title "Local Black Leaders in the South, 1867-1875: An Essay Toward the Reconstruction of Reconstruction History."

The manuscript was typed by Gail C. Sheldon and Anne P. Larkin, and Sharon Kurpita assisted in my search of newspapers on microfilm.

Miriam Sper Magdol read the manuscript sympathetically and criticly and asked challenging questions that pointed the way to clarity.

I am grateful to all of those persons named here who have knowingly or unknowingly helped to produce this book. I alone am responsible for any features that deserve criticism and correction.

Edward Magdol

Potsdam, New York
May 1976

About the Author

Edward Magdol, associate professor of history, S.U.N.Y., Potsdam, has specialized in the study of American social history. He has written articles for such journals as the *Journal of Social History* and *Societas—A Review of Social History*. He is also the author of the political biography *Owen Lovejoy, Abolitionist in Congress.*

A RIGHT TO THE LAND

Introduction

The actions in these essays occurred during the Reconstruction era. In traditional histories that period began in 1865 at the end of Civil War hostilities. But reconstruction for the freedmen began instead very soon after the outbreak of hostilities in 1861. Slaves emancipated themselves in Virginia in the late spring and summer of 1861, and in 1862 in the lower Mississippi Valley and along the Atlantic coast from North Carolina to Florida. Four important and critical years of slave activity remain neglected in Afro-American history, if Reconstruction is considered to have begun in 1865. This volume, therefore, is guided by the concept of slaves emancipating themselves and affecting the arrangement and reconstruction of Southern society before the war was over. In following this line, these essays emphasize the continuing process of change in which the freed people were the subjects and objects of action. Consequently, they no longer appear episodically and discontinuously. The recurrence of the same or similar behavior, not only between 1865 and 1877 but also between 1861 and 1867-1868, tends to bolster the notion of continuity and typicality in that freedman conduct.

Typicality is further strengthened by enlarging the geographical arena of the process. Thus this work does not confine itself to one state or another but ranges across the entire South. Similarities and differences emerge, but the former prevail. For example, in the simultaneous appearance of an Afro-American artisan leadership in freedmen communities after the passage of the 1867 Reconstruction Acts, there is more than localized political history. Similarly, when freed people collectively attempted to purchase, lease, or migrate to land and establish communities as far flung as those in Arkansas, Florida, Mississippi, Georgia, Kansas and South Carolina, from 1863 to 1880 and later, we see more than a number of isolated and spasmodic phenomena of economic history. When considered in the wider context of nineteenth-century working-class structure, the several Southern Afro-American artisan leaders take on greater social and ethnocultural dimensions. The collective hunger for and pursuit of land similarly fit into the larger context of an American nineteenth-century agrarian aspiration, shared by Afro-Americans as well as by landless Irish Americans. Moreover, in a western hemispheric postemancipation context North American freedmen appear to share values and goals with Caribbean and South American counterparts. Therefore, the active roles freed people played in the Reconstruction era deserve more attention than they have previously received.

The subjects of these essays, freed black lower classes and the institutions they created or adopted, pose problems for some recent interpretations of slavery. The difficulty for such reconstructions lies in the evidence that freedmen did not conform to the image of a collapsed slave population. The logical outcome of these theories would be a final step of surrender, in which slaves would have been so overwhelmed by their bondage and the masters' dominance that they would have been incapable of self-defined activities. However, the evidence contradicts such a theoretical consequence of slavery. When the antebellum system is refracted through the freedmen's thought and behavior, it becomes difficult to accept theories of infantilization or of the slaves' surrender to the masters' paternalism or of the slaves' internalization of the masters' Puritan work ethic. Self-assertive freedmen embarrass such theories. Black artisans and field laborers displayed little if any evidence of childlike dependence upon their old masters. Instead, they made clear in their self-emancipation that they opposed their old masters. One strong indication was the move to expropriate or expect the expropriation of the former slaveowners' lands. Another was the movement to gain the right to vote and then to exercise it in 1867 and 1868. Moreover, the internal relationship between laborers and artisan or the artisan-preacher leadership continued one developed in the slave quarters. Masters may have fastened bonds upon the plantation, but within it slaves made their own choices.

The slave community that the bonds men and women constructed was relatively powerless against the masters. Nevertheless, it was the slaves' own adaptive strategy to deal with the master and his system. The community proved to be a school for self-definition, as postemancipation experience confirmed. Freed people reassembling their broken families and recreating their communities refute theories of their depersonalization. Moreover, they did anything but surrender to paternalism when they refused to contract for field labor in the old ways in the fall and winter of 1865. That they were forced to go to work on employers' terms was due more to the U.S. government's abandonment of the freedmen's cause.

Above all, freed people made massive efforts to be independent of their old masters and of their culture. Freed laborers expressed a keen self- and class consciousness squarely at odds both with their old masters and some of their new "guardians." These continuing exhibitions of self-determination, which are the subjects of the following pages, make Elkins's depersonalization thesis less believable. They also topple the Fogel and Engerman concept of a slave Horatio Alger. Finally, they deny Genovese's paternalistic planter class its easy "hegemony" over the slave community and its preacher-artisan leadership.[1]

Elkins hypothesized through the extended metaphor of the Nazi concentration camp a system of North American slavery so absolutely closed that its inmates, the slaves, were forced to become sambos. These were the typical products of the system, according to Elkins, individuals utterly infantilized, docile, and dependent upon their masters for their ideas, values, and existence. The masters became the significant others who provided the sole models for slave learning. The rigidity of the system was due in part to the absence of institutional constraints on the masters' absolutism, such as those supposedly imposed upon Latin American slavery by the Catholic Church and the Spanish crown.

The freed people who emerged from slavery in the United States could not have done so as the products of the world Elkins constructed. He is basically correct in affirming the harshness of the system, which Kenneth Stampp had also demonstrated. Nevertheless, fugitive freed people by the hundreds and thousands and who eventually numbered a million before the end of the Civil War stole away from the plantations, whether or not abandoned by their owners.[2] Such freedmen, one-fourth of the total slave population, little resembled those infantilized and dependent beings in the Elkins thesis. Even though many blacks appeared to wartime philanthropic whites and teachers and missionaries to be pitifully destitute as they trundled into contraband refuges on mules, wagons, and on foot, those slaves had made decisions or had been forced to take action for which no dominant master prepared them. Going to work and providing their own means of subsistence by their labor, as they had during slavery days, but now paid wages under the new order, these laborers, carpenters, seamstresses, draymen, laundresses, cooks, servants, and field workers prevent belief in the doctrine of their debased personalities. Individual cases are credible, but a *typical* sambo is not.

The freed people's behavior from 1861 onward indicates that damaging as slavery was to the condition and self-esteem of many, the freed man and woman generally maintained a strong self-concept. As Chapter 2 in this book shows, the freedmen's self-emancipation was more than a physical one, more than a new and broader mobility. Moreover, freedmen raised individual awareness to the level of community consciousness. They proceeded to reconstruct their communities along lines not entirely preconditioned or dictated by former masters or new allies and guardians from the North. Their design drew upon experiences both in slavery and the old slave quarters and as amended by experiences in the contraband camps, freedmen's villages, and other settlements. They chose institutions that had served antebellum free black communities—the church, the school, and the mutual-benefit society. They also adopted the political party and the mass meeting and the convention. This particularly emphasizes their adaptability, considering that the masters had denied them access to, and attempted to keep them ignorant of, such democratic American institutions

Some freedmen had derived benefits while slaves from association with free blacks in cities and plantations. Ira Berlin's sophisticated study of antebellum free blacks in the South demonstrates that their communities reinforced slaves.[3] In itself this is a valuable contribution, for it provides us with yet another refutation of the Elkins's thesis, a "significant other" who was not the master. We should not reject the possible ambivalence of some free blacks who thus strengthened the slave's psyche; they were themselves the master's progeny. All was not harmonious between free blacks and slaves. Nevertheless, their roles ran against the master's purposes. Notwithstanding tensions between newly freed people and the somewhat aloof antebellum free black men, as Berlin skillfully portrays the relationship, they enjoyed powerful affinities. Significantly, those Southern free blacks had sustained communities and learned lessons that Reconstruction era freedmen adopted and applied to their own endeavors. Dominant whites also applied lessons about separation and division of lower classes along ethnic fault lines, those cultural crevices tending to separate one ethnic or religious group from another. That merely underscores for our attention a *modus operandi* of slaveowner rule and of other oligarchis. What remains most significant is the constancy of self-defined thought and behavior during the slave's metamorphosis into a freedman.

The authors of *Time on the Cross* constructed a model of slavery in which slaves internalized the master's work ethic, an upwardly mobile slave who believed in progress like any nineteenth-century American middle-class person. Slaves and masters shared the same ideology and the goals of efficiency and productivity. Master's positive incentives, and some necessary disciplinary whipping, brought diligent and valorous deeds of labor and production in response. Fogel and Engerman create an incredibly halcyonic aura about the plantation that is at odds with the history of slave resistance, discontent, and disbelief in the masters' world views and practices. On the contrary, freedmen reflected the rejection rather than the internalization of the masters' philosophy. Fogel and Engerman reduced the plantation relationship to an economic one, an inevitable consequence of their econometric methodology and the kinds of economic questions it is designed to service. Plantation realities are skewed as a result of their approach, indeed even turned on their head.

The freedmen furnish better information about their independent minds and their rejection of the masters' work ethic than does a panoply of computers. Three examples among many others in the following pages especially illustrate this. One is furnished by Richmond tobacco factory workers making modest wage proposals; another by Savannah dock workers proud of their designation "laborers" rather than "porters"; and a third by Liberty County, Georgia, field laborers, seeking decent working conditions and havens for their aged relatives and describing themselves as "a Working Class of People." The slaves did not learn these concepts from the masters. These self-concepts arose from their independent thought processes based on their interactions with masters and employers and with slave and free artisans, laborers, and others. The Fogel and Engerman system suffers from an inability to reconcile its putative harmoniousness with its rapid collapse when alienated slaves emancipated themselves. These alleged black beneficiaries of the system turned it topsy-turvy once the guns began to shoot in 1861 and, afterward, in the vicinity of their plantations. Having nurtured the concept of freedom within slavery, they attempted to realize it after helping to destroy the system. The masters did not teach the slaves to love freedom and to overthrow their world. Slaves had developed their own notions of worthiness and progress.

More elaborate refutations of the Fogel and Engerman model of slavery are best left to the brilliant critiques by Herbert G. Gutman, Peter

Temin and Paul David, and other economic and social historians.[4] However, the several studies in this book demonstrate that freedmen did not come from the world created by Fogel and Engerman's econometric calculations. Slave and freed artisans pose problems for their doctrines, as the reader may observe in this volume.

Genovese's interpretation of slavery is more subtle, plausible, and richly textured than the others. Yet in a most fundamental way it differs little from the Elkins thesis. Genovese constructs a model of a porous, symbiotic system within which slaves did indeed make a world of their own, but basically they did so by internalizing and surrendering to the master's paternalism. The failure of slave resistance is ascribed to a crisis of slave leadership, a failure of slave preachers to transform their support in the slave quarters into effective political action.

Unlike the other two interpretations, this one recognizes and understands more of the artisans' leadership role. Genovese concedes that in the emancipation years, artisans "gave a good account of themselves." But he does not explain how and why they should have done so if they were among those preachers who had failed to lead the slave quarters to open resistance. Preachers and artisans frequently were the same individuals. Genovese charged the preachers with having surrendered "the principle of political leadership and authority."[5] He attributed that surrender explicitly to the black preacher's lack of a prophetic tradition; implicitly, because the preacher-artisans bought the boss's ideology of paternalism. Individual cases of preacher-artisan sellout may be found; a general case against the preacher, and his alter ego and counterpart, the artisan, is not plausible. It would have to face the fact that throughout the South freed preacher and artisan leaders became the special targets of planter-sanctioned violence. The Reverends Richard Burke in Alabama, Benjamin Bethea in Lumberton, North Carolina, who appear later in this volume, and Reverend William Thornton of Hampton, Virginia, were at least three of that class of preachers. Thornton, for example, was told by a white man that he faced death for a speech he had made at a public meeting on January 1, 1866 (the anniversary of the Emancipation Proclamation): "We hope the time will come," the white man said, "that these Yankees will be away from here, and then we will settle with you preachers."[6]

The general attack on the freed people in the emancipation era indicates that the planter class wished to maintain its control not by the pow-

er of its ideas and values but by intensifying the physical force and violence used during slavery. In this regard Genovese's concept of hegemony
is incomplete. His view that the masters maintained their domination by
their world view—their humane paternalism—and that the slaves internalized and acquiesced in it is contradicted by both the masters' behavior
and that of the slaves. The breakage of families by sale and by force, and
the masters' use of flogging and night patrols as well as other coercive
measures, on the one side, and the slaves' manifold resistance, on the other, contest Genovese's hegemony.

The validity of his theory rests on the supposed slave internalization
of the masters' values and world view. However, the slaves were resistant
(as well as accommodating) during slavery, and they rejected this kind
of paternalism again in 1861 after assessing the existing power relationship between themselves and the masters. This indicates that the slaves
held an alternative and oppositional world view. Because Genovese's concept of hegemony is basically static and totalitarian, it misses that reality
within the complex and changing plantation relationships. Raymond
Williams offers a more dynamic model of hegemony: "We have to emphasize that hegemony is not singular; indeed that its own internal structures are highly complex, and have continually to be renewed, recreated
and defended; and by the same token, that *they can be continually challenged and in certain respects modified*" (my emphasis). *Roll, Jordan,
Roll* addresses some of these complexities but ultimately resolves them
in favor of the masters' reigning and unchanging world view. On the contrary, the slaves and freed people in the transition period suggest more
subtle and profound oppositional thought and behavior than Genovese's
theory recognizes.[7]

It is simply too difficult to execute the maneuver—to leap from
Genovese's master-sanctioned autonomous slave to the freed men and
women who people this book. They were not stamped from a single die.
They utilized various modes of action and expression. Most significantly,
they gave ample evidence of a prophetic tradition that took Moses and
the Exodus as models for their millenarian aspirations. The single-minded
concerns of the freedmen communities to obtain land upon which to
realize their deliverance and the prophecies of their teachers—Prophet
Nat Turner among them—suggest that Genovese has underestimated this
aspect of slave culture: Masters preached obedience and subservience;
many slaves preached flight, freedom, and change. Freedmen clearly dem-

onstrated that they had listened to their own prophets even though they had been forced to hear their master's voices.

The black laborers' self-assertions from 1861 onward were continuations by better means of their warfare against the masters. Their cautious assessment of the chances for successful emancipation before the Civil War suggests political acumen—a sober assessment of the relationship of forces, as it were, informed the slaves' collective actions or inactions. After the war the freedmen's use of the Republican party and the Union or Loyal Leagues was largely self-determined. Freedmen frequently demonstrated that they had not caved in to antebellum bosses or postwar plantation operators. Their declarations of religious independence, their search for land and community, their political actions did not occur because they ate the poisoned apple of paternalism or swallowed the line of upward social mobility during slavery or delivered their personalities into their masters' hands.

In this connection it is useful to consider the thoughts of a literary artist and an anthropologist. Ralph Ellison, writing about black musicians and black creativity, reminded Le Roi Jones that "Slavery was a most vicious system and those who endured and survived it a tough people, but it was not (and this is important for Negroes to remember for the sake of their own sense of who and what their grandparents were) a state of absolute repression."[8] As the several essays in this volume attempt to show, creativity and technique developed in the slave quarters and in the fields and shops (that is, the creation of community) were used in social interactions during the postemancipation period.

It makes a significant difference in one's perception of Afro-American history if the focus moves from enslavement and victimization (wretched as they were) or from the search for African origins (frustrating for the searcher, after new ways have supplanted them) to the manner in which enslaved and newly emancipated people *used* their material and ideological resources. Sidney W. Mintz, who has studied Afro-Caribbean and Afro-American cultures and societies with meticulous care, asserts that:

> we must conceptualize Afro-American cultures not simply as historically derived bodies of materials, as patterns of and for behavior, but also as materials actively employed by organized human groupings in particular social contexts. Without the dimension of human action, of choices made and pursued—of maneuver—cul-

ture could be regarded as a lifeless collection of habits, superstitions, and artifacts. Instead, we see that culture is used.[9]

The enslaved Africans in the Americas were compelled to use their culture in reordering their world to make it viable. They were forced to redefine themselves, and to do so it was necessary to reconstitute a community. The African village, family, and kinship system that New World slavery disrupted and dispersed had defined the person. Inasmuch as self-awareness is "a generic human trait,"[10] the first Africans in the Americas and succeeding generations of enslaved and then emancipated Afro-Americans were inspired by their needs and their consciousness to reconstitute cultures and communities. The slaves made linguistic adaptations, mastered new skills, and devised varieties of resistant behavior. The slaves achieved a partial solution to their problems of existence by pressing against their masters in many ways and above all by preserving to the best of their abilities an internal institution of their culture. That was the very process of community making. It remains a potent institution that appears to have been neglected by Elkins's hypothesis.

The international and internal American slave trades constantly threatened the fixity of slave communities by their disruptions of tribal groups, slave families, and kinship networks. But slaves found constant reinforcement from traditional African morality. Essentially it was a societal rather than a spiritual morality, a morality of conduct rather than one of being.[11] Such a morality must be informed by experience and consciousness. Among slaves and freedmen, an ethos of mutuality was the expression of that consciousness and morality. Even though weakened by the external force represented by the slaveowners and a resultant tension within the slave community, the bondsmen's sense of community and mutual aid remained strong enough to carry generations through slavery. That ethos of mutuality, based ultimately on bonds of real and fictive kinship, shaped the process of making and remaking community in the Reconstruction era. It probably was the most potent instrument patterning Afro-American culture and community since then. While religion continuously furnished an influential organizing principle, kinship and mutuality appear to have been its equal and probably were more compelling imperatives of the freedmen's culture and community.

Patriarchy was an influential accompanying force in the community process during slavery and emancipation. It reemerged from obscurity when slaves relieved themselves of the stress put upon their communities by the breakage of families and kin groups and by the duress of planter social control. As the revitalized freed people found openings in wartime and postemancipation society, they endeavored to enlarge them. Many of the experiences noted in this book make those hidden elements of patriarchy more visible: headmen of groups of families making labor contracts or seeking homesteads together; some slave artisan "uncles" emerging as political leaders and testing the democratic electoral process; others starting new churches according to their own visions, not those of European-Americans; and others leading their wives, children, and communities in search of a New Canaan, migrating from Georgia and the Carolinas to Mississippi and Florida, and from Mississippi, Louisiana, and Texas to Kansas.

A new set of social relations faced the freedmen. They used their culture to respond to the new ways. Rather than abandon their hopes to receive land grants, freedmen resisted contracting to labor for others under unfair terms. They especially resisted and avoided the gang system of labor that had prevailed during slavery. No doubt many continued to display that subservient mien common to slaves, serfs, and other powerless peoples. But increasingly and creatively, freedmen sought to establish new relationships independent of masters and employers. Land became a key instrument to gain that independence. When it was not forthcoming, many settled for sharecropping as a partial realization of ownership, at least of a measure of self-management. This is evident in the pattern of labor contracts between 1865 and 1868.

In striving to obtain a homestead of twenty or forty acres (but more frequently no larger than one- or two-acre provision ground and yard), the emancipated person appeared to be returning to the settlement pattern of the plantation slave community. The masters had made a tactical concession in granting the slave garden patch. But the slave considered it to be his by right—by "manorial right," as the historian Willie Lee Rose explains.[12] The slave regarded it as family property and extralegally passed it along within his kinship groupings. The possession of a cabin and vegetable garden patch probably taught its owner the need to become an independent farmer. It may have inspired the fervent longing for and expectation of the masters' lands in forty-acre lots in 1865. But there was more than economic significance to that slave "ownership." It was the repository of family and community history. Within it, as within the house and yard of Caribbean peasantries, life was lived, birth and marriage and the events of nature's calendar were celebrated, and death and burial were used to link generations. The home place that so many refused to leave in the ebb and flow of Civil War and that became virtually a universal goal of a dispersed freed people was often that remembered cabin and garden in the slave settlement.

The home place was a freedman's family objective. And the collective desires of families, arising from the experiences of the plantation or farm, were to strengthen a community, to settle together in villages and in household groupings. This appears to be the meaning of freedmen's efforts toward such objectives, as the several examples in this book demonstrate. The ultimate expression of communal movements was the exodus of 1879-1880. Like the others that culminated in it, it was a subject and an object of the revitalization of a people.

Much in these essays is explained by the concept of revitalization, which was proposed by Anthony F. C. Wallace to denote a process of cultural-system change. It referred particularly to a variety of cultural innovation movements. Some of them have been religious revivalist, messianic, utopian, communitarian, revolutionary, or charismatic. The concept is based on an analogy between a culture and an individual psyche, in which stress is an important feature. Stress triggers the process by which an individual searches his "mazeway" (or "mental image") in order to reduce the stress. He seeks a mode of action that will change his mazeway by changing the *"Gestalt* of his image of self, society, and culture, of nature and body, and ways of action." He may also attempt to change reality and bring it into congruence with his mazeway. That effort to reduce stress is "revitalization effort," and when it is conducted by a group of individuals, it becomes a "revitalization movement." Wallace offers a useful definition in this statement: "A revitalization movement is defined as a deliberate, organized, conscious effort by members of a society to construct a more satisfying culture."[13]

Revitalization movements have occurred throughout history. They appear to be the responses of lower classes and indigenous populations to confinement and subordination by more powerful classes. In other words, revitalization movements are marked by communal and/or class differentiation, resistance, and conflict. They may utilize elements of external as well as internal cultures or syntheses of them as mechanisms. Afro-American slaves conformed to that unexceptional pattern of self-defined activity. As freedmen they merely enlarged the arena of their adaptive strategies.

In this connection an additional guide to our understanding is the commentary of Leonard B. Glick, an anthropologist at the University of Wisconsin:

> Often people perceive a need for more than ordinary amounts of change in their worlds, and . . . at such times they are likely to mobilize every form of leverage at their command to gain unity with their own kind, purpose in their lives, and control over their own destinies.[14]

This the Southern black people attempted to do, even in the unfavorable circumstances created by a government retreating from the revolutionary democratic policies adopted during the war and Reconstruction era. President Lincoln in 1862 hesitated to take such extreme and revolutionary measures as immediate and uncompensated emancipation and recruitment of black soldiers. Two years later he led the fight for the Thirteenth Amendment, applauded the recruitment of black soldiers, and was prepared to enfranchise blacks who had served in the military forces and those who were literate. Lincoln gave credit for his transformation to events that controlled him. Among the critical events were the actions of freed people emancipating themselves and beginning to affect the rearrangement of Southern society. The retreat of some in the government and the frustration of the revolution under way only set in bolder relief the self-defining role of the freedmen.

In conclusion, then, these are the concepts that lie at the base of this book. Slaves chose adaptive strategies in making their own community out of European and African cultural components. At the center of their world view was the need to survive and struggle for freedom from bondage. They erected their own defenses against a harshly exploitative system. They resisted with such means as they could marshal. These proved meager and insufficient to overthrow the system. The line of attack had to be more subtle, therefore, and expressed itself in continuing incidents of open and masked resistance as well as in the slave community's internal relationships, culture, and aspirations. An ethos of mutuality informed the slaves' relationships with one another and with free blacks. The two groups held consanguinial and cultural ties, the latter in great part the result of racial oppression.

Slaves took a large part in shaping their world by their self-emancipation. In that process they enjoyed a revitalization. This is not meant to impose an exotic character upon these laboring people. They were not super men and women in their strivings, nor were they objects of pity and paternalism. They were a working class of people seeking social justice. They affected the reconstruction of Southern society, and their history deserves continuing study and appreciation.

As freedmen they set themselves the task of transformation into independent farmers. They largely failed to achieve that objective. However, out of the wreck of Reconstruction they salvaged elements of their former community to create a new one, reflecting their own designs and their own Afro-American identities.

The essays that follow contain a considerable amount of evidence that validates these concepts. They conform to a chronological pattern that begins with slavery and proceeds through the stages in the growth of the freedmen's community from self-emancipation in 1861-1862, through contraband camp existence in 1862-1864; freedmen's village formation in 1862-1865; struggle for the land in 1865-1866; participation in Reconstruction political affairs in 1865-1868; efforts to buy land collectively in 1863-1874; and communal migration in 1878-1881. The final chapter attempts to emphasize the survival of the freedmen's community.

The Legacy of the Slave Community

> While slaves, of course, their days were claimed by the masters; and consequently they contracted a habit of transacting their own private business after nightfall. If you remember that a whole community was thus forced to provide for its interests after sunset, you will see what a singular state of affairs obtained in this way. —Charles Nordhoff, *The Freedmen of South Carolina*, p. 21.

Despite its repressions and brutalities, and indeed in spite of its relaxations, American slavery failed to prevent the emergence of a self-defined slave community. Whether masters were benign paternalists or rapacious brutes, Afro-American slaves in their quarters fashioned a culture that sustained them as individuals and informed their creation of a community for their survival. Their common bondage was their common bond, and it dictated their strategies for survival in a collectivity.

They learned to cope and to hope for freedom. When they decided the chances were good for their release from bondage, they seized the moment. The obvious improvement in the odds for successful self-emancipation came with the outbreak of the Civil War and its resultant stress in the planters' hegemony. Slaves could observe and analyze and had indeed developed a shrewd appraisal of the slaveowners and the other whites in the world around them. They had utilized an "underground railroad" in a widespread network of free black and slave communities to combat the master class before the war. Within weeks after the firing on Fort Sumter, slaves calculated that the time was right that their homes should come within the orbit of Union military power. They packed their meager possessions, loaded wagons, horses, and mules, or tramped on foot to make their way with their kin toward U.S. Army camps, forts, and other federal establishments.[1] They knew on the "day of gunshoot," on the day master and mistress fled, or by untold signs and portents that the road to freedom was open. But not all slaves chose to run away to freedom. Despite the burdens of bondage, a home place, even in paltry slave quarters, was familiar, settled. Thousands chose to remain on the home place. Exodus and flight were expressions of resistance to and negation of slavery. But staying, on the other hand, need not have been a sign of resignation or docility.

One force appeared to be most influential in both these modes of behavior—the force of community and family ties. That community was created out of their needs during two centuries in an alien culture and out of their memories of various African tribal experiences and cultures. Before the end of the Civil War the slave community transformed itself into an Afro-American freed people's community.

In order to support their postwar way of life, black freed people sought a material base, the ownership of land. For this reason, its acquisition became the principal issue for them. Martin R. Delany made it clear in July 1865 when he addressed a crowded audience of freedmen in the Baptist Brick Church on St. Helena Island in the South Carolina Sea Islands. Then a major of the 104th Colored Infantry Regiment and an agent of the Freedmen's Bureau, Delany said, "Now I will come to the main purpose for which I have come to see you. As before the whole *South* depended upon you, now the *whole country* will depend upon you. I give you an advice how to get along. Get up a community and get all the lands you can—if you cannot get any singly."[2] What the black major meant by a "community" may have been an association or a specific organization for the purpose. He may have meant the kind of community normally assumed to be a neighborhood, settlement, or village. He did not define the idea or enlarge upon it in the speech. But he articulated what was in the minds of freedmen in many places in the South. During that first summer of legal freedom, in 1865, they were caught in a major struggle over ownership of land with former plantation owners. The Johnson administration had reversed orders setting aside a southern coastal strip of land for freedmen occupation. Black people who had settled on those seized plantations, or who hoped to settle on them, were being evicted and barred from possession. Delany's words became a guiding slogan. Moreover the major sounded the theme of this book: the connection between land and the making of the freedmen's community. It is well known that the freedmen lost that struggle for land. However, it is too little known how profound was their desire and how serious and advanced their efforts to acquire land in order to realize the American nineteenth-century dream:

an independent homestead in their own version of the happy "republican township." That process is a significant chapter in American history.

The roots of the freedmen's community lay in the slave and in the urban free black communities. Some aspects of the aid rendered by the antebellum free blacks have been noted. A fuller treatment has been produced by Ira Berlin in *Slaves Without Masters*. He explores and explains the tensions between Southern free and slave Afro-Americans and the support that free blacks gave to slave blacks. The literature about North American slavery is growing, as scholars probe deeper into the little-known eighteenth-century experiences. Therefore, it is not necessary here to duplicate that work. However, it will be useful to reiterate those features of slave life that fed the growth of freedmen communities.

George Rawick, examining more than 2,000 narratives of ex-slaves that were recorded during the 1920s and 1930s, found the creation of the slave community to have been a "process which largely went on outside of work relations." He aptly entitled his work, *From Sundown to Sunup*.[3] John Blassingame took another route into the slaves' world.[4] He relied on autobiographies of former slaves written during the nineteenth century, sometimes as part of an abolitionist propaganda thrust, and on many biographies of whites and travelers' accounts. He did not neglect to review traditional sources of antebellum history, such as plantation records, which conveyed the planter's point of view. Through Blassingame's studies emerged a clearly defined slave community making itself out of rich African cultural components retained and altered to fit the slaves' needs. Genovese's *Roll, Jordan, Roll* is replete with vivid examples furnished by plantation records and planters' diaries and by the slave narratives. His treatment is more sophisticated and more comprehensive than the others. He reveals what he regards as the weaknesses and failures as well as the strengths and successes of the slaves in making their world within that of the masters. But there is no doubt that the slaves made the best of their circumstances and created a community within their severely restricted conditions. Genovese's adherence to a belief in an omnipotent planter class distorts the mass of evidence in his work that attests to a less absolute power. But more important, his prodigious scholarship has produced a volume full of examples of the slaves' resourcefulness and creativity in fashioning their world.

Rawick discerned a convergence of culture and society, African past and American plantation present, in which slaves, continuously fashioned a way of life necessary to define themselves, their children, and their community. It should be added that the process did not go unaided by the planters. They made of the captive Africans a labor force sufficient to sustain their own rich habits of living or even to maintain a comfortable level of progress for the vast number of less than aristocratic slave-owners. They did more. They helped to create a people tied not only to their persons but to the land and at the same time denied the slaves a right to that land for themselves. Their concessions to slave subsistence by the provisions of garden patches behind the slave quarters were prudent but paltry in this context. Yet they unconsciously created a major component of the community that would strive to make itself in post-Civil War America. They brought forth a landless people hungering for land of their own. If peasants around the world historically strove for agrarian independence, former slaves equaled them in their reach for land and, above all, community.[5]

The role of Africa was powerful in the making of the slave community, if only for the cushion that African agricultural society provided to the profound shock of enslavement and removal to the New World in the dawn of the modern era and in following centuries. The village was the physical center of West African society and contained family units whose heads made community decisions. Villages were linked by family connections into a collectivity. The basic unit of the village was the extended family, dependent on the land and the hard work entailed in its cultivation and fructification. Everyone in the village was a landowner through membership in a family of the village. The land was sacred and therefore inalienable. Much control of the land was exercised by the elders of local kinship groups or by ritual leaders. Although an individual claimed exclusive ownership of his produce on the parcel of land he worked, the land remained the property of the family and village. If the extended family fell on bad times and failed to produce sufficient foodstuffs for itself or for the market, it could sustain itself by participating in larger cooperative agricultural units. A variety of such communal production units was found among the Dahomean, Nupe, Jukun, and Mossi peoples. In addition, Melville Herskovits, studying Dahomey ways of life, identified African plantation systems resembling those later to be found in the New World. On both sides of the Atlantic the modes of production shared the features of specialization, complexity, and class structure.[6]

The New World plantation work experience in itself thus was no extraordinary shock to the enslaved. They had known slavery, or a special type of African servitude better called "unfree status." They had known long hours of hard work breaking soil, planting seeds, tending crops, and uprooting weeds. Work on the land was familiar, and work in gangs was known to them in their homelands. The true shock came in the disruption of the whole way of life based on the land, the breakup of familial, communal, religious, and communicative bonds that linked living people in a settled pattern from day to day, season to season, year to year, generation to generation. In order to survive the attack, African slaves in America struggled to preserve what they could.

Europeans entering the modern capitalist era in the fifteenth and sixteenth centuries required labor to exploit the abundant New World lands. The transatlantic slave trade became the conduit for the shipment of at least 9 million Africans over four and one-half centuries.[7] Europeans in great numbers also were used to meet the demand. Among them, Irish laborers sent to North America and the Caribbean islands were bought and sold like chattel but were relieved of a permanent slave or indentured status by the imposition of a racial and permanent slavery upon Africans instead.

Captured African laborers came to the Americas with capabilities and skills. Knowledge of rice culture and boatsmanship, for example, made many slaves valuable to South Carolina's proprietors in 1769 and after. Newspaper advertisements describing runaway African slave artisans clearly indicated their attainments in a variety of trades important to the North American British colonies. Not all slaves came with skills at hand, but many were taught their trades during the eighteenth century on the plantations and in towns. Their productivity was significant in the economic and political growth of the colonies. The Americans owed much to the slave labor contribution when they became strong enough to challenge British mercantilism. After independence, however, slaveowner restrictions in the nineteenth century reduced the numbers and proportions of slave artisans in the free black and slave adult male populations. They lagged far behind those of native-born and immigrant whites. Field laborers made up the bulk of the slave population.[8]

The industrial nature of plantation agriculture throughout the New World utilized the gang system. In the nineteenth-century American South, it prevailed over the relatively less rigid task system. The latter was more adaptable to rice cultivation along the coastal areas. Gang labor became the mode of production on tobacco, cotton, and sugar plantations. Close and severe supervision by whip- and pistol-toting overseers and their subalterns, the black gang drivers, made such a daylong labor onerous to say the least.

One example of how a slave's day was filled may be read in the reports of Frederick Law Olmsted. While traveling in Mississippi in the 1850s, he spent some time on a large, successful, and efficient cotton plantation that made wealthy an absentee owner who lived several hundred miles away. While the 135 slaves included servants, cooks, and seamstresses, and a blacksmith, a carpenter, and a wheelwright, 67 were field hands. They were divided into hoe gang and plow gang. Olmsted saw thirty plows

> moving together, turning the earth from the cotton plants, and from thirty to forty hoers, the latter mainly women, with a black driver walking about among them with a whip, which he often cracked at them, sometimes allowing the lash to fall lightly on their shoulders. He was constantly urging them also with his voice. All worked very steadily.

Even the rare visit of a stranger failed to disturb the routine, none so much as glancing at him.[9]

The slaves ate a snack before daylight in their cabins, at about five o'clock at this season, and went to the fields. Dinner arrived at noon in a cart. The hoe gang stopped only long enough to eat, in the field. The plow gang drove its teams to "weather houses," open sheds where they ate and where their mules were fed. "Water toters" attended to gangs in the fields. Labor went on until the slaves could not see well in the dusk or darkness. No other food or rest was provided until the laborers returned to their cabins. The driver blew a bugle at 9:30 P.M. and a half-hour later visited each cabin to be sure that "its occupants were at rest." They were "at liberty" until summoned in the morning. They had gardens and raised greens for themselves to supplement the weekly ration of a peck of corn and four pounds of pork per person.[10]

There were many variants of this large plantation pattern. Treatment by overseers and drivers varied with the planter's dictates, needs, and the pressures or lack of them put upon him by market conditions or slave behavior. As for the slaves, they appear to have been driven harder during the picking season. They also ran away in larger numbers at such seasons, hid out in swamps or forests, and returned after the harvest to face punishment by whipping. Although masters came to rely upon the gang system, it proved to be anathema to slaves. On plantations in Mississippi and Arkansas, as on coastal South Carolina Sea Islands, the gang system aroused the slaves' deepest hatred. It was an arduous existence that they shared. It became the first object of their ire and independence and stimulated them to circumvent and escape it. Although slaves laboring on Louisiana sugar plantations enjoyed more flexibility than those in cotton agriculture, they too rebelled against the system early in 1862, when Union forces invaded and captured New Orleans. At about the same time, April 1862, South Carolina Sea Island blacks refused to continue working in the old ways under Northern employers who even paid wages.[11]

After arriving in the slave ships with very little material possessions, and with only memories of kin and home and of the shock of enslavement, the blacks sought to make strategic adaptations to new social relationships and environments. In African societies "there was no distinction between sacred and secular activities." But under the domination of Christian masters in America they were forced away from such a unitary way of life. Slaves who knew other gods nevertheless later adapted Christianity to their needs, plumbed its depths, and practiced it in their own furtive praise meetings and night sings free from the master's eyes and ears. They enriched the service with a form of circle dance preserved in their memories from Africa. In the late eighteenth and in the nineteenth centuries some Christian masters permitted their slaves to sit in their churches to hear preaching and to pray and sing hymns. Others forbade slaves to go to church. In any event slaves found their own time between sundown and sunup to create their own church and their own prayers. As one former slave remembered it, "Massa never 'lowed us slaves to go to church but they have big holes in the fields they gits down in and prays. They done that way 'cause the white folks didn't want them to pray. They used to pray for freedom." That prayer was informed by their bondage and by what they heard from the white man's religion about salvation and deliverance, about the Israelites in Egypt, about a heaven in which one escaped earth's trials and tribulations. There was a message of hope in resistance as well as in resignation. Slaves did not content themselves with their masters' religion, however. They injected into it an element identified with Africa, in which the congregation became the Afro-American community, "a sacred family, in which the preacher is the leader and head of the community." In the Old World the elder was in contact with the "Unknown" and demonstrated his superior power in his relationship with his community. Slave preachers became leaders of the transatlantic slave collectivity, in tune with its profoundest wish. As one exuberant preacher prayed, unmindful of a white man present, "Free indeed, free from death, free from hell, free from work, free from white folks, free from everything."[12]

Furthermore, some black people seem to have blended a West African god into their stories of conversion to Christianity. Such accounts usually involve the person's "death" and fall into a hell or into a hole or pit. Always a "little man" appeared as a messenger from heaven, saying, in some versions, "Arise and follow me for I am the Way, the Truth and the Light." The West African counterpart of the little man is the Yoruba god Elegba or Legba. Like Hermes, he too comes as a messenger and mediator between men and gods. Thus did slaves produce this among other syncretisms, further suggesting a role for Africa. The extent of African cultural retentions should nevertheless be measured cautiously. While few slaves may have been converted to Christianity by the end of the eighteenth century, it is clear that direct knowledge of Africa was supplanted by acculturation to English ways. The confluence of African and Anglo-American cultures created the Afro-American by the end of that century.[13]

The immediate as well as the extended family proved to be resilient mechanisms in making and maintaining the slave community. While purely West African polygynous forms of marriage and family were not retained in American slavery, slaves substituted a variety of relationships. Through them they reared children and transmitted to them codes of conduct for survival and values for living. More than forty years ago E. Franklin Frazier, a descendant of slaves and an eminent sociologist, reviewed published slave autobiographies for material to write his pioneering article "The Negro Slave Family." Together with the plainly repressive and proscriptive features of chattel slavery, he found, slaves did have some degree of social maneuverability. "Social interaction within their own world on the plantation created a social life among them with nearly all the features of any society," he wrote. He found a wide variety of slave families reflecting in part different strata of slaves. He differentiated them along occupational lines; he also distinguished among them by their status, depending on the types of plantation settings in which couples lived. Rawick's study of the slave narratives collected in the 1930s unearthed "a variety of socially approved and culturally sanctioned relationships."

Not only did he find the monogamous marriage sanctioned and encouraged by paternalistic masters, but he also found a considerable range of
slave-determined structures and some "less structured sexual contacts
which led to the birth of progeny."[14] Among the more distinctive marks
of slave choice in the marriage ceremony was the broomstick wedding.
A man and woman jumped over the broomstick to solemnize their union,
in many cases a choice of their own preference and not necessarily that
of the masters.

The slaves' choice was emphasized by the register of freed people's
marriages in Washington, D.C., between 1865 and 1867. Of the 848 unions
recorded, 421, or nearly one-half, had been performed without a formal
marriage ceremony. Some of these couples had lived as man and wife for
more than forty years during slavery. The other half of the marriages had
been performed by a minister or a priest, or a master reading from a paper.[15] Jumping over the broomstick and the unions made without a formal ceremony signify a notable break with the masters and their paternalism.

The concept is further weakened by evidence of the masters' separation of marriages and families. Slave unions proved to be durable when
they were not broken by death and other natural causes or by separation
through the sale of slaves. The 1864 and 1865 Mississippi and Louisiana
Freedmen's Bureau marriage registers reveal that the masters, not the slaves
displayed little regard for the sanctity of marriage. Force, or the master's
sales, broke up one-fourth of the slave marriages of persons recording
their new unions in those registers. A report from Vicksburg in March
1865 provides a further sampling. Between April 10 and November 1,
1864, a total of 2,912 persons were registered as the partners in 1,456
marriages. Five hundred and fifty-two persons had been sold or driven
away from their mates during slavery. They comprised 18.9 percent of
this limited sample and underscored the slaves' belief in the institution
of marriage and the masters' violations of it.[16] Those broken marriages
revealed that the banner raised to symbolize the masters' paternalism
and hegemony was a tattered pennant.

The slave family, adapting itself to plantation slavery conditions,
proved more potent a force for survival than generations of scholars believed possible. In fact the prevailing impression of the "pathological"
black family stems from ignorance of its strengths. The supposed fragil-
ity or debility in maintaining relationships of tenderness, care, and love

for mates, children, and parents has been used unjustly and cruelly to blame twentieth-century blacks for their poverty and so-called disorganization. The problems facing black people in slavery, as well as in modern capitalist society, are exploitation, deprivation, and racism. Nevertheless, during their enslavement Afro-Americans made of their several modes of family structure an instrument for survival and for creating community. In it there were important roles to be played by child-caring grannies, older children caring for younger ones, as well as by their mothers and fathers. In addition, supportive roles were played by significant others outside the immediate family, especially by the respected slave artisans. The slave father, who has been unjustly deposed by friend and foe alike from his positive family leadership role, should be considered in the light of Blassingame's and Rawick's conclusions. They find evidence of slave fathers providing for their families through hunting, fishing, gardening, working to provide extra income, building and furnishing the interiors of slave cabins to make them more comfortable, and giving gifts to wives and children. The affection of slave fathers for their children was not destroyed, and their protective arms were not broken, despite the slave-owner's domination over all he surveyed. Published slave autobiographies reveal that fathers as well as mothers taught their children obedience and submission as a means of survival. They also taught their children to be proud and defiant, and children could only be impressed by the models created by runaways, and "bad" slaves, who, if they did not put "massa" on, dickered with him for improved working and living conditions. "Fathers were loved and respected because of their physical strength, courage and compassion," Blassingame observed. But slavery was incapable of permitting a fully autonomous immediate family existence, and the impact of the slaveowners' system required another strategy of the enslaved. That was the larger family, the community.[17]

Slaves maintained elaborate kinship networks, according to Herbert Gutman's studies. These relationships persisted even in the face of the masters' separations of wives and husbands, mothers and children, fathers and wives and children. New alliances between men and women sold and separated from original unions produced children. They were loved and treated like the offspring of first unions. The masters cared little for the effects of their sales and separations upon slaves. But the kin of the victims surely did. The consciousness of their relationships proved a binding force of the slave community. Moreover, their actions in caring for the children and aged members of their households and of their slave quarter settlements were enduring instruments of individual and community survival. The first actions of freedmen in the 1860s verify this heritage, but the eighteenth-century Maryland slaves' complex networks of blood kin and of slaves on neighboring plantations indicate the early establishment of such slave communities.[18] We have yet to learn the specific ways in which the extended family network operated. But on such a base, one can assume, nineteenth-century Afro-Americans developed identities and relationships to other slaves through kinship groupings that were independent of the masters' world views and hegemony.

In that connection an element of the slave strategy was a type of fictive kinship. This was illustrated by Frederick Douglass's experience on Colonel Lloyd's expansive Maryland plantation. In his boyhood there, Douglass's "uncles" were the skilled slave craftsmen. Uncle Toney was a blacksmith, Uncle Harry, a cartwright, and Uncle Abel, a shoemaker. They probably were not blood relatives. Nevertheless they were respected by the younger slaves "according to plantation etiquette." With evident pride, Douglass wrote:

> Strange and even ridiculous as it may seem, among a people so uncultivated and with so many stern trials to look in the face, there is not to be found among any people a more rigid enforcement of the law of respect to elders than is maintained among them. I set this down as partly constitutional with the colored race and party conventional. There is no better material in the world for making a gentleman than is furnished in the African.[19]

It was neither strange nor ridiculous, unless, perhaps, the viewer was an outsider. Most striking about Douglass's statement was the "constitutional" and "conventional" behavior that suggests a code persistent among Afro-Americans, and particularly among slaves. These artisan uncles of the nineteenth-century slave community represented more than traditional elders commanding ritual deference. They were a particular historical product of the slave community and of the imperatives of a slave system whose masters in the eighteenth century were compelled to seek economic independence from British manufacturers. Forced to train bound laboring people in skills to attain that independence, slaveowners liberalized their treatment and their conceptions of their skilled male slaves. These black carpenters, blacksmiths, wheelwrights, masons, coopers, shoemakers, and tailors gained a degree of freedom of motion. Their duties and their products demanded respect from the masters and from everyone else on the plantation. They learned to speak and sometimes read and write English. During and after the Revolutionary War, they learned about the new democratic institutions. The attempted slave revolt in 1800, led by the blacksmith Gabriel, demonstrated considerable political sophistication and a positive self-concept among the slaves who collaborated with the artisan leader and organizer.[20]

Later, when Douglass was a boy observing his uncles, these skilled men proved to be models for slave children to emulate. Their self-esteem burst the confinements, as another slave artisan later testified. James W. C. Pennington, a blacksmith, was the son of a slave blacksmith. He became famous as a fugitive and later as a leading abolitionist in the North and in England. He had great reverence for his father, and it was put to the test when the elder Pennington was beaten and humiliated by his master before other slaves. The experience was all the more shocking to the younger Pennington because he had resigned himself, through his self-esteem, to slavery. The paradox is best explained in his own words:

> I had always aimed to be trustworthy; and feeling a high degree of mechanical pride, I had aimed to do my work with dispatch and skill; my blacksmith's pride and trade was one thing that had reconciled me so long to remain a slave. I sought to distinguish myself in the finer branches of the business by invention and finish; I frequently tried my hand at making guns and pistols, putting blades in pen-knives, making fancy hammers, hatchets, sword-cases, etc., etc. . . .[21]

His father's humiliation convinced him that he must break with slavery, escape, and bring his family out of bondage. The elder man was obviously one of those respected men—doubtless an uncle, in the special sense we have previously mentioned, as well as a father, a significant figure in the slave community, an artisan.

Just as the younger blacksmith's penchant for creativity, his pride in "invention and finish," sustained him, the slave community as such was forced to be creative in order to survive the rigors of the system. Slave spirituals stand out as an instrument of endurance, a unique cultural expression. The form of that invention, an adaptation of African call and response between group and leader, provided creativity for both the individual and the community. The ease with which the same spiritual could be varied in tempo, mood, and emphasis, as well as in minor alterations of words, signified its adaptability. As a communications system, the slave's spirituals leaped over the walls of confinement. Above all, they were the slaves' testament to their own high self-esteem as well as to the worth of their own community veiled from the slaveowners.[22]

Rejecting the masters' religion as given by them, the slaves created their own belief in deliverance. Undoubtedly escape and sorrow and otherworldliness can be detected in the spirituals. Yet, on closer examination, it is clear that the songs express, through vivid and vigorous imagery and analogy, the present, the problems and relationships of the slaves' real world. The "lessons" of obedience of servants to masters, which slaves were taught from the New Testament, were simply omitted and rejected. Instead, with an Olympian sense of humor, they chose to sing about those worldly men rising from the pages of the Old Testament, Moses, Daniel, Joshua, Jonah. They were delivered, lived to see Pharoah's army drowned, were sprung from the lion's den or the belly of a whale. Why not every man? That was one aspect of the slaves' verbal, poetic expression of their world view. As for notions of a moral economy, which they failed to find in the master-slave relationship, one must listen to a song Douglass remembered:

> We raise de wheat
> Dey gib us de corn
> We bake de bread
> Dey gib us de cruss
> We siff de meal
> Dey gib us de huss
> We peal de meat
> Dey gib us de skin
> And dat's de way
> Day takes us in

And they had a sense of time and history, within which there was a remembered culture. Rather than the pitiable slave tossed helplessly between two cultures, we find him still conscious of Africa, as in this song:

> Working all day,
> And part of the night
> And up before the morning light
>
> CHORUS: When will Jehovah hear our cry,
>   And free the sons of Africa?

but conscious as well of their Afro-American identities in this rousing song, modeled on a national patriotic song, that speaks of Africa in American cadences:

> Hail! all hail! ye Afric clan
> Ye oppressed, ye Afric band,
> Who toil and sweat in slavery bound
> And when your health and strength are gone
> Are left to hunger and to mourn,
> Let independence be your aim,
> Ever mindful what 'tis worth,
> Pledge your bodies for the prize,
> Pile them even to the skies!

It has been attributed to Denmark Vesey and was sung by *slaves* off the coast near Charleston, South Carolina.

That sense of brotherhood, of shared values and aspirations, was creatively expressed in folktales and anecdotes. As in the slave music, a bitter irony tinged the tales. These entertainments of the slaves were infused with a controlled sense of outrage. It came through as amiable humor, as a soft monitory stroke across the cheek of the master. This is especially the mood in the John and Master stories, and in the Br'er Rabbit tales modeled on the African trickster tales, ultimately deriving from the tradition that gave us Aesop's fables. In the American setting the David-slew-Goliath theme pulses beneath the surface of the stories. Realistically, slaves like John did not permanently or often gain the upper hand over massa. Yet it served as ego-building nourishment to tell the story. The symbolism of the tales had meaning to a community that identified with the spunky rabbit and the thinly armored John playing his games, outsmarting and smarting from the master's power and strategies. The

folktales served as a community defense mechanism, as a community
mirror of its positive self-esteem. They were part of the slaves' symbolic
language.

Black English, however, was the real language that slaves created. Varieties of it were spread through what its leading scholar calls, "primarily
Black community process." Similarly, Lawrence Levine, studying slave
music, asserted that it was "created or constantly recreated through a
communal process." Recent advances in the study of black English demonstrate that it was not confined to the Gullah dialect in the Carolina
Sea Islands. That was only one type among several found throughout
the New World where West African peoples were transported. Slaves
creolized the language. In New York, for example, Sojourner Truth spoke
a black English. Northern nineteenth-century Afro-Americans spoke virtually the same dialect as Southern blacks but less creolized. Blacks in
Nova Scotia as well as in Kentucky used versions of black English. Thus,
wherever there was Afro-American community, slave or free, black English was a distinctive means of communication.[23]

No part of the slave experience was greater than the whole. However,
one part that emphasizes the slave's sense of community is his resistance
and flight from the system. An individual fugitive depended first on the
slaves in his own quarters to keep the secret of his departure if they knew
it beforehand, and then to cover up his disappearance for as long as they
were able. Runaways, resourceful as they may have been, depended on
free black communities and some white abolitionists, above the Ohio
River or north of Chesapeake Bay, all the way to Syracuse, Boston, New
York, Philadelphia, Chicago, and Detroit, and ultimately Canada. Furthermore, bands of slaves made the escape effort, some succeeding. Occasionally, as in the case of William and Ellen Craft, husband and wife
made their escape through clever disguises. The cost of slave resistance
and day-to-day disobedience and sabotage and in disappearance has not
been measured or quantified. The slaves' effectiveness in breaking down
the system was clear in the masters' slave codes and patrols, in his political discomfort in the face of combined slave assault and Northern capitalist and abolitionist challenge.[24]

The slaves' harassment of the masters in dozens of seemingly petty
ways required some mechanism of community. It is difficult to find
more than the occasional description of that link between individual
slave rebel and his peers, as in Douglass's, Pennington's, and other for-

mer slaves' autobiographies. However, struggle against the slave system reached its highest point of community action in the establishment of runaway settlements. These risky enterprises depended on group solidarity and in turn upon a collective consciousness. Such maroon communities, as they were called in the Caribbean and Latin American countries, were created by determined slaves and their families throughout the New World, from Brazil to Cuba and Jamaica, to British colonial North America. They persisted within the United States down through the Civil War. The first known maroon community in the English colonies appeared in Virginia in 1672, almost at the same time that black African indentured servants increasingly were being depressed into chattel slavery. They chose the safety of swamps, bayous, forests, and mountain hideouts. One type of fugitive community served as a base for attacks on nearby plantations. These outlaws raided to obtain food, animals, supplies necessary for subsistence, and to run off other slaves. The grand march attempted by a collectivity of South Carolina slaves from Stono toward the swamps of Florida in 1739 summoned slaves along the way and was signaled by the drum in a celebratory mien expressing cherished African customs. Many cases of resistant and aggressive slave outlaw communities show that they unnerved masters and fortified their own ties to one another.[25]

The leaders of maroon settlements can be likened to Robin Hood, a social bandit who expressed his people's protest against oppression. These primitive rebels, to use Eric Hobsbawm's phrase, appeared throughout the world to represent peasant and other rural poor folk against feudal lords, plantation gentry, and the armed forces and police of the modern bourgeois democratic state. These outlaws served in their roles for relatively short periods of time, practicing brigandage in a daring and swift fashion. They proved no match for the superior strength of ruling classes in such combat. Yet they proved to be important in sustaining hope for justice among their constituencies and in enjoying a reciprocal community sanction, approval, and support.[26]

A second type of maroon community took the form of a permanent settlement. One such "town" of black fugitives flourished on the South Carolina side of the Savannah River in the 1760s. Approximately forty men, women, and children subsisted by raiding Georgia plantations. Hidden in a swamp, the community was built up around a "Square consisting of four Houses 17 feet long and 14 wide." A kind of military organization was maintained but proved insufficient to resist a posse of white planters that broke it up. A similar experiment was reported in 1827 in Louisiana. A black woman who had been absent for sixteen years returned to her master in New Orleans and reported a maroon community of sixty persons eight miles north of the city. A community of "Mulattoes, Free Negroes, and notorious Harbourers of run-away Slaves" near the Peedee River in South Carolina was reported in 1768. The suggestion of a multiethnic community is one of many that led one scholar to conclude that the close relationship in the southern back country between lower classes and outlaws was so large that in effect it constituted a separate society. The persistence of such a pattern of multiethnic lower-class community was indicated by the outlaw role of Henry Berry Lowry, an Anglo-Indian carpenter, and blacks, Indians, and some poor whites in Robeson County, North Carolina, in the Reconstruction years. The reappearance of maroon and outlaw communities in the slave experience over two centuries strongly suggests their fixed place in slave consciousness.[27]

No account of resistant community would be complete without mention at least of the prolonged struggle of fugitive slaves and the Seminole Indians in Florida. The Second Seminole War (1835-1842) was actually a defensive effort of these two groups against the attacks and pursuits of the U.S. armed forces. Most significantly, the blacks in the Seminole country maintained their own villages, despite their purported slave condition under Seminole masters. They lived in their own well-built houses, raised crops and cotton, and owned herds of livestock. Their bondage was in name only. They shared a preindustrial culture with the Seminoles. Moreover, the blacks were protected by the Indians in exchange for "tribute" paid at harvest and butchering times. The war cost the U.S. government more than $40 million and the lives of about 1,500 soldiers. At stake was the blacks' freedom and the Indians' retention of traditional lands, which could only be protected by their common struggle.[28]

The well-developed free black urban communities of Baltimore, Richmond, St. Louis, and Charleston sustained the needy and proved vital as havens for runaways. They also provided way stations for adapting to life away from the plantation. In St. Louis the antebellum community under the leadership of Reverend John Berry Meachum bought slaves and freed them. The fugitives obtained jobs and learned trades from people like Meachum, who was a carpenter and a cooper. Free and quasi-free blacks in Petersburg, Richmond, and Williamsburg, Virginia, by the end of the eighteenth century maintained an underground community furnishing refuge for runaways. By 1835 Baltimore's black community had thirty-five benevolent associations, with about 35 to 150 members in each. Several held interest-bearing accounts in local white-run banks. The strength of the community lay in its mere existence: slaveholders in Eastern Shore counties and in southern Maryland considered such a large settlement of free blacks to be anathema. Even in the Deep South free blacks practiced mutual aid. In Columbia, South Carolina, the black members of the Presbyterian church bought an elderly slave woman out of slavery and supported her through the Civil War years. The family that owned her sold her for $5 at auction when she became too old to work. The Irishman who had purchased her resold her to the black people when he discovered his "bad bargain." In and about Beaufort, South Carolina, where slaveowners probably felt secure about contacts between free and slave, a mutual-aid society served both classes. It should not surprise us that its president was Prince Rivers, the articulate slave coachman and later sergeant of the South Carolina First Volunteers.[29]

By the beginning of the Civil War, slaves had created a community within their quarters and in the process of struggling for their freedom. Any experience of 200 years could not be without its human shortcomings. In this connection an observation by Sidney Mintz about Caribbean slavery systems is equally applicable to the North American institution. After noting the myriad ways of resistance to slavery, he writes:

> But there was also accommodation, submission, degradation, and self-hatred. Moreover, it is clear that some of the most effective forms of *resistance* were built upon prior *adaptation,* involving the slaves in processes of culture change and retention of a complicated kind. To write of all adaptive mechanisms as a loss of will to resist is tantamount to a denial of creative energies to the slaves themselves.

However much the accommodation of slaves appears as a gross weakness, it pales in the face of the voluminous evidence of survival, self-reproduction, and determination to remake a community after the destruction of slavery. The signs of vitality were evident during the slave experience. Above all, the slaves' creation of their own culture demolishes theories of their infantilization and total dependence upon their masters.[30]

We have seen how the artisans in the slave community furnished at least one variant of a set of significant others. Moreover, proud and self-confident blacks, fugitive slaves, maroon communities, rebel conspirators and leaders, slave preachers, and clandestine teachers—all combine to refute the concept of an absolutely closed society or one totally dominated by benevolent aristocrats. The persistence of African notions or their transformation to meet the needs of slaves were not the creations of depersonalized beings. Nor, of course, were the richly contrived, complex, and varied spirituals and tales dependent upon the masters alone. The readiness with which slaves in Gabriel's conspiracy adopted his leadership based on American political concepts suggests some inspiration from the masters' ideology. At the same time, slaves used that liberal ideology against the masters themselves. In the history of slavery this was yet another demonstration that the slave was not content only to receive action upon himself but that he was the originator of action.

We could profitably follow Marc Bloch's guidance as a master historian who taught that history is the study of man in society over time.[31] Each man is not a grain of sand sifting through the hands of rulers and masters, and historians. He is a man in society making himself and his collectivity. The slave, although relatively powerless, was an actor and a subject in history and not merely a victim and an object. He was oppressed but found ways in which to reduce the weight of the masters on his back and even to exert pressure against the masters. He was a creator, and his much confined community was his greatest creation in preparing the way to freedom.

The Habits of Mutuality

Master give me over to de National Freedmen's Bureau and I was bound out to a Cherokee woman named Lizzie McGee. Then one day one of my uncles named Wash Sheppard come and tried to get me to go live with him. He say he wanted to get de family all together again. He had run off after he was sold and joined de North army and was discharged at Fort Scott, Kansas, and he said lots of freedmen was living close to each other up by Coffeyville in de Coo-ee-scoo-ee district. —Morris Sheppard, in Norman Yetman, ed., *Voices from Slavery* (New York: Holt, Rinehart and Winston, 1970), p. 273.

In many cases the negroes act like children, roving around the country, caring nothing for the future, not even knowing one day what they are to eat the next. They also seem to think that in their present condition as freemen their former masters and present employers should address them in a more respectful manner. —Charles H. Gilchrist, Colonel 50th U.S. Colored Infantry Commanding (1865).

"The desire for improvement seems to be universal with the freedmen." [In the absence of a school in Brookhaven, Mississippi] the freedmen organized "an association for improvement politically and socially with weekly meetings at which those who can read do so from such Books and Papers as they have for the benefit of the rest." —Freedmen's Bureau Agent, Brookhaven, Mississippi, September 1867 Report.

Without a strong sense of their own worth as individuals and without
their own community and culture to sustain a positive self-concept, it
is inconceivable that slaves in America could have emancipated themselves
as they did. Their massive entry into contraband camps was not merely
an accident of military fortunes and misfortunes; slaves read the signs and
made their own decisions about the link between the military situation
and their own freedom. Indeed, if slavery had so demolished their identities as the Elkins thesis claims, then it would be even more difficult to explain the enlistment of 200,000 black men in the Union army and navy
and their successful performance. The sambo thesis cannot abide the notion of a slave community and its ethos of mutuality, nor the many applications of that spirit in the midst of war, emancipation, and Reconstruction. Nor can the powerful efforts of freed people to reconstruct a
world of their own after slavery fit the surrealistic portrait of a social
landscape strewn with defeated and depersonalized victims.

Freed people gave the lie in many ways to prevailing contemporary
middle-class sentiments about their alleged lack of readiness for a place
in American society. Some of the more important of them, in the process of making a community, will be discussed in this chapter. First, it
appears necessary to trace the line of mutual aid and self-help that informed Africans at home as well as in Europe and the New World. Their
institutionalized benevolence was crucial in making the Afro-American
community. Then we will move back and forth across the former slave
states and over the post-Civil War years to examine the freedmen's positive self-concept as expressed in his political activity in 1865 and after
1867, his attitudes toward and patterns of work, self-support activities,
marriage and family, and love of his home place (and his stubborn insistence on leaving his old plantation quarters to test his freedom).
Some consideration of the debate among white liberals and others ner-
vous over the freedmen's capabilities will nicely fulfill one of Bloch's
expectations of the historian. The debate will permit us to "wring from
them [the documents] further confessions which they had never intended to give."[1] Finally, the freedmen's uses of church, benevolent society,
school, cooperative enterprise, and bank will be considered.

Sometime during the Great Depression in the United States, an aged
black farmer attended a lecture on cooperative efforts in general and farmers' cooperatives in particular. Afterward, he was reported to have said,

"We's don' it befo'—that's nothing new—but us tho't it was only for sweet charity's sake."[2] He may or may not have had in mind a tradition that could be traced to African roots. At any rate, the old man testified to the durability of that ethos of mutuality that traveled across the Atlantic and proved an instrument of black survival and renewal.

At times the evidence of such activity is skimpy, whereas at other times the evidence, as in nineteenth-century America, is abundant. In the black diaspora, an early expression of self-help and mutual aid occurred in 1472 when black freedmen *(negres libertes)* in Valencia, Spain, petitioned for permission from Don Fernando to establish a charitable brotherhood and society. A group of some forty freedmen asked that they be granted a charter, a meeting place for their society in Valencia, the right to collect dues from members, and a royal banner to display in their meeting place. Above all the *cofradia* stipulated that it would aid the poor, the sick, and the wretched, who are in great need *("los cofrades enfermos, pobres, y miserables. . . ")*. The brotherhood appears to have been granted its requests and may have been a prototype for others in the Iberian Peninsula during the height of the transatlantic slave-trading era. A similar society appears to have been established in Cadiz late in the sixteenth century. The heightened group consciousness is suggested by the inclusion in its membership of black slaves as well as freedmen and whites *(La cofradia de los Morenos de Cadiz)*. Black brotherhoods appeared in eighteenth- and nineteenth-century Brazil. They cushioned blacks and mulattoes from the harshly competitive white-dominated world. Providing funds for the sick and for burials was their common function. However, some brotherhoods, particularly one in Rio de Janeiro, granted loans to brothers to purchase their freedom. They were numerous and widespread and were found in both rural and urban settings.[3]

Those Afro-Iberian benevolent societies probably demonstrated continuity with African cultures. The likelihood gains support from evidence of the cooperative tradition in West African agriculture and survivals or variants of it in the New World. Herskovits reminds us of "tree-felling parties of the Surinam Bush Negroes, the *combites* of the Haitian peasant, and in various forms of group labor in agriculture, fishing, house raising, and the like encountered in Jamaica, Trinidad, the French West Indies, and elsewhere." Moreover, an institution of thrift clubs that thrives today throughout the world appears to have been utilized in Africa in the eighteenth century. Twentieth-century rotating credit associations are

not exclusively African in origin, for they proliferate in Asian societies
as well. But their presence as *esusu,* as they were known to Yoruba peoples in Nigeria, and their appearance in the West Indies as *asusu* or *susu,*
suggest some line of transmission westward to the Caribbean. Their similar characteristics in both hemispheres, that is, of an association of con-
tributing participants to a fund that each receives in rotation, is further
evidence of the tradition of cooperation. Yet it must be conceded that
the rotating credit association did not appear among North American
black people. On the other hand, free Afro-Americans carried on the
tradition of mutual aid in their own fashion.[4]

The seed of a flourishing Afro-American institution of benevolence
and cooperation during the nineteenth century was planted at Philadelphia in 1787 by two energetic and articulate black men, Richard
Allen and Absalom Jones. They had been slaves who had hired out
their time and purchased their freedom with their earnings. Allen saw-
ed wood, made bricks, and later became a shoemaker; Jones packed and
stored goods in a shop. They worshiped at St. George's Methodist Church.
When white members saw a rapid growth of black faces Sunday after
Sunday, they attempted to segregate the blacks—newcomers and old-
timers—to the gallery. This was in the era of Pennsylvania's gradual
abolition of slavery after 1780 and a black migration to Philadelphia.
Allen and Jones organized their black brothers in a protest walkout.

The small group met on April 12, 1787, and organized the Free
African Society, a nonsectarian association that would provide mutual
aid to the sick and to widows and fatherless children. This was one great
step toward organized black social life. But it was not unique. A year
later the Philadelphia group was in correspondence with the Negro Union
of Newport, Rhode Island, and with groups of free blacks in Boston and
other places. In 1798 the Sons of Africa Society was organized in Boston
as a mutual-benefit association, and in 1808 New York blacks succeeded
in incorporating the New York African Society for Mutual Relief. An
African Educational and Benevolent Society was formed in Chillicothe,
Ohio, in 1827, and in Providence, Rhode Island, in 1828. Three years
later the Peace and Benevolent Society of Afric-Americans appeared in
New Haven. And, as already mentioned, the free black community of
Baltimore had, by 1835, a well-organized benevolence establishment.
It was probably only second to Philadelphia's, which by 1847 counted
106 societies, whose membership consisted of 4,904 persons, or one-

half the adult population. The tradition was advanced by Baltimore's black ship caulkers, who organized a pioneer trade union and benefi-cial society in 1838. Through collective bargaining the Association of Black Caulkers won for its members a relatively high wage scale and con-trol over work in the shipyards through the Civil War years. In this func-tion as well as in its practical benevolence, the association, like thousands since the first Free African Society, preserved the tradition of coopera-tion and community self-help. The several examples cited in this survey are of course limited mainly to the antebellum northern urban community. And they do not include the variety of other cultural, social, fraternal, political, and economic organizations that gave a rich associational tex-ture to free black communities.[5]

Outstanding in that context was the black abolitionist movement nur-tured by the northern urban black communities. It coexisted with reli-gious and benevolent institutions and with self-help and self-improvement societies. When the impact of an emergent industrial society was felt in the 1830s and 1840s, many American social thinkers advocated an agrar-ian communalism. Black leadership also advocated landownership as the guarantee of independence and was encouraged by the example of a group that had prospered on its farms in Mercer County, Ohio, from 1837 to 1843. In the latter year the National Negro Convention at Buffalo, New York, heard a report from a committee on agriculture that recommended the establishment of agricultural communities by twenty family units. It was further recommended that these groups settle on adjoining tracts of land and cooperate in creating schools, churches, roads, and flour and sawmills as community endeavors. The profits earned would be shared in accordance with individual investment. Some few white families would be permitted to participate in order to avoid the charges that a segregated community was being contemplated.[6] Essentially here was a blueprint for black independence and community. Moreover, like other midcentury Americans anxious about the threat of land monopoly to their future wel-fare, some leading Afro-Americans centered their attention and their hopes upon the farm homesteads as a basis of community. Their formula was to organize communities to realize their freedom from the bondage of dis-crimination in the North, and to provide some haven for fugitive slaves fearful of recapture and return to the slave states. Some successful but short-lived efforts along these guidelines occurred in Canada.[7] Somewhat romantic and precious, tentative and experimental, these Canadian organized communities fared little better than the communitarian efforts of white perfectionists in the United States. Their hope to reconstruct society by withdrawing from it and its struggles was in the end naive and contributed greatly to their frustrations and failures. Yet they left a legacy of communal endeavor. It would be recalled in the Civil War and the Reconstruction era, when the building of a new society in the South was a paramount task and when the new freedom of Afro-Americans revitalized their effort to organize their own communities.

IN POLITICS

Electoral activity is a classic form of American politics. Casting a ballot is the act of decision and participation in the democratic process. But so is the mass meeting and the convention, the petition and the parade. The Civil War fed the hope of black people that the long-denied right to vote could be gained. Lacking it, they participated nevertheless in other forms of political action. For them, in this respect, 1865 was a critical year. With the end of the fighting, and even before the guns ceased shooting, black men pressed for their suffrage. The initiative may well have been taken in the 1864 National Colored Men's Convention in Syracuse. There the resolution was to organize Equal Rights Leagues in the North to struggle for Afro-American suffrage.[8]

Throughout the year, beginning on January 9, 1865, in New Orleans, blacks in southern cities met in organized fashion to declare their demands. New Orleans black men had however been active and articulate in the city since Union control was achieved in 1862. Norfolk blacks also had earlier attempted to assert themselves through a kind of political demonstration. In December 1862, hearing of President Lincoln's Emancipation Proclamation scheduled for January 1, they asked permission of General Viele to "make a procession with flags, and other demonstrations, on New Years day."[9] The general agreed, and the demonstration took place although the celebration was soured by the realization that the proclamation excepted certain counties. But in 1865 Norfolk black men poured out in meeting after meeting to express their demands. Free people followed the same route toward suffrage in meetings and organization in Petersburg and Richmond, Virginia, Savannah, Vicksburg, Nashville, Charleston, Raleigh, and Wilmington, North Carolina, and in 1866 in St. Louis, Little Rock, Baltimore and in Florida.[10] Much of this activity occurred in the face of black codes designed to reduce freed people to slavery and peonage, and while the Republican party in the North and in Congress debated the question of black enfranchisement, this activity across the South was demonstrating the key role that freedmen could play in Reconstruction. President Johnson strove to frustrate that objective while radicals like Thaddeus Stevens and Charles Sumner led the party and congressional struggle for black male suffrage. Without the demonstrated political consciousness of the freed people, their base would indeed have been too weak to realize their aim of remaking Southern society. Thus did the freedmen's self-assertion in politics make a difference to the future not only of their own emerging community but also to that of the United States as well.

Alongside the Fourteenth Amendment, added to the Constitution primarily to protect the rights of freedmen, there ought to be a place for this call for a committee of Wilmington, North Carolina, freedmen to their state convention at Raleigh in 1865:

> These are the times foretold by the Prophets, 'When a Nation shall be born in a day,' the good time coming. Four millions of chattels, branded mercantile commodity, shake off the bands, drop the chains, and rise up in the dignity of men. The time has arrived when we can strike one blow to secure those rights of Freemen that have been so long withheld from us.[11]

An "Address from the Colored Citizens of Norfolk, Virginia to the People of the United States" claimed equal rights for blacks and warned of the danger to the United States in denying suffrage to freedmen. The address rallied black people to be active and self-reliant in the crisis and urged them to form labor associations to protect their wages and contracts with planters. Similarly, the address urged black people to form land associations in which they could amass funds through installment payments until enough was acquired to purchase land in the name of the association. It would hold a mortgage on such lands and would turn them over to investing members who would pay off principal and interest and receive clear titles.[12] Richmond and Petersburg mass meetings issued similar claims on equal rights but appear to have said nothing about land.

During June 1865, the Richmond black community was preoccupied with protesting the reelection of a secessionist as mayor and the persecu-

tion of blacks by police and military authorities. The campaign was successful in removing the mayor and lifting the discriminatory laws. The
Richmond community was constantly active and alert in this period, for
we find it again mounting a campaign in 1867 to protest discrimination
on streetcars. A firm working-class base to the political assertions of the
black community in 1865 is suggested by the strike of Richmond tobacco factory workers for decent wages. Their self-concept seems to have
remained undamaged despite their distressful conditions. "They say we
will starve through laziness that is not so," they asserted. "But it is true
we will starve at our present wages. They say we will steal we can say for
ourselves we had rather work for our living." These were the people who
closed down the city's tobacco factories on August 1, 1867, in order to
attend en masse the Virginia State Republican Convention.[13] Although
the vigorous activity of 1865 registered the claims and protests of freed
people across the South, victory was not automatic nor immediate. The
assertions of black communities however did have impact in the political crisis of the nation during 1866. Not only was there a limited fran-
chise for blacks included in the Fourteenth Amendment, but when it
was rejected by the Southern states under ex-Confederate leadership and
with the encouragement of President Johnson, Congress was driven to
guarantee full black adult male suffrage in the 1867 Reconstruction Acts.

In black communities, both in the cities and in the countryside, men
and women who had been slaves only two, three, and four years earlier
reenacted some of the scenes of the American Revolution. Long lines of
them, preceded by fife and drum and an American flag, marched to the
polls to vote for delegates to new state constitutional conventions, then
for representatives in 1868 in new state governments and in Congress.
Black men organized under the Republican party banner and the Union
League. The latter, at first a secret fraternal and political society, recruited thousands of black freedmen and, along with black churches, became
a center of Reconstruction era black community life. From its ranks
came an indigenous leadership whose courage and boldness frightened
and threatened white planter social and political domination. The transformation from slave to solon was a revolutionary change in the South.
It was met with terrorism fostered by the Ku Klux Klan. The counter-
revolution brutally halted the new black community advance by killing
and maiming the preachers, artisans, and farm laborers who dared to assert their own program of emancipation.

However, the determination of freedmen to make the enfranchisement in the Reconstruction Acts come alive prompted them to guard against the terrorists. Thus the histories of Southern states and the documents on which they are based are replete with examples of armed contingents of freedmen accompanying their people to the polls and to election rallies. These were frequently the very occasions on which disfranchised and disgruntled whites retaliated. Freedmen nevertheless displayed a militancy that left their opponents certain in their paranoia that blacks meant to conduct a race war. Actually, the South was experiencing a democratic political revolution the main burden of which was carried at this time by black men with support from a minority of white Southerners. A Democratic newspaper in North Carolina drew a somewhat exaggerated but instructive picture of such a display of freedmen assertiveness in politics: A "most pitiful and Godforsaken looking set of negroes . . . " came into Lexington, North Carolina, in September 1868. They wore shoulder straps in "mock military style" and carried sabers at their waists. They moved through the streets in a "self-important manner." In their parade after noon the van was taken by a buggy drawn by two horses. A black man carrying the U.S. flag rode in the buggy. A farm wagon drawn by a mule followed and carried the band producing what the newspaper reported as discordant music—three fiddles, an old drum, and several iron triangles. The reporter deplored what he charged was the free flow of whiskey, the passage of money from one man to another, and the mingling of white and black Radical Republicans while the speeches rang from the platform in the public square. Most distressing was the reported demagogic promise to freedmen by politicians of sixty, not the usual forty, acres of land. The quest for landownership proved to be a powerful motivation for freedmen participation in politics. What had been denied by the failure to confiscate slaveowners' lands in the settlement of the war, it appeared, might be attained by political action. In order to make this part of their emancipation real, freed people defied employers and would quit work to attend political meetings and go to the polls.[14]

One Alabama freedman took his rights seriously. Determined to leave the plantation and attend political meetings, he told his employer that he was not working for wages but was a part owner of the crop. "As I have all the rights that you or any other man has," he asserted, "I shall not suffer them abridged." On Election Day in 1868 Frances Butler Leigh, to her dismay, failed to prevent blacks on Butler Island, off the

coast of Georgia, from going to vote in Darien, on the mainland. There
was "not a negro in the field," and even the "half-wit who took care of
the cows" went with the others to vote. But they did return next day
to finish their tasks. Near Apling, in the same state, freedmen's "enthu-
siasm knew no bounds. The great mass resisted every attempt to intimi-
date them, and marched boldly to the polls. . . ." About one hundred
armed men walked twelve miles to Apling, the county seat, and arrived
soaking wet from wading through rain-swollen creeks, then cast their ballots for Republicans. In Yazoo, Mississippi, it was hazardous for blacks
to wear Grant and Colfax buttons. And even when some were beaten
and stripped of the buttons, they still insisted on wearing them at all
costs, for failure to do so meant almost "a voluntary return to slavery."
Some struck back at their attackers and created cases for the Freedmen's
Bureau agent to settle. Freed women defiantly wore campaign buttons
when their husbands feared to do so in the presence of "old massa and
missus." Some women walked sometimes twenty or thirty miles into
town to get a button and "wear it openly, in defiance of husband, master, mistress, or overseer." A leader of Yazoo black people, Foote, wore
not only one but two and insisted on walking on the sidewalk in defiance
of orders to "walk in the middle of the street, where other niggers go."
At Livingston, Alabama, freedmen voters, with arms, bugles, drums, and
fifes, marched to the polls. For some leaders defiance resulted in their
being beaten or killed by night riders. Thousands of other freedmen who
disobeyed orders and warnings to remain in the fields but who quit to
attend political rallies, as in Mississippi, were discharged without pay.
The planters retaliated in the same manner when they learned that their
field laborers joined the Union Leagues or voted the Republican ticket.[15]

Freedmen devised many modes of resistance to their oppression by
hooded gangs or respectable planters and pillars of the community. Open,
organized militant action occurred in South Carolina, Georgia, Alabama,
and Mississippi. When freedmen decided to fight back, they did so not
as self-appointed heroes but as leaders of black lower-class communities.
Some exceeded what contemporary whites might have been willing to
tolerate. One such instance was in the so-called riot at Hunnicutt's Crossing in the upcountry Pickens district of South Carolina in 1867. A
white man had been killed by a band of armed and violent black freedmen. There appeared to be an implication of the local Union League,
led by Nat Frazier. During a heated meeting with a white man whom he

was cursing for not joining it, he was asked the purpose of the organization. He replied, "It was to put South Carolina back into its proper place. We intend to have land, and we intend to send men to Congress to make laws for us; and if they don't act in the way we desire, we intend to kill them." Later he repeated, "We intend to have land, and to have some of the white men where they had us."[16] The white reign of terror lasted at least ten years but failed to reduce freed people to total submission. Resistance in one or another form continued throughout the Reconstruction era. As for their role as voters, freed people went to the polls despite the violence. Eventually, after 1870, their numbers at the ballot boxes diminished, but they never permitted themselves to be destroyed as a political body. Their survival through this era of violent repression makes a mockery of those theories of slave depersonalization and of a negative black self-concept.

An older scholarship in Reconstruction history portrayed the freedmen as ignorant tools of carpetbagger and scalawag manipulation. This was supposed to explain the mass turnouts of black men at the polls after 1867. Defenders of Southern white supremacy attempted to show that black voters knew nothing about the voting process and were used to advance the interests of Northern whites. It is clear that the loss of control over the black laboring force frustrated and enraged most of the former dominant classes in the South. They and their apologists, therefore, used the manipulation theory to cover their failure to honor black capabilities. Two examples will serve to show that freedmen, while obviously following the lead of the Republican party (the party of emancipation), made their own assessments and determinations in politics. During the 1867 struggles to establish and elect a Republican party slate in Virginia, a newspaper correspondent asked a group of blacks whether they would vote for Northerners who were living in their midst. The leader of the group replied, "Well, the northern men who are worthy can get office at home; those who are unworthy we don't want." Several hundred miles away in Alabama, George Houston, a former slave tailor and a Reconstruction era leader of a freedmen's community, refused to be led into testifying before a congressional committee that Northerners had "used" him.[17]

Not all freedmen spoke in such determined and independent fashion. Some chose to be Democrats or recanted their Republican radicalism and appeared to be Democrats or were bribed to switch parties. Benjamin Leonard, a mechanic and gunsmith of Bluffport, Alabama, ceased his political activity when threatened with the loss of white patronage in his trade. More than that, he signed a public statement of recantation prepared by a white man. Some charged but did not offer proof that Leonard's renunciation was worth $1,000. Two black Democrats in a town divided by the Georgia and Alabama boundary were rewarded with suits of clothing, and one of them, a mechanic, received a tool chest for marching in a Democratic parade. Other black Democrats were subjected to scorn, harassment, and violence by the larger segments of their black communities.[18]

Those thousands of freed people who made up the local Union Leagues and Republican party organizations, indeed even some of those who were persuaded or bribed into appearing as Democrats, made important choices based on their perceptions of the importance of political activity to achiev desired goals. Those objectives were understood and articulated by freed people: to be free, to live decently and peaceably, to gain a good educatio to own land and become economically independent, to live in communities that were familiar and established or that were newly established, as we shall see later, and were worth developing as they wished to develop them.

AT WORK

The Richmond tobacco workers had clearly demonstrated their own interpretation of the work ethic. Other freed people in the countryside still clung to preindustrial attitudes toward work. They merely chose to work at the rhythms suitable to their needs, spiritual as well as material. They did work, after all, gathering fat bales of cotton, sheaves of tobacco leaf, cribs of corn, and hogsheads of sugar. They were not indolent, lazy, or useless, as some exasperated planters and employers insisted. It was only their manner and attitude toward work that stood between them and their employers. And it was their own needs, their own bodies, and minds to which they ministered by their absences from the fields. Ferrying or rowing across a swamp creek or from the Georgia Sea Islands to the mainland in order to vote was one expression about the of priorities of work and civic duty. To be sure, the loss was calculated in the plantation counting room. When it occurred, such behavior by laborers offended the directors of a systematic capitalist agriculture. In 1866 a a Tensas Parish, Louisiana, plantation, for example, freedmen worked in the morning but quit in the afternoon. An eyewitness reported that "they assembled and joined in singing, praying and shouting, and 'the spirit of the Lord come down mightily and smote them.' " He could not but regret that the afternoon was lost to labor.

A Northern planter in Georgia found that singing songs at work was a pastime of freedmen and that they would "drop the shovel and the hoe" and sing a religious song. "They claimed the privilege of carrying their guns to the fields, in order to shoot a stray rabbit, or squirrel, that might cross their path." When they were prohibited from carrying the guns with them while at work, the freedmen protested that it was a "great encroachment upon their rights as freemen." When they deemed it necessary for their physical welfare to declare a holiday, they did so, once on a Saturday morning at the height of cotton planting. They were offered two holidays *after* the cotton was planted, but they refused. The same planter found some self-satisfaction in the diligent labor of his hands in the cotton-gathering season. He worked alongside them sometimes for an hour or two by moonlight and found "it is so much more comfortable working then, than in the heat of the day." With incentive payments such as holidays and presumably cash rewards, he stimulated them to more labor. A firm advocate of "free labor" and an abolitionist, the planter seemed smug in noting that the laborers strained to meet his approval. When treated fairly, freedmen appreciated and honored work. "It rejoices my heart, to watch them coming home from the field at night, singing, laughing, and joking; and their children running to meet them. 'O,' say they, 'it feels so good to be treated like a man, and to feel that we have no master.' " At another time during the closing days of the war, a British antislavery newspaper correspondent reported meeting a party of twenty-five women and children as they entered U.S. military lines, and on their way to Washington. When asked where they were going, they replied, "Oh, we's going Washington to Uncle Abraham, he'll take care of us and git us work." The problem, as one Louisiana sugar planter discovered during the busy and critical grinding days, was that newly freed blacks were most troublesome. They made their own decisions about work.[19]

The attitude toward work was far different when the freedmen's own crops or farms were involved. Near Fernandina, Florida, one proud freedman boasted of his ability to work hard and raise bountiful crops. "I've got a handsome piece both side ob de road. I chose him dere purpose to hurt deir feelings; to be riding long de road and see de nigger crop a flour-

ishing; for dey tells me dere won't no cotton go to market from de niggers dis year." He chuckled as he explained this to a Northern white
schoolteacher. "We'll show 'em how de nigger can work de farm for himself."[20] Farther north on the South Carolina coastal island of Edisto, militant freedmen who had resisted surrender of their lands to returning
prewar planters and former masters, declared at a meeting that they all
expected to work for a living.[21] Also, when earlier in the war U.S. troops
evacuated blacks from Barnwell and Hall Island to Port Royal Island, the
former slaves left behind crops of corn, potatoes, and cotton. When it
was determined that no Confederates were on the islands, they sought
and obtained permission to return to tend the standing crops. A Northern journalist marveled at "this independent colony" working for
months without a guiding superintendent and "without the slightest encouragement or pay." Later he saw their cotton in the gin house at
Beaufort.[22] During the now famous "rehearsal for reconstruction" in
the Sea Islands, after November 1861, freed people perplexed Yankee
entrepreneurs like Edward S. Philbrick intent on turning out large cash
crops of cotton with "modern" cash incentives. The field laborers preferred to defy his management and plant their corn and melons down
the rows between the cotton plants and harvest them as they pleased.
Once William C. Gannett went into the fields and pulled up much of
the corn himself after failing to persuade the freed people to do so.
Their rage was visible and one, Tony, stormed out on the field with a
club and carving knife, "brandishing them and swearing that he would
have his blood." Tony did not go near Gannett and appeared by afternoon to have resigned himself to the situation. On another plantation,
John, with nine acres of cotton to work, planted a thousand watermel-
on vines. He was a vexatious man to the landlord. When the men were
paid, the young New England schoolteacher William Allen asked what
right the men had to plant corn and melons on Philbrick's land when
they were hired to work cotton. The reply was a larger one than the
good-natured reprimand was intended to elicit. "Man! don't talk 'bout
Mr. Phelbrick [sic] lan'. Mr. Phelbrick no right to de lan.' "[23]

And that occurred in June 1864, more than a year before Thaddeus
Stevens campaigning for a party colleague in Pennsylvania proposed his
sweeping plan of confiscation and redistribution of rebel lands in forty-
acre tracts. Several years later, when planters in their consternation proposed to replace blacks by importing Europeans and Chinese to work the

fields, freedmen organized in protest. For example, at Frankfort, Kentucky, a meeting of black laborers objected and resolved to "earnestly recommend to our people industry, economy and a faithful observance of contracts when correctly and strictly made." Fayette County freedmen in the same state declared in a meeting that they were ready to contract with farmers, "for we have been raised to work, and it don't go hard with us." These black former soldiers established an "Intelligence Office" and labor agency and placed 3,000 men in jobs during the first half of 1869 "into every cornfield and almost every occupation of trust in Kentucky." Freed laborers understood the limits of their power to compel a redistribution of land, and they also understood the alternative, the necessity to contract for labor. They also did not easily yield to the planter's superior power. Freedmen sought four basic conditions in their contracts, as early as 1864 in Louisiana: (1) flogging must cease as a punishment; (2) they would work only when well treated; (3) there should be no separation of families; and (4) their children should be provided with an education in schools. At that time these conditions were the freed people's rejoinder to Union General Nathaniel P. Banks's labor codes, which were thinly disguised slave conditions. The freed people declared their familial and parental responsibilities and their self-emancipation. At this critical moment of societal change freedmen planned their future by looking at their past, revealing their historical sense. They contradicted theories of irreversible damage to their personalities inflicted by slavery.[24]

Former slaves having to provide for themselves and their families, perhaps remembering negotiations with masters before emancipation, organized and bargained with their prospective employers. When pressed by necessity, they went on strike to obtain concessions and tolerable wages and working conditions. Field laborers, washerwomen, ironworkers, longshoremen, and sawmill workers went on strike and formed unions and protective associations. Like other early forms of working-class organization, most of them combined economic and benevolent functions, the latter appearing to be most important.

In September 1865 about forty Savannah dock workers, finding wages of $1.50 a day intolerable in the face of rising prices and taxes, and of rents that were doubled by a combination of landlords, forcefully attempted to threaten fellow longshoremen to make them quit work. The competition for older dock workers provided by an influx of laborers who came in from the country "to avoid starvation" and who were willing to work for lower pay was an additional cause of the outburst. While the editor of the *Savannah Daily Republican* berated the would-be strikers for demanding compensation for labor '*vi et armis*', he appeared to be pleased that a squad of soldiers had broken up the demonstration and marched the leaders to the guardhouse. A meeting next day of the Savannah Union League unanimously condemned the "unlawful means" resorted to by their "deluded brethren," thanked the editor of the newspape for his concern, but proceeded to point out tactfully but firmly the real grievances that had sparked the attempted strike. A sense of working-class discipline informed the statement that called for organization and redress through legal means rather than through coercion of fellow workers. The best way to prevent a recurrence, the resolution stated, was

> to protect ourselves against the combinations of those unfriendly to us in the city and other portions of the State, to manage the rates of labor and to maintain our rights in all respects is in harmony with all the laws of the country and of God, to organize ourselves into associations whereby we may in the best manner avail ourselves of the means of enlightment, of industry, of mutual help and protection within our reach.

Specifically, the Union League was the organization recommended. Although neither the editor nor the dock workers directly mentioned the "free labor system," they obviously had divergent views of its meaning.[25]

In 1863 field laborers in St. Bernard Parish, Louisiana, demonstratively differed with General Banks's draconian "free labor" regulations. A black preacher-blacksmith led them in a strike to demand full pay and passes to travel to New Orleans when they wished to do so. Ideas of freedom and autonomy had apparently been germinating in the slave quarters. In August 1863 plantation laborers in the same parish armed themselves with lead-headed clubs, drove off the overseers, and elected two "colonels" to lead them and to proclaim their self-government. Similar quavers were felt in other Louisiana parishes as the laborers made distinctions between bound and free labor and especially between their concept of freedom and those of General Banks, who continued to practice bondage in all but name after the Union forces were in control.[26]

In some cases strikes by one group of black workers were elevated into community struggles. When Mobile dock workers went on strike in 1867, for example, for a wage increase from twenty-five to fifty cents an hour, the activities spread to other workers. The dock workers lost their strike, but the local newspaper reported that "a growing feeling of dissatisfaction and discontent" spread to "the entire negro laboring population" including those who worked on the levee, in sawmills, and among day laborers and occasional workers.[27] Ten years later cotton pickers in the Combahee River district of South Carolina struck for cash wages instead of provisions and a promise of profit sharing. The black political leader R. B. Elliott found that the strikers were making a community affair of their struggle. "All classes of workmen are compelled to demand higher wages, and women and children are now beaten as well as men," he reported.[28] In 1866 the white cotton planter William Elliott discovered during his strained negotiation with reluctant laborers what might have been in the freedman's mind. When the Combahee black workers refused to contract with him, Elliott tried to break their solidarity by negotiating with Jacob, a "faithful" former slave, but he failed. Jacob's back stiffened, and he spurned the offer to plant five or six acres of cotton for half a share. He preferred working two acres and having "all the provisions he may make for himself." For Jacob that was just compensation for past service to the Elliotts. The planter felt this was grossly ungrateful and bitterly complained that Jacob "is eaten up with self-esteem and selfishness." Ultimately, Jacob was converted, and he aided in bringing about an agreement between Elliott and the laborers on three of his plantations.[29] Freed laborers demonstrated their serious commitment to solidarity, as in the case of a group of men in Cherokee County, Alabama. They had bound themselves under penalty of fifty lashes on the naked back not to work during the harvest for less than $2 a day.[30] The habits of mutuality could embrace the blood oath or its equivalent.

The critical point in time when freedmen asserted their claims and disclosed their attitudes toward work was in the summer and autumn of 1865. The myth created by the first Reconstruction historians was that freedmen refused to work, were shiftless, lazy, and ran off to a life of hedonistic dissipation in the cities. We now know better. We now know that freedmen were testing their freedom by some spatial mobility and were searching for members of their families separated during slavery and the upheavals of war. Above all, the growing refusal to make contracts for work in the coming year of 1866 made the long summer and autumn of 1865 appear to be the decline and fall of the former slave. Even friends of the freedmen among white antislavery people looked "charitably" on their alleged weaknesses and believed they had to be taught to work and to adjust to the new society. The truth of the matter was that in the countryside black people were expecting a redistribution of their former masters' lands.[31] Freedmen made this the point on which they determined to fight to the best of their abilities and their meager material resources. General Ulysses Grant in December 1865 was only half right when he said, "The effect of the belief in the division of lands is idleness and accumulation in camps, towns, and cities."[32] We shall attempt a closer look at this confrontation of freedmen with the land question in Chapter 6. Meanwhile, during what appears to have been a potentially revolutionary situation, particularly along the coast from Virginia to Florida, the freedmen gave evidence of their lofty self-concept and their urgent desire to settle in communities of their own.

OF PRIDE AND PRUDENCE

Freedmen continually demonstrated a sense of pride in themselves and in their people as a community. Although much charitable work was accomplished on behalf of the freed people by Northern church groups and philanthropic organizations, there were distinctive black efforts. Among them were the African Civilization Society, which recruited and sent black teachers to the South, the African Methodist Episcopal Church, the African Methodist Episcopal Zion Church, and their agencies. The African Freedmen's Commission appears to have been a consortium. At one of its meetings in New York City the Right Reverend J. J. Clinton, Bishop of the African Methodist Episcopal Zion (AMEZ) Church and president of the commission, reported on its work. He made a striking assertion that black teachers of black children were better than white teachers. He cited the example of two schools in Norfolk, taught by black teachers, whose pupils outperformed those taught by whites in every examination. Bishop Clinton declared, "The reason was the colored people felt a pride in doing good for their own people."[33] Probably the most telling evidence of black pride was in the insistence of thousands of freed people upon paying for the education of their children. The earnestness of older black people in building and sustaining schools was compensation for their sense of loss at having been denied education and a sign of their determination to gain a better life for their children. They felt a deep pride. Sometimes it was excessive, as in the case of the old man who told a class of Vicksburg, Mississippi, schoolchildren that study in early life was important, that their eyesight was better than that of their white friends and they must make the most of it. Above all, he added quietly, "Your intellects are also superior." The amens were "very hearty."[34]

Freedmen's pride expressed itself in the desire of black people to earn their own living and avoid dependence upon philanthropy. Joseph Warren, chaplain and freedmen superintendent, reported this about his charges at Vicksburg.[35] General Rufus Saxton on the Sea Islands and Colonel John Eaton in the Mississippi Valley, both with great responsibilities for the welfare of thousands of freed people, testified on more than one occasion to this quality in them. Saxton emphasized the freed people's self-reliance. He explained after the war to a Northern journalist that when young black men in the Sea Islands volunteered for the army and received a $300 bounty, in many cases they decided to give $200 of it to their families or used the money to stock farms or invest in government bonds.[36]

The American Freedmen's Inquiry Commission in 1863 found stiking confirmation of this self-reliance in Louisville and St. Louis. In the first they learned that very few blacks were dependent upon public support. "They are very much like Jews and Quakers in that respect—they take care of one another," a doctor testified. Not 1 out of 200 blacks was in the poorhouse, he explained. Finally, he declared, "They have a great deal of personal pride." In St. Louis the three-man commission learned from the pastor of the Colored Baptist Church that the black community practiced mutual aid for its needy members. "We have always done that," said the Reverend Edward L. Woodson, "because we don't like to have the white people think we can't take care of ourselves." Woodson was himself an example of proud and successful self-reliance. He had been a slave who hired out his time, bought himself, his wife and fourteen children, and five or six other persons. Farther west, in Kansas, Colonel Richard J. Hinton, who had been a close friend of John Brown, told the commision about a striking transformation in freedmen. He found that among the slaves who came into his command area, the most intelligent and self-reliant were those from western Missouri bordering on Kansas, the Indian Territory, and Arkansas. Those who came from the extreme northeast corner of Texas and the Red River country of Louisiana at first meeting appeared "much more stupid and stolid . . . and they were much black-er." But as he came to know them better, he realized that the stupidity was assumed. Though they were supposedly not as bright as the frontier blacks and "they had a heavier look and they cringed more," after a few days in the army "they appeared as bright as anybody, walked straight and looked right out of their eyes at you." This confirmed his opinion about assumed stupidity, but he seems not to have explained to himself the put-on, the self-protective sambo veneer. It was an old paradox that puzzled Hinton the abolitionist and former Chartist: The freedman frequently was forced to hide his pride beneath a heavy cloak of prudence.[37]

Among the seemingly trivial ways in which pride was expressed was the one of dress. A black woman in the Yorktown, Virginia, contraband settlement explained this to the good people who had come from Philadelphia to aid the former slaves. The Friends society for the relief of freedmen had sent clothing. It was satisfactory except for a shipment of sturdy gray flannel dresses. The black woman found them repugnant and preferred to buy garments of less durable materials, even second hand. The flannel dress was rejected because it was made of the material worn during slavery. "We's *free* now, missus, isn't we? Den we don wan to war *dat* kine o' stuff no more. We's allers had to wear dat," was the explanation, "and we wants to dress like de white folks now."[38] The Quaker woman who heard this understood, but other whites did not. An officer of black troops camped at Corinth, Mississippi, told the American Freedmen's Inquiry Commission (AFIC) he could see a desire to gain property among some freedpeople but he could also see others who cared less. The preferred to spend their money on "clothes and things of fancy."[39] When the commissioners asked a Virginia supervisor of contraband camps about the money-saving habits of his charges, he too reported that they preferre to spend on "gaudy dress and good things to eat, that is life's luxuries."[40] General Saxton affirmed a diversity of habits but stated that "not all of them, as is frequently asserted, think only of today."[41] (He was particularly impressed with the growth of the South Carolina Freedmen's Saving Bank, which he had founded in 1864 for his troops.) At the height of Kl terror in 1871, Caroline Smith, a freed woman of Walton County, Georg discovered from the lashing she received that the so-called luxuries of life were more expensive than the mere money cost. "The colored peopl she told a congressional investigating committee, "dare not dress up ther selves and fix up, like they thought anything of themselves."[42] The person obviously made the dress speak for him or her. Although friendly an sympathetic army officers and philanthropic workers wondered and per haps fretted about freedmen's habits and Klansmen tried to regulate pride out of existence, freed people quite simply rediscovered themselves or felt freer to express themselves in ways that often were denied under their old masters. That positive self-identification was indirectly stated by an eighty-year-old former Virginia slave in Washington, D.C.: "I had a kind master, who nebber persecuted nor 'bused me, like some did, and dere was good Christian people dere; but somehow dey nebber seem to tink we cul'd folks hab any souls nor any human feelin's like white folks."[43] That they believed firmly in the equality of their souls with those of white folks is suggested by a Virginia historian's observation. Under the indoctrination of Northern schoolteachers in their midst, he wrote, "negroes began to talk a great deal of their desire to be 'treated as a man and a brother.' "[44]

STAYING HOME

Before emancipation, for most slaves there was no place like home. For many of them home meant the community built up of families in the slave quarters and the visiting slaves from the mansions who socialized with them. The anguish of separation, when it occurred, only made the memory of the meager hearth in the slave cabin all the more bitter sweet. It was after all a yearning for the loved ones, the respected uncles and grandparents, the mothers and fathers, sisters and brothers left behind. And it was sometimes the memory of the master's favors, especially if they had been granted to a slave as a child. It was no wonder then that when the institution crumbled under the guns and under the steady departure of slaves, there remained with many slaves a fondness for the home place. For many slaves there was no such separation and anguish. Many stayed where they were while the war was in progress and remained after the fighting to make their peace with their former masters. Many left temporarily to test their freedom and returned. Some who had been removed with their masters as a consequence of the economic dictates of the cotton market hoped someday to go back to old Virginia or some other seaboard state.

Freed people sought to lease or buy the plantations wherever they happened to be at the moment. Others feared to do so because it might mean buying lands far away from the old home settlements. During the summer of 1865 the Texas lowlands were crowded with freedmen who

had been moved there from the east by their masters. They demonstrated their dissatisfaction by ignoring the inducements of their former masters to work there. They desired to go home to Virginia and other Southern states where they were raised.[45] But even closer to their homes, in
Maryland, where a group of 800 worked on government farms, some refused to stay. They were especially offended by rigid rules much like
those governing the old plantations during slavery times. And some did
want to go home to Virginia.[46] This love of home had been noted in
South Carolina's Sea Islands. There, federal officials and philanthropic
volunteers and teachers observed the attachment to home. Perhaps the
most perceptive statement about it was made by A. D. Smith, chairman
of the board of the U.S. Direct Tax Commissioners for South Carolina.
The freed people did not want to move away, he reported; they wanted
to stay if they could be protected and free. Therefore, they needed the
family organized, and *"they must have land, land."* The government
must give them permanent titles—"a mere military title furnished no security, no permanence."[47] Farther south, in Louisiana, a sixty-year-old
man told a traveling New York journalist, "What's de use of being free
if you don't own land enough to be buried in? Might juss as well stay
slave all yo' days." Another man, who had saved four or five hundred
dollars, only wanted to buy four or five acres of land "dat I can build
me a little house on and call my home."[48]

RAISING A FAMILY

Getting a home and owning some land were not of course ends in them
selves. With them, however, a family could settle and plan, perform necessary tasks, live and love, and try to build a community with other families. The powerful bond of kinship had not been destroyed during slavery
times. Men and women made valiant efforts to find and reunite with mem
bers of their families separated by sale or removal. When some of the
first runaways during the war risked their lives to reach U.S. Army camps,
they tested the promise of freedom made by the army's presence. But
they soon dissappeared only to return with wives and children. Some
found their first opportunities to look for loved ones within the contraband camps set up by the government. And scores of them wanted to
bring them out of the plantations into the camps. In 1863 Colonel J. M.
Alexander at Corinth, Mississippi, was overwhelmed by the problem this

created for him. "The greatest difficulty I have now with the Soldiers [1st Alabama Infantry Colored Troops] is their constant application to get their Wives or Children from the Country."[49] Not too far away, and a few weeks after the fall of Vicksburg, at least one "contraband" in the U.S. Navy on the Mississippi River applied for a pass from his commanding officer. He was Edward Jones, a crewman of the *Carondolet,* and to whom Rear Admiral David D. Porter had given a two-week pass to search for his family.[50] Charles Nordhoff, visiting South Carolina in 1863, reported that ten men from a place a hundred miles inland were sent back as spies by General David Hunter. They returned to his headquarters at Hilton Head Island with a satisfactory report *and* with their wives and children. Throughout his stay in the Sea Islands, Nordhoff paid attention to these family attachments. His conclusion was that "Men who return to the enemy's lines to steal off their wives and children do not lack enterprise."[51] Had he been exposed to the depersonalization theories, he might have countered with the cases he witnessed. Nor was he the only commentator on this strong family bond that was unbroken through slavery and emancipation. On separate occasions two eminent Southerners testified about it. James Speed told the Freedmen's Inquiry Commission in Louisville that he had been brought up on his father's farm with a black family. When pressed with a specific question—"I mean in regard to the family relations, Did they keep up family relations?"—Speed said, "Oh, yes, when the father came back at night he went to the house. They always took their supper together. I don't know that they had a regular table and a family meal, but the father always went home and was with the family at night."[52] Eight years later former Georgia Governor Joseph E. Brown told a congressional committee, "I should say that the majority of them, where they are of proper age, have families, and the husband and wife live together; and I think a majority of them during the time of slavery did so."[53] Out in the Cherokee Nation, frequent cases of Indian and black intermarriage were noted, despite a Cherokee law banning such amalgamation.[54] When 3,000 black people gathered in a St. Louis hall in January 1865, one of the handbills displayed on the walls read: "Our wives and children are free."[55]

As soon as they were able to solemnize or formalize their marriages, freedmen and women seized the opportunity. In the Mississippi Valley, once the Union forces secured it in 1863, black people flocked into their arms. Men were recruited into the newly authorized black regiments. And they swamped their officers with requests for permission to get married. John Eaton professed to an inability to carry out completely an order with respect to men and women living together. But he did report that "Respect for family relation has been quickened, and is keeping pace with the rapid growth of respect for themselves."[56] His subordinate superintendents of freedmen encouraged and aided correspondence between soldiers and their wives. Besides, Eaton stated, "The difficulties and expense of travel do not prevent soldiers' wives at Helena [Arkansas] from visiting their husbands at Fort Smith."[57] After the war thousands of marriages and "cohabitations" begun in slavery, as well as new unions, were formalized in army-supervised ceremonies in the former Confederate states.[58] But a precedent had been set as early as September 1861 when hundreds of freed people took their vows in mass ceremonies at Fortress Monroe, Virginia.[59]

Freed people confirmed their parental and familial responsibilities. First, there were countless numbers of men in and out of the army who went on hazardous reconnoitering missions, accomplished their tasks, and returned with their families to havens in the Union army camps.[60] And again, when black children in Conecuh and Montgomery counties, Alabama, for example, were kept in apprenticeship status, a euphemism for continued involuntary servitude, freedmen became indignant. No amount of money could induce them to permit the master-apprentice relationship even where the children were well treated.[61]

The deep-seated concern for children and aged members of the community was best expressed by freedmen in Liberty County, Georgia, in a letter to the Freedmen's Bureau. It began, "We the people of Liberty county, State of Georgia . . ." and asked for advice about the conditions of their employment by their former owners. They were "put in confusion" on learning that only the prime hands would be hired and that their infirm mothers and fathers and their children would not be provided for. Moreover, their existence as a community was threatened. "Our *School* that was established in the county are *Broken up and We are Destitute of Religious Worship.*" They feared that their children would not be *"Allowed to educate or Learn More than they were permitted in slavery."* These freedmen were willing to work under fair conditions but not under terms taking them back to slavery. "We are A Working Class of People and We are Willing and are Desirous to work for A Fair Compensation," they declared.[62] These concerns mark the people who express them so distinctly as normal human beings, neither depressed nonpersons nor romantic hero figures. Indeed had they been either of the two, they most likely would have been unable to reconcile themselves to contract with their former masters and at the same time seek redress against their unfairness.

During the 1870s, rural black lower-class families in Louisa County, Virginia, similarly took care of their own aged dependents as well as homeless individuals outside of their own families. Census data of 1880 showed that black households frequently also took in mothers and mothers-in-law. The poverty of the black community in this tobacco county was marked. Mutual-aid organizations such as the Order of Saint Luke and the Order of Good Samaritans provided some relief. So did the Freedmen's Bureau and the County officials. But after the Bureau was dissolved in 1869, the black farm people could rely on only one resource, their kinship networks. Augmented and extended families became "their brothers' keepers," thus adding instrumental roles to their normal affectional roles, according to one scholar, while white poor families adhered more to nuclear forms.[63]

Since neither white nor black middle-class families were burdened by such additional functions, these Louisa County lower-class blacks appeared to have responded not only to their poverty and economic circumstances but to cultural patterns. Recent research suggests that black family structures of considerable complexity and variety and their mutual-aid roles predate the American slave experience. The traditional Ashanti family, for example, has been defined as the several households making up a community. Numerous examples of extended and augmented families among rural blacks in the 1920s and 1930s as well as in the 1880s suggest continuity.[64] Direct evidence of an unbroken experience over time is at best suggestive. However, the most significant feature of the experience is the freed people's mutual interdependence.

Another illustration of normal parental and familial concerns expressed early in the Reconstruction era was the " 'quirin' letter." Such letters supplied the names and ages of the mother, father, and child sought by a freed person, including such identifying clues as the name of the former owner. These letters were forwarded to one church after another, where they would be read to the congregations, who were then asked to supply any information about the missing persons. They told where relatives could be reached and proved successful in reuniting families after

distant separations. A similar agency for reuniting families was provided
by the New Orleans *Tribune,* a newspaper published by mulattoes. The
newspaper listed the names of persons for whom letters were received
in the Freedmen's Bureau headquarters in the city. Another means of
locating separated children and parents was through paid advertising in
black newspapers.[65] Here are two examples from the Nashville *Colored
Tennessean,* on October 7, 1865:

Information Wanted

INFORMATION is wanted of ANN ELIZABETH, granddaughter
of Susan Hineway. She was sold by George Cunningham to J.
Jordan, and by him sold to J. Sykes of Columbus, Miss. Sykes
was a relative of the Seviers of that place. Any one who can give
me information as to the where-abouts of said Ann Elizabeth,
will confer a great favor by addressing Colored Tennessean box
1150.

P.S. her mother's name was Lithy Jane Johnson.

                                                        C. J. JOHNSON

Sept. 30. — 3m

Information Wanted

OF MY WIFE, LUCY BLAIR, who I left in Jonesboro, Washington
County, East Tennessee, four years ago. She was then living with
William Blair. I was raised by John Blair. I am a wagon maker by
trade, and would be thankful for any information respecting her
whereabouts. I am in Nashville, Tenn. on Gay street, north of the
Statehouse. Address me or the Colored Tennessean, Nashville,
Tenn. Box 1150.

                                                        HENRY HILL

Jy 29 — 3m

Mississippi Valley men and women searching for one another to rebuild
their families; Combahee River cotton laborers setting out to make a liveli-
hood; Liberty County freedmen returning to their old masters in a new
employee-employer bond but protesting the denial of access to schools

and churches and care for their elderly and children; Richmond tobacco factory workers demanding a living wage; Jacob on the Elliott plantations holding out for his own terms; Tensas Parish field laborers quitting work to sing, pray, and shout; a Fernandina, Florida, black farmer teasing unfriendly whites and boasting of his flourishing crops; Tony brandishing a knife in anger over the uprooting of his corn and melons; a Yorktown black woman who spurned sturdy flannel dresses that reminded her of slavery; fiery Nat Frazier; oath-bound Cherokee County harvesters; long lines of black voters filing into the polling places behind the American flag, drum, fife, and fiddle; and George Houston, the tailor, who distinguished between shoddy and quality politicians—all of these were the manifestations of freedmen's self-esteem. They demonstrated the strengths and weaknesses of slaves making themselves free and creating their world. They seemed to have few doubts about their capabilities. Moreover, their actions reflected their habits of mutuality. Africa and America, the tribal village and the extended family, the plantation slave quarters, and the masters, too, reinforced those habits that were reshaped to serve the emergent freedmen community.

Taking Care of Themselves 3

The opinion and feeling among the negroes throughout this district, comprising the counties of Claiborne,
Copiah, Lawrence, Covington, Jones, Wayne, Jefferson, Franklin, Pike, Marion, Perry, Greene, Adams,
Wilkinson, Amite, Hancock, Harrison, and Jackson,
and Concordia and Tensas parishes, Louisiana, are almost unanimous on one point, viz: they will remain
on their old places this year for a support, and such
remuneration as the crop raised can give them, but
next year they will leave and make other arrangements.
They say that they have tried their old masters, know
what they require, and how they will be treated, and
unless they are now free, they will try some other
place and some other way of working. They take this
view not because they are tired of work, or because
they want to be idle, but because they are free and
want to find out in what their freedom consists. —
George D. Reynolds, Major, 6th United States Colored Heavy Artillery, and Acting Assistant Commissioner, Bureau of Freedmen, &c., Southern District of Mississippi, Natchez, Mississippi, September
25, 1865.

As the number of contrabands multiplied rapidly in late 1862 and early
1863, the army commanders were forced to provide for them. But a nag-
ging question remained with policy makers in Washington and among
journalists. Could the freedmen take care of themselves? Would they become a continual burden upon the government? The American Freedmen's Inquiry Commission, made up of Samuel Gridley Howe, Robert
Dale Owen, and James McKaye, was empowered to investigate and report to Secretary of War Stanton.[1] In the course of their inquiry and of

numerous probes by journalists and other visitors to the South, much was revealed about American middle-class attitudes. And much was discovered about the capabilities of the former slaves. Much too was revealed about the freedmen's self-supporting activities, as we shall see later. Charles Nordhoff spent some time in the South Carolina Sea Islands. There he found not the alleged "idle, dissolute, worthless set of creatures, who are supported at an enormous expense by an abolition government, etc., etc.," but a hard-working and productive and self-supportive people.[2] Thomas Carney, governor of Kansas, at about the same time assured the AFIC that 15,000-20,000 freed people then in his state differed not at all from whites. "That is, as their material interests dictate," the governor said, "they manifest a disposition to go where they can be most successful in maintaining themselves." The lazy and shiftless were to be found, to be sure, but Carney believed their proportions to be not greater among blacks than among whites.[3]

An army officer at Leavenworth testified to the courageous, capable, and industrious blacks in the state. These former Cherokee slaves "are the smartest blacks I ever saw fresh from the shackles," he declared. "Here in Ks. the colored man & colored families are indeed prosperous and happy."[4] When Captain Richard J. Hinton fresh from Kansas met with the commissioners in New York in December 1863, he cited a corroborating experience of a year earlier. Following the battle of Prairie Grove and after his march to Van Buren, General Blunt provided about 400 black men, women, and children with horses and mules taken from the Confederates and gave them subsistence. Put in charge of a blacksmith who had been a slave in Van Buren, they were told to go to Fort Scott. There Hinton met them and was given the responsibility of learning their numbers and provisions and of helping them to find work. They apparently scattered, many going into Kansas with most of their property. Hinton knew about fifty of them in Leavenworth, families headed by "blacksmiths, carpenters, and masons . . . who have obtained work, taken care of themselves, and are doing well." The blacksmith in charge of the original group purchased a lot and built a shop and cabin. In addition Hinton said he had heard directly that about 200 men, women, and children were working on farms and doing well. The remainder, mostly young men, went into the army as teamsters or soldiers. By the fall of 1863 the black community in Leavenworth numbered over 2,000. Nine-tenths of them had been slaves within the preceding four years. Hinton found an "astonishing number" who owned their own homes.[5]

John Eaton's responsibility for freedmen welfare covered a large area in Mississippi, Arkansas, and Tennessee. In 1863 he testified about the black people's ideas of freedom: There was a general idea that it would come as a result of the war. "They wished to be free from the necessity of working for others," he wrote, "but not from the necessity of working for themselves." Some had been accumulating money for many months before making their flight to freedom. He concluded that the majority "disappeared from official notice by fusing in with the general population" and were profitably employed to their own and the community's advantage.[6]

Many of the men found jobs as stevedores and as waiters on steamboats. But about 1,000 were employed in woodyards established by the freedmen's camp commanders. In addition, private business interests started woodyards and employed about 500 freedmen. The wood they cut from the abundant supply of trees along the Mississippi River and on the islands in it furnished fuel to steamboats and thus was an important commercial product. The district under Colonel Samuel Thomas in 1864 delivered 60,000 cords of wood to boats and gave freedmen earnings of more than $120,000. These former slaves had brought wagons and gear and teams from their plantations and used them in the woodyards. The government saved money because their use was not charged. Also, thousands of cords of wood were "a clean gift from the negroes to the Government." Men and women shared the work, the men chopping and hauling, the women "loading, unloading and cording" the wood when it arrived in the yard. Wood depots were located near camps, such as those at Young's Point, Paw Paw Island, Omega Landing, and Island 102. The income from the sale of wood significantly contributed to the livelihood of the families, which also raised their own food. The people depended less and less each month on government rations. Besides, a surplus went into the Freedmen's Fund. From it would come money to build schools and provide medicine. Eaton estimated that a well-managed policy of establishing woodyards would enhance self-support for 12,000 freed people in the Mississippi Valley.[7]

A small number of freedmen also supported themselves in this department by leasing and working five-acre tracts from the government. These were either abandoned plantations or lands confiscated under U.S. tax law. Some men obtained larger tracts, and their earnings were significant. For Eaton and others the amounts represented the measure of their capability for self-support. Robert Miner, for example, near Milliken's Bend, cultivated eighty acres of corn. In the Helena, Arkansas, district four men sold their crops for from $4,000 to $8,000. Many averaged $500, a considerable sum for that period. These were fortunate men, for they sold before the worm attacked crops in the area. There could be no question about their shrewdness and industriousness in managing these enterprises.[8] J. A. Saxton, father of the general who headed the Freedmen's Bureau in South Carolina and Georgia, supported that opinion. After a visit to St. Helena Island, he wrote, "In the Management of their own lands or business, no people could be more industrious or shrewd." When they could afford to do so, they were eager to obtain modern equipment and use new methods in cultivation.[9]

By early July 1864, Eaton reported, 7,000 acres were leased and cultivated by black people, some of whom managed 300- and 400-acre tracts. In sum, of the 113,000 freed people for whom he was responsible, Eaton reported 62,000 as self-supporting "the same as any industrial class anywhere else—as planters, mechanics, barbers, hackmen, draymen, etc., conducting enterprises on their own responsibility or working as hired laborers."[10]

From South Carolina and Georgia came similar testimony of industriousness and self-support. The commissioners learned that it was common for black men to be managers of rice plantations in Georgia and South Carolina. Around Savannah the "slaves" had property of their own. Many had garden patches in which they raised produce for sale in the city on Sundays.[11] Frederick A. Eustis, son of a Confederate general who had owned 116 slaves and a plantation on Ladies Island, gave conflicting testimony. Lying was the freedmen's worst habit, he asserted, but he also said that the freedman "has a profound sense of law—the greatest respect for it—and also a sense of justice." He concluded that they are a great deal more industrious than they used to be."[12]

When they arrived in Louisville, Kentucky, the AFIC heard complaints from an unnamed black man, and from many others, that restrictive laws prevented a black man from keeping "a tavern, or grocery store, or drygoods store." With respect to working in a shop with black men, however, there was less prejudice from whites in Louisville than from those in the free states. "A colored man can have a mechanics shop, and work in it," he stated. Black people can take care of themselves, he assured the inquirers. Most had worked on boats on the river until the previous year and were now going into the tobacco factories. As for himself, because his boat was too big to run in the summer, he wanted to find some trade into which he could put his money during the off season. He appeared no less an entrepreneur than familiar New England types.[13]

But his optimism could not be shared by Richard Holcombe, a Bladen Springs, Alabama, freedman. Holcombe had leased a building in the village so that he could pursue his trade of boot- and shoemaker. One month later a gang of five white men took him and his wife out of doors, demolished the shop and its materials, and whipped the two people in a woods two miles away. Holcombe, who was regarded by other whites with great respect before and after slavery, testified that the gang told him they had nothing against him "except that I was working for myself and not living with any white man . . . and [they] did not intend to let us live by ourselves." The city of Vicksburg passed ordinances aimed at the same goal of black subordination. As Samuel Thomas, assistant commissioner of the Freedmen's Bureau in Mississippi stated, the aim was "to drive out all independent negro labor." Draymen and hackmen were required to post bonds of $500 plus a license fee, and be freeholders. Slavery made the latter status virtually impossible, and state laws now prohibited blacks from owning land or holding property. Licensing was used to limit other trades sought by blacks.[14]

Sometime after passage of the second Freedmen's Bureau bill, of June 11, 1866, and of the Civil Rights Act passed earlier that year, Savannah laborers protested a local ordinance and mayoral action that would require them to wear a badge labeling them as "Porters." James Mackey of the Union League and 200 others petitioned against the designation, for in their opinion they were laborers and obviously proud of the identity. Fully conscious of their rights as citizens, they cited the Civil Rights Act, which guaranteed them the right to " 'make and enforce contracts' on the docks," Georgia statutes, and other federal laws. They contended that the mayor labored under a "misconception of the word *Porter* in the city laws which we have had no voice in enacting; notwithstanding 'all just laws, derive their powers from the consent of the governed.' " Finally, they asked for military protection against the "unconstitutional statutes, ordinances, regulations or custom not yet recognized by the Congress of the United States," lest they be reduced to paupers. It is fair to assume that the legal citations in the petition may have been more the work of the petitioners' attorney, the black radical lawyer A. Alporea

Bradley, who signed the protest in that capacity. More important was the use of the Union League as an independent organization of dock workers, as in the dock strike of 1865, quite unlike the stereotype of a Northern white tool of black manipulation. Perhaps it was such class-conscious and proud men who prompted William Allen to observe in 1865 that about the only ones whom the victorious North could depend upon for loyal Southern allies were the mechanics of Savannah.[15]

Not all the responses to an AFIC questionnaire were optimistic or positive about the freedmen's capability to endure free enterprise. The officer of the 8th Louisiana Colored Regiment stationed at Milliken's Bend, Louisiana, regarded the freed people as "valuable members of this community." But on the question of industriousness and self-support, Colonel H. Scofield wrote that the black people had enjoyed only one summer of freedom, under many disadvantages. "Too many seemed satisfied with a bare subsistence." He held out hope, however, that they would do better when they had homes and " a greater stimulus to industry." In this regard, two of the Kansas respondents to the AFIC held similar opinions. One suggested that Texas be made a "National Home for the freedmen of America." Hinton, too, believed that land should be "farmed out to them."[16]

Where this had been done, in the Sea Islands in 1863, for example, and where freedmen had purchased plantations, the optimism about their capabilities had been borne out. This was, of course, an issue among the freedmen's aid society workers who had come south with high purpose; it was not an issue for the freedmen there. But in order to stimulate support back home in New England, in Philadelphia, New York, and other areas north of the Mason-Dixon line, freedmen's aid workers in the islands reported on the successes. Reuben Tomlinson was the government's superintendent of freedmen in St. Helena and Ladies islands. His report recounted the amounts of cotton raised and sold by industrious freedmen farmers and their families. On one plantation the people earned enough to pay a handsome $400 (a bale of cotton) to the Rev. Dr. Solomon Peck for his advice and help, sent for a shipment of lumber from the north to build houses on lots made by dividing the plantation among them. Tomlinson also detailed the earnings of those who worked the cotton fields for others: For example, two elderly laborers, Anthony, aged over sixty, and Venus, aged over seventy, received $194.80 exclusive of their provision crop; on the Coffin Point plantation, Aaron and Judy received

Figure 1. "TEACHING THE FREEDMEN." From J. T. Trowbridge, *The South, a Tour of Its Battle Fields and Ruined Cities. . .* (Hartford, 1866)

Figure 2. "SLABTOWN," the freedmen's village near Hampton, Virginia

$136.48; Abel and family, $210.57; Amaretta and family, $335.24; Leah and Peter, $99.38; Hackliss and Phillis, $175.32; Frank and family, $181.93 George and family, $174.60; Miller and family, $188.67. Several other families earned from $50 to $100, all of these independent of the provision crops. And there were others in Tomlinson's brief catalog. All in all, he wanted everyone to know of the freedmen's industriousness and hence of their capability to function in his world of free enterprise. In a concluding paragraph, Tomlinson grew almost rhapsodic at the consumeristic prospect. But the figures reveal more than dollar amounts accumulated. They tell us of families laboring together, improving their material conditions, laying aside money that might hopefully be used to purchase a farm or a few acres for a homestead of their own.[17]

As we look back through the eyes of contemporary abolitionists come to do a good work among the freedmen, we are struck by their apparent naivete. Their sense of wonder at the successes and attainments of black people actually reveal a kind of ethnocentrism mixed with a real understanding of the freed people's true capabilities. A dedicated U.S. Army surgeon, Dr. A. Pettijohn, stationed at Alexandria, Virginia, revealed both tendencies in 1864. He described with sympathy and admiration the 1,200 schoolchildren in day schools, their parents in night schools, and their avid attention to learning. That he had to speak "soberly" in giving his "candid opinion" suggests that he feared for his credibility among the readers of the *Freedmen's Advocate*. But soberly and candidly he believed that "they are just as capable of learning the arts and sciences as the Anglo-American." For proof he listed the many kinds of artisans among the freedmen, and asserted that they handled mechanical tools "with as much facility . . . and evince as much ingenuity, as the white race." Dr. Pettijohn saw no need for experimental villages of contrabands, such as the one at Alexandria, where they would be taught trades and how to support themselves, at heavy government expense. They were already well qualified but needed only protection and prompt and fair payment. After all, hundreds of the contrabands had built their own homes in the Alexandria village and had paid for them, "besides supporting their families." His summary opinion was that "Many of the freedmen are worth more today than some of their superintendents." Having said that about their abilities, he appeared not to realize the condescension and white supremacy in declaring:

It makes the heart of the philanthropist rejoice to see the light of education gradually penetrating the minds of these poor little sable sons and daughters of oppression, and dispelling and rolling back the accumulated darkness and superstition of ages, and piercing the future of these children of Africa with rays of light and hope, that they, in time, may grow up to the full stature of educated and enlightened American citizens.[18]

Despite this clouded vision, the doctor did inform us of the freedmen's indisputable attainments.

Not far away, Charles Francis Adams, Jr., commander of a black cavalry unit stationed at Point Lookout, Maryland, took time in 1864 to reflect on the matter in a letter to his father. This young member of the antislavery Adamses was pained to think that unlike other oppressed peoples, such as the French peasants in 1789, the Africans in Haiti and San Domingo, "our Africans" did not rise up, even after arms had been thrust into their hands, and retaliate against cruel treatment. He could only conclude that the 200 years of American slavery had been patriarchal. The slaves had become "as a whole, not overworked, well fed and contented—greedy animals." Only this war and the teachings of the army would save them. With proper officers, blacks would make good soldiers in infantry but not in cavalry. In the latter they would be called upon to perform individual acts of valor beyond their will or capacity, according to Adams. Nevertheless, the young officer believed in the transformation of men fashioned by 200 years of cruel oppression into good soldiers. The army in peacetime would become the school in which "every soldier made a mechanic" would perform in the most disciplined fashion. Yet he claimed that his men did learn to take care of themselves at Point Lookout. "You cannot realize the industry, versatility and ingenuity called forth," he told his father. With only axes and nails supplied by the army, they were forced to fell trees, make their own lumber and shingles, and build stables and houses. "Every blacksmith, every carpenter, every shoemaker, every tailor, and every clerk," he boasted "is constantly busy and those who can do nothing else dig and carry until they can do something better." He even invented tasks "simply as discipline." The men baked bricks, made good pumps for the wells, built chimneys, and made plaster and mortar from the mud. The large open fireplace in his quarters showed "no little ingenuity and skilled labor." Compulsive and perfectionist, young Adams saw no contradiction between his men's skilled and controlled labor and his deprecation of their soldierly capabilities. He had only to be in touch with a fellow officer in the Sea Islands, Colonel Thomas Wentworth Higginson, to confront stories of valorous ex-slave infantrymen. There the 1st South Carolina Volunteers under his command raided Confederate strongholds. Higginson went into daring expeditions with his men; indeed, their courageous scouting had led the way for the regiment in the Florida and Georgia river campaigns. Higginson's classic book about his regiment is a sensitive appreciation of the men that is at odds with the perception of the younger Adams. Moreover, freedmen contradicted the cavalry officer's views in many ways.[19]

When freedmen did speak on the question, their statements were unequivocal, self-confident, trusting in the cooperation of the U.S. government and its officers. The 800 free families residing at the freedmen's village at Hampton, Virginia, enlighten us on this question. They lived and worked there, went to school, built five churches and paid their pastors, and operated a community-owned store. They lacked only the fee to obtain the lands nearby that they eagerly sought to convert into permanent homesteads. Spokesmen unhesitatingly asserted that if the farms of the former owners were operated in superior fashion before the war, then now their fields would "yield better, richer and heavier crops twice told than were ever known before under the system of slavery." Thirty-seven of the people attending the meeting at which these words were spoken had been raised on the farms. They knew that free black labor, with all its continuing deprivations, was superior to slave labor. "Those who assert that we are not capable of maintaining ourselves," they declared, "either wickedly misrepresent and malign us or . . . are grossly ignorant of our capabilities." They were confident of their ability to "build up a city upon our lands, as soon and as well, as orderly, as prosperous, as religious, as patriotic and as intelligent as could be done by any other people."[20]

Even more blunt and certain of themselves were the spirited editors of the New Orleans *Tribune*. The black community of that city had received the cooperation and help of white Treasury Department and army officers in January 1865. The free black editors were duly appreciative of that collaboration in their organization of equal rights and other associations. However, they rejected the tutorial stance of white friends. "We have asserted our manhood and we will do it again. We need friends, it is true; but we do not need tutors. The age of guardianship is past forever. We now think for ourselves, and we shall act for ourselves."[21] The bitter fact for the Hampton freedmen was that their declaration of independence came too late. President Johnson's policy of restoring property to former Confederates was well under way, and even the freedmen's offer of a liberal sum of money to the former owners to settle their claims proved to be of no avail. Such agonizing rebuffs proved as costly to the future of the South as the perennial refusal to honor the freedmen's demonstrated capabilities. Liberal Northerner and conservative Southerner alike misconstrued the freedman. Encrusted racist ideology distorted their vision of living reality.

Fresh from slavery, the black people were revitalized by their struggles to rediscover and redefine themselves and to establish stable communities. Their self-perception was implicit in their behavior. Their actions reflected a desire for self-improvement. As the Hampton freedmen had promised, they would build a city unsurpassed in America, provided the remaining fetters on their freedom were removed. Never completely losing sight of their African heritage, within slavery they had created a new community and a new identity, that of the Afro-American. They brought a synthesis of African and Euro-American cultural components with them into freedom. They defied and disproved friend and foe alike who doubted their capability to be free, to be as independent as any people could be in postwar Southern society undergoing the stress and conflict of change on a grand scale.

The freedmen began their own reconstruction when they entered contraband camps and freedmen villages. There, jointly with the army and the freedmen aid societies, freed people maintained the camps, reunited families, and participated in the first steps toward making the freedmen's community. Before we take a closer look at those settlements, let us consider some other ways in which freedmen fashioned and used instruments of self-help and cultural independence. Together with their positive self-perception and their demonstrated self-support activities, these expressed the ethos of mutuality that would help to carry them through an unexpected inferno.

Churches formed the hub in the wheel of black community life. Freed people worshiped in them, heard political as well religious themes presented in their ministers' sermons, listened to the reading of " 'quirin' " letters, organized benevolent societies and schools, witnessed dramatic productions, and attended concerts. Freed people gathered in their churches for all these reasons and for the opportunity it gave to meet friends and relatives. The churches of black people were truly social centers, community centers. Reflecting on the church at the end of the nineteenth century, a Georgia black minister declared, "It is [the black man's] only institution and forms the center of his public life. He turns to it not only for his spiritual wants, but looks forward to it as the center of his civilization." The centrality of the black church is revealed in the experience of a Northern missionary. He had difficulty in 1869 in establishing services among Southern blacks. Unless he had a black church available, he could not make progress. "He cannot preach to the colored people," a correspondent reported; "neither can he organize schools among them."[22]

During slavery, masters were solicitous of their slaves' spiritual needs and provided churches and opportunities for worship. But these too frequently were under the direct control and surveillance of the masters. Especially after the Nat Turner insurrection of 1831, masters became even more uneasy about unsupervised slave gatherings, such as those in churches. They tightened their grip on the churches in order to maintain their social control over their laboring population. When emancipation opened up the way to a new life, freed people brought their churches out into the open, free from both the control of whites and the solicitous concern they expressed. Thus the Reconstruction years witnessed an exodus remarkable for the volume, speed, and ease with which it progressed. The emergence of the freedmen's churches provided a dynamic thrust to the making of the freedmen's community. South Carolina historians Simkins and Woody were not overstating the case when they wrote, "The winning of religious independence was perhaps the most momentous social change of Reconstruction."[23] Its revolutionary significance is even greater when considered in the context of freedmen's assertions of political independence and their determination to achieve an independent economic base on the land.

The coincidence of the freed people's movements for religious and political independence is not accidental. It occurred, to be sure, after Congress passed the Reconstruction Acts in 1867. But both the religious and the political movements were reconstructive endeavors made *by* the freed people. There are two indicators of the intimate connection between these two forms of community definition. One is in the roles of freedmen clergy. The second is in the political uses made of the churches. In addition, the process of separation as freedmen conducted it tells us much about their self-reliance.

Whites complained during the Reconstruction era that black preachers were becoming too political and therefore were posing a threat to white supremacy. Although their apprehension was exaggerated (for not all black clergy were political leaders), their appraisal was close to the mark. A Lumberton, North Carolina, freedman, Benjamin Bethea, was slain by Klansmen because he had not only preached the Gospel but also Radical Republican politics. His crime was that he had brought "politics and the wrongs of the colored people into his prayers."[24] Others like Bethea were to be found throughout the rural South. They were former slaves, artisans, and farmers and former servants and field laborers. We shall meet some of them again as we examine the matter of local black leadership. Many suffered persecution for their leadership roles as influential political and religious men in their communities. They led a movement of cultural independence and resistance.

Even before the Reconstruction Acts enfranchised the freedmen, the struggle to win the right to vote was backed by the black churches. They were established churches that had been central to the lives of free black communities during slavery. In 1865, when most Southern states enacted proscriptive black codes and virtually restored slavery, the black churches were probably the only places secure and suitable enough to house significant rallies and meetings. Thus in the 1865 campaign for suffrage the following churches served as meeting halls: in Norfolk, the Baptist Church, the Bute Street African Methodist Episcopal Church, the Catherine Street Baptist Church; in Petersburg, the Union Street Methodist Church; in Nashville, the AME Church; and in Charleston, the Zion Church.[25] Two years later we find black churches hosting Union League or Loyal League meetings of freedmen. Among the Baptist preachers who combined secular with clerical roles and whose churches were used for these purposes, were Richard Burke in Gainesville, Alabama; Romulus Moore in Columbia County, Georgia; Thomas M. Allen in Butts County, Georgia; and Elias Hill in Clay Hill District, South Carolina.[26] The Methodist minister J. Aaron Moore in Meridian, Mississippi, was, like some of the others, a state legislator and a local political leader. His church was a community center. Similar situations were to be found in Huntsville, Alabama, and Aberdeen, Mississippi, amid the plantations and rural settlements of freed people, in the world of the former field slaves.[27]

Separation from white-dominated congregations moved rapidly, as the reformation and establishment of black Baptist churches demonstrates.

As the largest denomination of black Christians in the South this was a significant movement. For example, in Virginia, by the end of 1866 every town and city of the state had separate black Baptist and Methodist congregations. A year later the Virginia State Baptist Association (black) was organized at Portsmouth.[28] Although there appears to have been a certain guarded cordiality and mutual willingness among North Carolina Baptists to separate along racial lines, the tempo of black removal suggests a quiet self-determination among freed people. The historian of that state's movement writes that between 1865 and 1867 "most Negroes desired freedom of religious action and departed." A general association of black Baptists was organized in 1867 and a state convention in 1869. The movement proceeded with little bitterness, indeed, probably with great consideration for one another among these black and white Christians.[29] State organizations, made up of hundreds of local churches and local associations, appeared in Arkansas in 1868, Alabama in 1868, Kentucky in 1869, and Mississippi and Tennessee in 1872. In South Carolina the secession of tens of thousands of black Baptists and the formation of their own churches was practically completed by 1874. Only 1,614 remained in the white churches.[30] Of course, this movement was not limited to the Baptists. Methodists and Congregationalists had similar experiences.[31]

The movement of freed people from the countryside to the larger town and cities placed a heavy responsibility on existing black churches. To the best of their abilities these churches provided shelter and immediate relief to their liberated brothers and sisters. Thus the Union Baptist Church of Baltimore grew from 200 to 926 members at the war's end. Freedmen seeking aid in Washington, D.C., flocked to the oldest black Baptist church in the city. The Nineteenth Street Baptist Church was reported to have added thousands to its membership lists. Petersburg Gillfield Baptist Church played a similar role. Its minister and his congregation organized the Gillfield Baptist Beneficial Society. A Richmond black church in 1865 organized a Freedmen's Aid Sewing Society, "for the benefit of the poor of our city."[32] This was in the tradition of the Free African Society and the earlier black churches in Philadelphia and Baltimore. A plea to New Orleans churches during the summer of 1865 for contributions of clothing to aid poor freedmen met no response from the white churches. The black churches gave fifty barrels (presumably used clothing) and ten boxes "full of good garments." These were sent into Louisiana's Red River

counties and other places in the state. The Freedmen's Bureau officer in
the city felt this showed there was no basis to stories that "negroes do
not pity one another."[33]

Savannah's long-established Baptist churches faced a great community
task when freedmen following General Sherman arrived in December
1864. When the general and Secretary of War Stanton met with black
community leaders there in January 1865, they conferred with twenty
ministers of Savannah's black churches. The spokesman was sixty-seven-
year-old Garrison Frazier, a recently ordained Baptist minister and only
eight years earlier a slave. Among them was Reverend Ulysses L. Houston,
another former slave who had bought his freedom. Later he would become
chairman of a convention of black ministers in the South Carolina and
Georgia Sea Islands. The men who conferred with Stanton and Sherman
declared their hopes for land and for the right to support themselves.
Theirs was a sweeping prescription for community that went far beyond
mere immediate welfare measures, however important in alleviating the
freedmen's distress.[34]

In answer to a question, Frazier replied that freed men and women
would prefer to live "by ourselves" rather than "scattered among the
whites." He believed it would take years for the white South to overcome
prejudice against blacks. Significantly, a similar view was expressed by
Foote hundreds of miles away in Yazoo, Mississippi. The Georgia Baptist
minister coupled his opinion with the desire to be self-sufficient on land.[35]

Freedmen demonstrated their self-reliance in the organization and construction of churches. The prospect of one day having a church building
of his own was a powerful stimulus to the freedman's energetic activity,
to his willingness to sacrifice to achieve that goal. Freedmen improvised
churches and pooled their small savings until they could construct impressive edifices. Some worshiped in the basements of white churches,
as in Raleigh, North Carolina, and Jackson, Mississippi, in boxcars in Atlanta, a tobacco warehouse in Danville, Virginia, improvised sheds and
"brush harbors" in many places in Mississippi and Georgia; in stables
and carpenter shops, even in an old slave pen in Savannah, and in the
homes of individuals. In Richmond, the Rising Mt. Zion Baptist Church
grew out of prayer meetings in a woman's home. Lime workers in the
same city meeting in a home in the early 1870s formed a Sunday school.[36]

The freedmen's spontaneity in establishing their own churches was
matched by their stubbornness. The Protestant Episcopal Church in Ala-

bama gave up trying to evangelize blacks because, "the ex-slaves would take neither their politics nor their religion from their former owners."[37] Even a friendly carpetbagger in Yazoo, Mississippi, appeared to be displeased that a local black leader had established an independent freedmen's center in the AME Church. The Northerner saw this as a segregation effort on the part of the blacks.[38] In some parts of Louisiana, French Roman Catholic planters had denied their slaves any other form of worship but theirs. After emancipation it was learned that these slaves had secretly maintained Baptist worship for many years. Long after emancipation, however, some black Baptist preachers sprinkled infants with water "as an act of the consecration of the child to the Lord."[39] In Thomasville, Georgia, late in 1865, black members of the Methodist Church decided to separate and build their own. Blacks in the Baptist church in the town decided that they too would separate. When they offered to buy the church building, the white members asked a price that appeared inflated. Moreover, the blacks insisted, they were two-thirds of the church membership and they claimed that two-thirds of the church building rightfully was theirs. In the county, by 1900, there were 98 black churches, most of them Baptist, for a population of 17,450 black people. That meant a church for about every 150 persons. The proliferation of these and other churches in that county and in other Southern localities was due in large measure to the spontaneous actions of "self-called" preachers.[40] Peter Kolchin has illuminated this for us in his study of the Alabama freedmen. Most black ministers, he points out, were former slaves, had no experience in the pulpit and were ordained in their late sixties. They were men of little wealth and little education. Thus, studying the 1870 census, he found that in a sample of six counties of black population density, eighteen of thirty-one such ministers had no real or personal property. Seven of them had a net worth of less than $500; three had between $500 and $1,000; and three exceeded $1,000.[41] When the first AME church conference of Savannah met in 1866, scarcely a man could read and write. "We had to get little white boys and poor white men to act as Secretaries of the Quarterly Conference," wrote one of the participants. Yet they persisted, studied, and learned to read and write and to build churches and organize the communities around them.[42]

The Baptist church afforded freedmen their greatest opportunities for spontaneous participation and leadership. The powerful and irresistible call to preach would instill confidence in a man, according to the Reverend W. H. Holloway of Thomas County, Georgia. He would then take

his family and relatives and move away to establish a new church in which
he could "make a better preach." Holloway believed that if the membership rolls of black churches were studied, they would show that many
churches were largely familial and that the first preacher "was some venerable patriarch." He believed that two-thirds of the churches had begun
in this manner.[43] Historians should of course pursue his recommendations
and research the data; meanwhile, his suggestion remains respectable and
valuable. It tends to support not only the idea of a positive self-perception
among freedmen but the activist role of black men in self-defined communities. It tends, too, to reinforce the concept of an unbroken habit
of mutuality and deepen it with the notion of family organization. Thus,
as its many expressions bear witness, the black church separation movement during Reconstruction emerges as central to the making of the freedmen's community.

Just as the church was nurtured in the underground of slavery, so was
the little known mutual-aid society. Both of them bore fruit in a freedmen's community. And the latter of the two is all the more striking,
since conventional histories tell us that masters maintained social services
for their slaves, the productive as well as the unproductive ones. True,
paternalism of this kind probably was well established, and it does go far
toward sustaining the masters' positive image in history. But the examples
of the *slave* mutual-aid societies that did exist certainly diminish the patriarchal postures of the plantation owners.

Prince Rivers, the sergeant of the 1st South Carolina Colored Regiment,
gained his prominence even earlier than the war years by his leadership
of such a slave mutual-aid society. Another wartime black hero, Robert
Smalls, told of similar societies in antebellum Charleston. Despite South
Carolina's legal prohibition against gatherings of more than four black
men without a white man present, Smalls said he belonged to *seven* societies organized to help "one another in sickness and distress." Thus
masters were not alone as a class in ignoring legal codes to suit their purposes. Slaves apparently found the means to protect their collective life
beyond the masters' laws and customs. Even so, Smalls made clear that
his clandestine associational experiences were limited to Charleston. He
did not believe that similar organizations existed on plantations except
for secret church societies.[44]

In this connection an Alabama Baptist deacon recalled that ten to
twenty years before emancipation slaves had organized a prayer band
to "pray for our freedom," which had met outside of town on Friday

nights under a large oak tree. They had a password, "the hindering cause."
Each slave softly uttered the phrase and was answered by others, "as he
came under the boughs of the tree," then sat in the bushes waiting the
hour for "united supplications."[45] Another Alabama black clergyman
recalled how fellow slaves, knowing that he could read, bought him a
Bible and had him read to them "the sayings of God." Their eagerness
was expressed in their working his patch in the one-acre "night farm"
slaves were allotted to raise provisions in order that he might continue
to study the Bible and read it to them.[46] This was the sort of information the American Freedmen's Inquiry Commission did not receive and
did not pass on. Its investigation and reports were based largely on free
black urban communities and army-supervised contraband camps. Nevertheless, the commission made a weighty contribution toward a policy
of aid in the transition from slavery to freedom. Its findings of self-support and self-sufficiency in New Orleans, Washington, Baltimore, Louisville, and in the Canadian free black communities indicated freedmen's
habits of mutuality.[47] The fact that free black communities supported
their own poor, that there were no beggars among them, and that they
were not to be found on county or parish relief rolls now appears to have
had counterparts deep in the heart of slave territory.

Emerging into legal freedom, former slaves applied the measures of
mutuality to one another, as in Nashville's Provident Association, with
its own coal and wood depots, soup kitchen, and physician.[48] A white
missionary in Norfolk was struck by the numbers of sick, of burials, and
of poor relief societies "in all the colored churches, no matter how poor
and beggarly the membership."[49] Similar groups could be found among
freedmen in relatively remote places such as Athens, Alabama; Aberdeen,
Mississippi, and Ocala, Florida.[50] In west central Georgia's Pike and Upson counties, freedmen organized equal rights associations that included
among their purposes "to establish schools, bury the dead, and employ
lawyers," "attend to the poor and sick . . . and cultivate good feeling between the freedmen and their former masters."[51] That there was a proliferation of benevolent and fraternal associations from Virginia to Texas
is apparent from the records of the Freedmen's Savings and Trust Company. Chartered by Congress in 1865 to serve freedmen, its deposit ledgers carried hundreds of churches and benevolent societies. If we take
Norfolk as one example, depositors included associations such as the Oystering, Laboring, Morning Glory, Baptist, National Workingmen's, Job

Benevolent, Laboring Mechanical, Catholic Benevolent, and Soldiers'
Aid Societies, among many others. We also find the Norfolk AME Church,
five Baptist churches, and a Presbyterian church keeping funds in the Norfolk branch of the Freedmen's Bank. A similar pattern of association depositors may be found in the bank's records for Tallahassee, Jacksonville,
Washington, New Orleans, which have been sampled for this study, and
probably in each of the fifteen branches across the South. The New Orleans
branch had a particularly rich variety of such depositors, which included
church, benevolent, fraternal, trade union, temperance, and building and
loan associations. Margaret Neary found these "Negro Business and Labor Clubs, Organizations and Unions, 1867-1874" in her search of the
Richmond, Virginia, branch records:

> Agricultural Association, Bakers' Society, Coopers' Society, Grand
> Lodge of Quarry Men, Lincoln Union Shoemakers, Manchester
> Laborers, Mechanics Union Society, National Laboring Club, Or-
> iginating Sons and Daughters of Business, Richmond Education
> Association, Stevedores' and Waggoners' Association, Tobacco Fac-
> tory Club, Tobacco Laborers Association, Union Laboring Branch,
> Union Laboring Class, and Warehouse Combined National.

She also discovered fifteen church and fraternal-aid groups, in the same
period.[52] From the "pony purse" for a specific and immediate relief problem to the established bank account for long-term purposes, it is obvious
that freedmen instrumentalized the benevolent society in the making of
their community. Moreover, there was a significant working-class component in that process.

The ill-fated Freedmen's Savings and Trust Company, was organized
first at Washington in 1865 and at other cities in the South within three
to five years later. A short life was guaranteed by the apparent misman-
agement and misconduct that resulted in the collapse of the institution
in 1874, robbing thousands of depositors of their savings and their hopes
to buy land and homes. Between the fall of 1866 and April 1867 depositors in the Charleston, South Carolina, branch had accumulated enough
to be able to draw $31,000 in order to pay U.S. tax commissioners for
land. The Beaufort, South Carolina, branch was expected at that date to
acquire 10,000 depositors from the 35,000 black people in the district,
a sanguine projection based on the rate of new depositors since the branch

was established. From Vicksburg, Mississippi, a newspaper reporter in 1871 wrote that "a great majority are saving as well as earning." His informants assured him that many were buying lands and others were "accumulating money" in the Freedmen's Savings Bank, with the intention of buying homes "at no distant day." The actuary of the bank in Washington reported in 1868 that "poor but industrious colored men" were constantly applying for loans, able to pay for money to "extend their frugal business" but holding no government bonds that they could offer as security. The actuary hoped that Congress would legislate authority to make such real-estate loans less difficult for freed people.[53]

It would be difficult to separate the two driving forces in the freed people's strivings, the desire for land and the desire for schools. Both served to build and strengthen families and communities. The measure of that ardor to learn may be taken in terms of the freed people's use of leisure time, such as it was, or in the moments they could snatch away from their tasks to study.[54] Freed adults flocked into evening and Sabbath schools to probe the supposed mysteries of the books. Black soldiers and working people took advantage of educational opportunities provided by philanthropic societies black and white and by the army and the Freedmen's Bureau. They also very significantly supported their own private black schools and teachers.

The depth of their commitment was caught in the word picture drawn by J. W. Alvord, Freedmen's Bureau inspector of schools, after a swing through all of the Southern states in 1865: ". . . the laboring classes . . . may be often seen during the intervals of toil, when off duty as servants, on steamboats, along the railroads, and when unemployed in the streets of the city or on plantations, with some fragment of a spelling book in their hands, earnestly at study." Two years earlier, when the journalist Nordhoff had visited in the South Carolina Sea Islands, he had described virtually the same scenes there.[55]

A New England man in St. Louis furnished another glimpse at the devotion of freedmen to learning. In the black-owned barber shop that he frequented, when some of the eight to ten journeymen and apprentices were not busy at their trade, there would be "more or less of reading or teaching" among them. "Sometimes I saw one reading the Bible, sometimes one poring over a spelling-book, sometimes a journeyman teaching an apprentice the first reading lessons in the primer, or hearing him recite a spelling lesson."[56]

Black soldiers recruited in the South were among the most enthusiastic searchers for knowledge. In each of the camps of the black regiments
at Port Hudson, a school was housed in the best-built cabin, according to
an officer.[57] Many of Florida's 1,044 freedmen recruits learned their
abc's in the army, and as early as 1863 soldiers were conducting schools
for the black troops.[58] At Fort Livingston an army surgeon with time on
his hands proposed to teach the black troops there. The officers sneered,
but the men readily accepted his offer. The doctor taught the ten bright-
est men for two hours a day. Each of them agreed to teach another class
of four for an equal period of time. They were most successful, and later
the surgeon learned that the pupils who had begun with the alphabet a
year earlier were now subscribing to over forty copies of *Harper's Weekly*
and *Frank Leslie's Weekly.*[59] Soldiers of the 62nd and 65th U.S. Colored
Infantry Regiments stationed in Texas in January 1866 exceeded even
this display of dedication. A spontaneous movement among the men of
the 62nd Regiment raised $4,000 and an additional $1,000 from the officers to establish a school for black people in Missouri. The enlisted men
of the 65th Regiment contributed $1,360. The result of their activity
was the establishment of Lincoln Institute in Jefferson City, a respected
institution of higher education known today as Lincoln University.[60] Alvord, generalizing on the basis of his tour of inspection, in 1865, asserted
that "Regiments of colored soldiers have nearly all made improvements
in learning."[61]

The children came first. Freed people made the school experience a
priority for their youngsters. Their readiness to pay tuition and to support teachers, black and white, was important to them. It was exhilara-
ting for the children to be learning to read and write, to solve problems
in arithmetic, to know the geography of their county and state, their
country and the world. "As the children repeat their lessons at home,"
Alvord reported, "parents become thoughtful, acquire many new ideas,
and are led to prize their families." While literacy was an important and
desirable objective for them, freedmen were concerned with additional
gains from learning to read and write. Plantation laborers near Savannah
were vexed to learn in February 1867 that the owner of the land on which
they worked reneged on a contract stipulation that they should control
all the houses. The special point of discontent was the denial of a house
for a teacher of their school, which would be discontinued as a result.
The owner said he needed the house for a family residence. The laborers

had other views: "He's no use for de house nohow. Dem sees how you's teachin we, an' gibin' we so much sense, dey's feared we git so wise dey can't cheat we." The people offered to leave the place, as the contract now "was not bind," if the owner refused to let the teacher stay. He did refuse when one of the freed people was sent to Savannah to state the case. There was "much mourning" over this rebuff and when the teacher advised them not to leave.[62]

The search for schools for their children led freedmen to take their families to the larger towns. But an experience in Louisiana in 1865 best illustrates the zeal for schools, especially among the middle and lower classes. A military order had suspended the collection of a general tax for black schools. This was regarded as a severe blow to the excellent system created by an order of General Nathaniel Banks in 1864. In its two years of existence the system had conducted 150 schools for black children, employed 265 teachers, many of them Southern whites, and taught 14,000 children. In addition 5,000 adults had received instruction, among them 1,000 soldiers. Freed people therefore considered it important enoug to their welfare to petition General E. S. Canby to collect a tax to support their own schools, and this already on top of the public school tax they were already paying and from which they derived no benefits. Wealthy creoles and the outspoken New Orleans *Tribune* opposed the added tax "on the ground that it was without representation." But the poorer and unschooled classes persisted in pouring in the petitions. "I saw one from the plantations across the river [from New Orleans]," wrote the Freedmen's Bureau's schools inspector, "at least thirty feet in length, representing ten thousand negroes. It was affecting to examine it to note the names and marks (x) of each, a long list of parents ignorant themselves but begging that their children might be educated." Although extremely poor, they promised they would pay for the schools. Moreover, the black children in the city schools sent in their own petition to the Freedmen's Bureau "praying . . . to sustain the colored schools of Louisiana."[63]

The mutual stimulation of parents and children led the elders to take an active part in the maintenance and multiplication of schools. Estimate of the amounts of money that freedmen spent on schools must be rough, but W. E. B. Du Bois developed some statistics in one of his *Atlanta Studies*. During 1866, he found, freedmen had contributed $18,500 to a

total of $224,359. More than $123,000 had come from the Freedmen's
Bureau, which had the primary responsibility under the 1866 law em-
powering it to support such schools. Private benevolent associations collected $82,000. School expenditures peaked in 1868, when out of a to-
tal $2,025,896, freedmen contributed $360,000. The Freedmen's Bureau
furnished $965,806, and benevolent associations, $700,000. As the to-
tals declined during the next two years to about $1.5 million in each
year, freedmen raised $190,000 in 1869 and $200,000 in 1870. By that
time public school systems were created by many of the Southern states
under Radical Republican and freedmen control. There may be some
underestimation of the total financial cost to the entire black community, for there is no differentiation along color lines among benevolent associations' contributions.[64] At least two Afro-American organizations
however did play a significant role in the maintenance of schools and
the supply of black teachers. One was the African Civilization Society,
with headquarters in Brooklyn, New York. Established in 1858 by Reverend Henry Highland Garnet and other Northern free blacks, the society espoused the rejection of the United States for its racial policies
and practices. These men had emerged as advocates of emigration from
a prolonged debate in the black community after the passage of the 1850
Fugitive Slave law. One destination was to be Africa. There educated and
Christian black men from America would start a new life by evangelizing
and "civilizing" a heathen and backward people. But the ambivalence of
their position was overcome by the outbreak of the Civil War: Their emi-
grationist objectives were reversed, and their subsequent action during the
war demonstrated that their fundamental objective, as ever, was a reformation of America. One significant step in that direction was their active role as individuals in recruiting black Union troops. They took a second step as an organization when they early began to send teachers to
freedmen's and contrabands' schools. The African Civilization Society
began its work in Washington, D.C., in January 1864 when it sent two
teachers there to organize a school of 250 students. The society enlarged
its work and by 1868 had furnished 129 black teachers and assistants for
8,000 children and adults. After extending its work in the District of Columbia and in Maryland and Virginia, the society went into North Carolina, South Carolina, Georgia, Mississippi, and Louisiana. The society published a weekly and a monthly journal. The latter, under the editorship

of Reverend Rufus L. Perry, general superintendent of schools for the
society, was sent to freed people. In many places, it was claimed, the monthly *Torchlight* served as a substitute for the primer.[65]

The Missionary Society of the AME Church was the other principal
Afro-American promoter and supporter of schools. The society collaborated with other organizations in supporting sixty schools. Forty thousand
children and adults attended the Sabbath schools connected with the
AME churches. From 1862 to 1867 the society received and spent
$36,383.[66] Such aid was well known in free black communities during
the antebellum period.

It was a revelation however to U.S. officials and philanthropic workers when they learned of schools taught and financed by blacks in Southern towns, some established before the war. Washington's blacks, for example, sent 1,400 students to twenty private schools supported by tuition payments in 1863.[67] Baltimore Afro-Americans had supported two
private schools for ten years by 1805, under a legacy of a black man. All
told, seven schools in the city were taught and entirely paid for by black
people.[68] Alvord reported similar private efforts in Halifax County, North
Carolina. He also received reports of independent black schools in Louisville, Nashville, Memphis, and Knoxville.[69] In addition, others reported
cases of freedmen raising money to purchase lots or to pay for buildings
to house schools in Columbia, South Carolina, and Canton, Mississippi.[70]
In Greenville, North Carolina, in the summer of 1865, blacks contributed
$60 per month to support teachers.[71] When General Charles Howard
visited Thomasville, Georgia, in December, he found a colored resident
teaching a school without even a suitable building. Leading black people
in town promised to repair a brick building located by Howard if they
could have it for a school.[72] During October 1865, private schools were
conducted by twelve black men and women teachers, including one army
sergeant, in a dozen Mississippi cities and towns. In Aberdeen, Mississippi,
freed people who worshiped in the basement of the Baptist church spent
their own money to furnish it for use as a schoolroom. The trustees, however, refused to give them that privilege.[73] In remote St. Mary's Parish,
Louisiana, where schools with white teachers had failed, a planter had
induced a young black woman to teach a school for which he paid the
rent. It was conveniently located near six plantations, and twenty-three
children from five to thirteen years old attended. The plantation laborers not only sent their children but paid a monthly tuition "out of their

hard-earned wages," according to the planter. It only proved to him that
a black woman with an ordinary education could educate twenty-three
"full blooded negro children who had never been ten miles from the plantation where they were born." Besides, he said, they could be taught as
much as any white child of the same age. Above all, he was convinced
that "with very little assistance, the *negroes will educate their own children*" (*his* emphasis).[74] An untold number of such arrangements between
planters and laborers were made in the South. Where labor was in great
demand in January 1866, as in Arkansas, planters paid relatively high
wages, plus board, and furnished cabins, fuel, medical attention, and
schools for the children of laborers.

When Alvord made his fifth semiannual report of freedmen's schools
on January 1, 1868, he could show that freedmen owned 364 school
buildings. This was sufficient answer to those who feared and predicted
that freed people "can't take care of themselves." They had surged forward toward the spelling book and readers, and where they could find
no teachers, they had devised ways to teach one another. Freed men and
women expressed "A willingness, even an *ambition*" to pay their own
way. As with the construction of their own churches, freed people improvised schoolrooms until something better could be built.[75] In Greensboro, North Carolina, for instance, with their Quaker teachers they shared old government wagon shops for schoolrooms. Freed people frequently said that if they were given a chance, "we want to show how much we
can do *ourselves*."[76] That independent spirit and the actions it inspired
among freed people in establishing and operating schools may indeed have
been challenged and stimulated by the Northern associations that sent
schoolmarms and masters. One of the most progressive achievements in
American society was the educational activity of the American Missionary Association, the Congregational Church, the Friends Society, the
American Freedmen's Union Commission, the boards of the Presbyterian
and Methodist Episcopal churches, and various Northern states' freedmen's
aid associations. It may be a tribute to their exemplary work that in some
places freed people tried to carry on and to maintain their own schools
and employ black teachers. Many of them taught in remote plantation
schools or in small towns and villages. There must have been hundreds of
places in which freed people, seemingly isolated from the affairs of centers such as Mobile or Savannah or New Orleans or Vicksburg fell on their
own resources to establish schools and create other community institu-

tions. The West Virginia village in which Booker T. Washington spent his childhood may serve as one example. When General Charles Howard stopped in Tinkersville, a freedmen's village in the Kanawha Valley salt-mining country during his inspection tour of 1867, these working people and others of neighboring villages had already established seven schools. In September 1865 when they had discovered a newcomer in their midst, a young light-colored ex-soldier from Ohio, who could read, the Tinkersville freed people hired him to be a teacher and paid him from their meager wages. Louis Harlan tells us in his biography of Washington that the Tinkersville folk opened the school as a strictly self-supportive effort. They had no assistance from "the local whites, the county, or township board of education, or the newly established Freedmen's Bureau in Washington." The school was in the home of Reverend Lewis Rice, or "Father Rice" as he was known throughout the Kanawha Valley, and the classroom was his bedroom rearranged to provide three or four hand-hewn benches for about thirty students. Rice was pastor of the African Zion Baptist Church in Tinkersville and appears to have been a leader of this community of salt furnace workers.[77] In Mississippi the Freedmen's Bureau educational officer believed that in similar cases in his state the sparse populations did not come to the attention of the Northern associations.[78] This would tend to support the idea of independent spontaneous activity in freedmen's communities.

Florida freedmen demonstrated a militant spirit of self-reliance. At Apalachicola a freedman tried to run a school at his own expense, with local black teachers even though they were untrained. Pensacola blacks preferred teachers of their own color, according to a white teacher. "Those fanatical colored men who belong to the so-called Equal Rights Club," he wrote, "opposed by every means in their power, the employment of Northern white teachers." At St. Augustine some black pupils left a free American Missionary Association school to attend "a tuition school taught by a Negro lady." The local school board in 1869 appointed black teachers rather than whites under pressure from the black community, according to an observer.[79] Inasmuch as these descriptions or reports were made by white persons, one of them apparently aggrieved, the issue may wrongly have been placed on color. It is clear that freed people were declaring their self-confidence and desire to conduct their own school affairs. It may also be possible that they made the decision to pay tuition turn on the question of color. But self-determination as persons may have been the ultimate and stronger motivation. Clearly, in all three of the Florida towns, freedmen's behavior sprang from group consciousness, but it should not be considered as exclusive. The importance of Northern men and women in the Reconstruction black educational process cannot be diminished. These visitors taught freed people to read and write and to enter a world wider than the plantation. They in turn were allowed to share the lives of freed people in meaningful ways. Above all, the freed people played a creative role in establishing schools and in sustaining another institution of their own—a legacy of old habits of mutuality.[80]

These pages have focused on those traits and activities that transformed slave and chattel into citizen and person; the slave quarters into freedmen's village, farm, and neighborhood. The rebirth of Afro-American community also occurred within the contraband camps and military freedmen's villages. It will strengthen our appreciation of the process of change to go with the fleeing slaves into those settlements.

The Rebirth of Community in Contraband Camp and Freedmen's Village

> ... and they have some very successful municipal governments on their various islands—formed and carried on by themselves. One (Skiddaway) has a black governor. —William F. Allen, Letters, July 1865.

The contraband camp was a contrivance of military commanders early in the war when confronted by the problem of human "property" in their midst. Some officers, respecting the rights of property owners and believing they had no authority to interfere with the return of fugitive slaves, were totally inhospitable to them. But when General Benjamin Butler at Fortress Monroe on the Virginia peninsula in June 1861 refused to return slaves to a Confederate officer who claimed them, he forced the government to formulate a policy covering such cases. While Congress grappled with the question during the next ten months, he and other officers "solved" the problem by declaring fugitives to be contraband of war. Their problem became much more complicated when they had to provide for the fugitives' welfare. Increasingly, the solution lay in paid employment to buttress freed people's self-support in aid of the military establishment that was their host and employer. A somewhat different approach was dictated by the particular situation in the Sea Islands after Union occupation in November 1861. There the masters fled and the slaves stayed. The former slave community was hardly disrupted. But, ironically, Union victories in the Mississippi Valley and the trans-Mississippi areas, and later in Sherman's march through Georgia and the Carolinas, disrupted former slave communities. The result was to place a great obligation upon the commanders to care for the freed people. For the fugitives and the uprooted the task was to find lost or temporarily

separated members of families, obtain food, shelter, work and to begin
life anew.

President Lincoln's Emancipation Proclamation of January 1, 1863,
the Confiscation Act of 1862, newly enacted federal tax laws, and above
all the decision to enlist black troops all contributed to the need for a
so-called contraband policy. The Emancipation Proclamation turned out
to be less of a paper tiger than some abolitionists had charged. In fact,
during the next year the proclamation was the authority for large-scale
emancipations by the marching Union army. Even before its announce-
ment, Union forces at Fernandina, Florida, in 1862 recruited black laborers, who then secured their freedom. Thousands were flocking into
Alexandria, Hampton, and Washington, D.C. At the mouth of the Mississippi after the capture of New Orleans in the spring of 1862, a whole
city and its surrounding regions were declared free by General Benjamin
F. Butler. When General Ulysses S. Grant secured Grand Junction, Mississippi, in November 1862, former slaves by the thousands sought freedom and his protection. After January 1, 1863, the proclamation enjoyed even greater application as Union troops battled eastward across the
South.[1]

Commanders appointed officers to supervise the work of "Negro Affairs." The responsibility fell largely into the hands of chaplains or others
normally regarded conversant with such matters as caring for homeless
and poor people. Grant appointed the chaplain of the 27th Ohio Volunteers, John Eaton, as his chief of Negro Affairs to supervise the massive
unmilitary job of social welfare throughout his western command. In the
other sectors, Rufus Saxton, Thomas Conway, Charles B. Wilder, Joseph
Warren, and Horace James, like Eaton, mixed pietistic and sentimental
rationales for their work with the sort of condescension and ethnocentrism displayed by most white officers. James later was to be exposed as
a selfish exploiter of the freed people under his charge in North Carolina.
He justified the shooting of a black man in his camp for disciplinary purposes. Wilder took advantage of his position to send two black men to
his New England home to substitute for his sons in the draft. Despite
these flagrant violations of trust, these superintendents paradoxically
performed useful services. They helped to lay the ground for freedom,
self-help and self-development. Although they deserve castigation, they
also revealed the flaws of American society. They especially reflected an
ambivalent abolitionist tradition, at best.

The superintendents obtained the active assistance of thousands of
black and white Americans who organized their support through their
churches and freedmen's aid societies. The contraband camps that they
governed became part of a temporary institution created by military men
to relieve themselves of a nonmilitary problem. The philanthropic shock
troops came south and performed their humanitarian services to relieve
the nation and themselves of a pressing moral burden. It is no surprise
then to find their version of the contraband camp experience primarily
depicting distressed, hapless victims in need of being uplifted and guided.
There was considerable chaos and desolation in the early days of some of
the camp experiences, particularly in the winter of 1862-1863 when Union forces penetrated the Confederacy's Mississippi Valley front. Grant's
perplexed attempts to take Vicksburg in the spring and early summer
were not made less difficult by considerations of what to do with thousands of slaves. Actually, there was some basis for perceiving the former
slaves as pitiable victims. When they arrived at the relatively secure havens behind the lines, the scene was one of wretchedness and disease, of
ignorance and suffering. But that was only one side of the story. In either
case—of the Negro Affairs officers confident of the freed people's capabilities for self-support or of those among the humanitarians who were
unconsciously racist in regarding their charges as inferior—the story usually has been told from their point of view. It should be fruitful therefore
in understanding the whole story to appreciate the experience from the
"victims' " point of view. They were active in their own reconstruction
and in the re-creation of community. In that process their longing for
landownership fed the roots of community and group consciousness.

The contraband camps and freedmen's villages brought hundreds of
people together in close quarters, providing propinquity as an element
of community. In the South Carolina Sea Island, freedmen's houses were
arranged along both sides of a street. Such a thoroughfare was an avenue
of trade and transport of men, women, and children, of crops, clothing,
and equipment. In this village street, army personnel and freed people
met and crossed paths with visitors, planters, and journalists. It was the
High Street and Main Street of several settlements of freed people who
went from their homes on the avenue to their fields and their fishing boat
and other jobs. Similarly, in the contraband camps such arrangements
were made by camp commanders or black or contraband affairs officers.
Indeed, more complicated grids of streets and avenues were laid out to

make a freed people's city at some places of refuge, such as at Roanoke Island, North Carolina.

One bond of community had already been established by color and by the slave's and later the freedmen's defense against white America's negative response to it. The common experience of slavery for most of the inhabitants of contraband camps and freedmen's villages further bound them together. The status of most of them as laborers tended to draw them together in common interest. After President Johnson's restoration policy in 1865, freedmen community and self-identity were stimulated if not determined by the need to defend the land on which they lived and labored. And, despite some disapproving opinions by Northern missionaries of their modes of worship, freed people clung to their own religious beliefs and practice. All told, their condition, status, experience, history, and ideology were potent forces operating toward cohesiveness and community.

Although energetic Union commanders had ordered houses and streets built for the freedmen, in the end it was these uprooted people who made their protectors' best-laid plans come into being. The villages of Slabtown and Acreville near Yorktown, Virginia, the city laid out at Roanoke Island, North Carolina, and the freedmen's villages of Alexandria and Hampton, Virginia, were constructed by black laborers and black and white craftsmen. Thousands of freed people lived in the homes built in those places. Near Hilton Head, freedmen occupied villages that they named after two generals concerned with their well-being, Saxtonville and Mitchelville (for General Ormsby Mitchel). As the caravans of fugitives from slavery and war daily arrived at Hampton, they received food and a place to rest in the hope that their freedom would become permanent. They built cabins and went to work at their trades, if they were trained, or at whatever they could do to earn wages. Hampton became well publicized in the press of the freedmen's aid societies as an example of the former slave's industriousness. By September 1865, after the U.S. government set aside 1,000 acres of adjoining farms abandoned by Jefferson B. Sinclair and Samuel K. Shields, 800 freedmen families had occupied the land, built or purchased homes, and laid out their settlement in streets "with order and regularity."[2] From New Bern and Roanoke Island, Horace James reported that every man in his charge knew how to build a house. He needed only protection. Of the 8,302 black people at New Bern in April 1863, 4,468 were males. Those between eighteen and sixty years of age totaled

2,730. An occupational census is unavailable, but James did report wages for "carpenters, joiners, glaziers, masons, caulkers, and engineers." Throughout his larger domain, James reported that other men were engaged in fishing, oystering, farming, turpentine and tar making, and other traditional trades such as barbering, driving teams of horses, baking, and storekeeping. The suggestion of some social stratification along occupational lines is strong. In addition to New Bern and Roanoke Island, freed people's settlements were located at other nearby North Carolina points: Beaufort, Washington, Plymouth, and Hatteras Inlet. These four accommodated 7,500 people. At Roanoke Island the 1000 persons settled there in July 1863 were spiritedly building houses and improving them and the one-acre plots that each family was allotted. The northern end of the island was cleared of a variety of pine trees; and streets were laid out along the sides of parallelograms. Women and children joined the men in the work of "the carpenter, the mason, and the gardener." They felled trees, cut boards, and rived shingles. Their ability to erect homes impressed James: "The Negro always builds his own house. Set him down where trees grow, give him an axe, a saw, a hammer, and twenty pounds of nails, and in a month his house is done." When he reported the progress of the settlement in 1864, he could state that 300 houses had been constructed, gardens prepared and planted, and the one-acre lots fenced. And most important of all as a mark of community, schools and churches were being constructed.[3] The freed people at Alexandria followed a similar pattern. Among the 7,000 there between the summer of 1863 and July 1864, some 700 to 800 houses had been built. The freed people were estimated to have spent $30,000 of their earnings in this enterprise. With the aid of philanthropic societies they had organized ten schools and constructed buildings for them. The largest they had built entirely themselves at a cost of $500 and owned it as their property. It was held by trustees whom they chose themselves.[4]

The first steps in the establishment and construction of other contraband settlements in the Washington area were taken by government and missionary society leaders. Freedmen who settled on the heights of the former George Washington and Robert E. Lee estates of Arlington in 1863 maintained a community for many years. The neat whitewashed one-story tenements that they rented were kept in good order. The village with its 1,200 residents continued even after the Freedmen's Bureau took over jurisdiction in 1865. Too little is known of the daily activity

and government there, but in December 1867 a hint of freedmen community organization was offered. The Bureau directed the freedmen's
village superintendent to prepare a room for a school to be taught by a
black teacher and to be "sustained by a Village Society." This was a
notable development for this group of former Maryland and Virginia
slaves. Community benefited from the formation of a Methodist and a
Baptist church, the latter under a black pastor. Moreover, the sense of
community and the practice of it must have been strengthened by the
variety of occupations and activities and the interdependence arising
from it. In addition to a school house that doubled as a place of religious
worship, the Quartermaster Department built a headquarters, commissary store, guardhouses, and workshops in which freed women and children were employed and taught trades. The men were employed as blacksmiths, carpenters, and wheelwrights. Contributions from Providence,
Rhode Island, provided funds to erect a home for aged and infirm freedmen. Much of the Lee estate was turned over to tillage by the freedmen,
who planted cereal grains. The village was designed to be a training school
and a way station on the route from slavery and destitution to freedom
and self-support. During 1867 its population was considerably reduced
by departures, presumably to more permanent residences and better economic arrangements in Virginia towns or in Washington.[5]

Not far away, at Anacostia in the District of Columbia, the Freedmen's
Bureau in 1868 purchased 375 acres of the Barry Farms. They were divided into one-acre lots and sold to freedmen at cost. A liberal payment
plan was devised, and each prospective purchaser received part of the
lumber necessary to build a home. By October, 359 lots had been sold
and 185 homes had been built. However, by that time 40 lots had been
forfeited when some ex-slaves withheld payment because they could not
be assured of clear titles to the lots. The early inhabitants displayed their
cooperativeness in purchasing lots for schools and churches by organized
community efforts. Day, night, and Sabbath schools were conducted by
black people, and one of their better-known teachers was Charles Douglass,
a son of Frederick Douglass. And when hostile whites harassed and as-
saulted Barry Farms black citizens, the freed people organized a secret
military organization to protect the community.[6]

The freedmen's village of Slabtown, near Yorktown, Virginia, began
with an officer's orders for cleanliness and orderliness among the dirty
and neglected troops and among the equally neglected contrabands hud-

dled there when he took over command in 1862. The freed people existed in makeshift shelters, were "supported in idleness on Government rations . . . in every stage of filth, poverty, disease and death," according to General Isaac J. Wistar. He and his engineer contingents laid out and built a village of about 400 cabins for the freed people. Materials came from the nearby woods and were made into logs and slabs, thus giving the place its name.[7] When a visitor named Kilham saw the village soon afterward, she was struck by the improvement in the condition of the people and in the attractiveness of the village. After first commenting on what she saw as childishness, she was impressed by their "wit to plan, the energy to carry out, and the stability to maintain, an undertaking like this settlement. It was entirely their own doings." Here too they had maintained their own store, church, doctor, and minister. The church was at the center of things, constructed from logs with the bark still on, just as the houses were made. Inside, Kilham was able to note pews made of rough boards on logs set upright and resting on an earthen floor. But from its rough midst she saw a pulpit that "rose like a piece of fairy work," doubtless produced by "a true artist soul." An evergreen was planted on each side of the pulpit, and an ivy "twined itself through the lattice work of the front." The glossy green against the brown wood were symbols of "everlasting spring," a beautiful expression of the faith and poetry that inspired the freedmen who designed and built this church. Kilham had been in almost every conceivable kind of Christian church or meeting house and was nowhere so deeply aware of the "Our Father" as in this little wilderness church, of the "poor and the needy." On her departure, Kilham could not refrain from noting that she was mystified about the name Slabtown. She had known of at least a dozen black people's settlements so named. Why could they not choose a prettier name, more appropriate to the character of the village, in this instance and in the others as well? But sympathetic reporter that she was, Kilham appears to have been ignorant of Shakespeare's question, "What's in a name?" and perhaps forgetful of her own observation, "This settlement was an independent one in every respect."[8]

   If names do convey a sense of a community, then two examples, one from Tennessee and one from Virginia, will be instructive. John Eaton drew attention in 1863 to a "little village known as Shiloah" near Memphis. The men worked for the army's engineer corps, their women and children received no rations, and it would appear, in this period before a superintendent of freedmen's affairs was assigned, that the freed people went hungry. But they were resourceful and independent and provided for themselves. They had a guard of their own and preachers of their own. A school was taught by a Northern woman, and the engineers were solicitous of their welfare. The village was built by the freedmen and accommodated about 2,000. Before Eaton could take charge, the village had deteriorated and he reported that it "became a den of thieves," in which even the teachers were implicated.[9] But far more honorable and durable was a Virginia freedmen's village near Richmond. After the war, freedmen led by an energetic carpenter and wheelwright, Henry Pryor, a former slave overseer on the Higginbottom estate, jointly purchased land and built homes and a village that they named Zion Town. Pryor built the six houses that accommodated the first eight families. The measure of their struggle for existence is indicated by the fact that not until 1885 did the community grow by the addition of seven families. But poor and slow in growth as this village of laborers remained, it was *Zion* Town.[10]

Farther west, around Little Rock, Arkansas, in 1864 freedmen built houses that clustered into villages. One was called Lickskillet and another Brownsville.[11] Similarly, black communities developed on the edges of other Southern cities, giving them black majorities by 1880. These were, according to E. M. Coulter, Wilmington, Charleston, Columbia, Macon, Savannah, Montgomery, Selma, and Shreveport. They were given names (probably by whites) such as Black Smoky, Black Centre, and Dark Town, not unlike the free black communities in the antebellum North, which were known as "little Africas" or "little Liberias."[12] Chattanooga also knew its freedmen's village, Contraband, with huts resembling those at Hampton, Virginia, and which the people had built. Simple and coarse, they were made of rails and mud. A chimney of sun-dried bricks and sticks was topped by a barrel. A roof of split slabs covered the dwelling.[13]

The process was repeated time after time and in various places throughout the conquered territories of the South. As Union armies occupied the Virginia peninsula, in 1861 and 1862, black people fled toward them. Not only was there a Slabtown and an Acreville (because an acre was allotted each dwelling), but in the vicinity a third contraband village was established. When Dr. Samuel G. Howe and Robert Dale Owen visited Uniontown in the spring of 1863, they found a village of 1,320 people under the charge of a Corporal Sykes. They saw a clean and orderly town laid in streets at right angles to a square appropriately named Washington Square. Sykes explained that the Army Quartermaster Corps had given permission to cut nearby timber and had supplied twenty kegs of nails and cutting and sawing tools. The freedmen had built seventy-eight dwellings that accommodated about fifteen persons in each.[14] There was yet another style of village genesis near Fort Nelson, Kentucky. There the missionary John G. Fee, who held 130 acres, sold them in small lots to freedmen. They established a village and built a church and a school with materials obtained from the local army commander.[15] Vicksburg, Mississippi, freedmen in 1865 were supported by their superintendent in their desire for landownership, or at least the right to rent significant numbers of acres, because they had already built homes and a school.[16] Not far away, in the neighborhood of Helena, Arkansas, a colony of freedmen at the mouth of the White River was under "nobody's management" but the freedmen themselves. As William Allen, the former teacher at St. Helena Island, South Carolina, made his tour of several such contraband camps in the Mississippi Valley, he noted that the White River group was a "self-governing community." Its members supported themselves with employment at the nearby army post. At Holly Springs, in September 1864, Allen found a community of 2,000 freed people living in log cabins huddled together, some with their own small gardens. But by this time the settlement was apparently on the way toward dissolution by the authorities. Freed people were being transferred to President's Island. Proceeding to that place, Allen saw a similar arrangement of houses close to one another but not so crowded as at Holly Springs. Some self-government was in operation here, for Allen met an old man, Stephen Wright, who had been put in charge of policing the camp. Things seemed neat and orderly in this village of 1,500 persons. As it was a Sunday and everything seemed quiet, Allen concluded that it was not a fair day to observe the settlement. He did record that there were a great many soldiers visiting their families in the cabins. The children in those families had the services of schools and five teachers. And the people had their "Praise-house," where Allen was privileged to hear an exhortation. His description is worth repeating for the light it sheds on the freed people's practice of religion in their own home communities. The exhorter talked very fast, "and in a sort of chanting tone, hardly ever varying from the harmonic tones, while the audience, by way of approval, hummed and murmured in harmony." He had heard the same among the freed people at Holly Springs, which, Allen pointed out, made the experience not unlike the one he was witnessing. The people sang two hymns, "a regular" one and "one of their own." He listened carefully to the latter and caught some of the words: "Brudder, guide me home and I am glad/Bright angels biddy me to come/What a happy time, chil'n/Let's go to God, Chil'n." A superintendent of freedmen at Holly Springs had earlier reported to his superior, John Eaton, that they had "correct notions of the Bible: justification, repentance, faith, holiness, heaven, hell." These freed people, he wrote, "are not troubled, like educated white men, with unbelief."[17]

One of the best organized and maintained freedmen's villages was the contraband camp at Corinth, Mississippi. General Grenville Dodge in command there had authorized its establishment in November 1862 when it became clear that he would be swamped by large numbers of runaway slaves. The chaplain of the 66th Illinois Volunteers, James M. Alexander, was given the responsibility for the camp. The black people were given tents at first and then were given tools to cut down trees and prepare lumber for cabins. They built a village laid out in streets and divided into four wards. The freed people built a school, a church, a commissary, a hospital, and an office. They dug a well at a cost of $50, which they paid. Freedmen's aid societies sent tools, seed, and other forms of aid. By April 1863 the Corinth freedmen's village contained 3,657 persons: 1,440 women, 658 men, and 1,559 children. The able-bodied men had been recruited into the army. The villagers had four of their own ministers. They paid a poll tax of a dollar a month. In the same spirit of self-help their men in the 1st Alabama Infantry of African Descent (because the Corinthians had come from Alabama) would tax themselves between fifty cents and a dolar to support teachers for each company in the regiment. The self-sufficiency of this community is further suggested by its inhabitants' occupations: 48 carpenters, 36 blacksmiths, 180 teamsters, 800 cooks, 150 laundresses, 80 seamstresses, and an unspecified number of shoemakers. Sixty freedmen maintained a guard even before a regiment had been organized. Schools were conducted during the day and religious meetings at night, all night; and when someone died, the freed people prayed and sang. Only 160 of the adults could read and 40 could write. This might have been a sufficient number to furnish a leadership group in the village, although we lack evidence of such a group in action. War disbanded the village. General William T. Sherman, taking up a command in the valley in January 1864, ordered

Corinth to be evacuated immediately and transported to Memphis. The 1,500 freed people who moved were reduced once again to living in tents amid squalor, some dying in the cold.[18]

Moving from plantation rigidities to contraband camp restrictions sometimes proved to be like going from the frying pan into the fire. Instances of harsh treatment of the freedmen by officers and men in the army were reported from the Fort Monroe, Virginia, district, and from the Clarksville, Tennessee, contraband camp, the first in 1862 and the latter in 1865. For a period in 1861, seventy-four men at Camp Butler, Newport News, Virginia, were denied full rations and pay by the sergeant who was their superintendent. An investigation resulted in his removal and correction of the situation. A report on conditions in the Clarksville camp revealed that freedmen were recruited into the army in April 1864, when the camp was established, only after receiving assurances that their wives and children would be "secure and comfortable." But instead, while the men were away on military duty, their families were "grossly neglected."[19]

While they existed, these freedmen villages with their basic institutions of schools, churches, homes, and gardens, also enjoyed some rudimentary measures of self-government. Not all such efforts succeeded, despite the sometimes sententious and solicitous attitudes of the contraband camp superintendents and freedmen's aid workers. Horace James reported a failure at Roanoke Island. Early in 1864 he had appointed a council of fifteen leading persons and instructed them to meet for the common welfare of this "African village." The council was to be a medium for communicating and enforcing James's rules and orders. He was "disappointed" in their unfamiliarity with making and receiving written communications and disingenuously wrote that they were "too ignorant to keep records." James erred in imposing a council rather than encouraging its election. Patronizingly, James wrote, "The sword to set them free, letters to make them citizens."[20] However, freedmen at Davis Bend, Mississippi, enjoyed successful government of their affairs, under army and navy protection. In this huge bend of the Mississippi River, where Jefferson and Joseph Davis's estates spread over a vast expanse, a freedmen's colony was established after Grant's hard-fought battle at Vicksburg. By the end of 1863, 600 freedmen were located at the Bend. Seventy-five of them managed to lease tracts of from five to a hundred acres in the face of the Treasury Department's favoritism to three or four white lessees who took almost all of the abandoned land under its jurisdiction. The freedmen raised profitable crops despite the army worm and the squabble over the lands between the Treasury and War departments. That success led military authorities in 1864 to divide up the land, lease it to partnerships or companies of freedmen, and to grant them a considerable measure of self-government and control. Although John Eaton and later Chaplain James A. Hawley, Freedmen's Bureau subcommissioner at the Bend, took pride in having encouraged freedmen's self-government, some of them may have followed a precedent set by the Davis brothers during the 1850s when they had granted their slaves "self-government." This consisted of a judicial system of black sheriffs, constables, judges, and juries. The latter was composed of "settled men" on the plantation, and the presiding judge was "an old Negro" who sat over a process in which witnesses were examined as in regular courts. Conviction by such a black jury led to the imposition of punishments. The system is reported to have survived down to 1862 when federal troops arrived. Under U.S. protection, freedmen elected sheriffs and judges and administered justice without interference from white officers. A three-man court was elected for a three-month term beginning in January 1865. Each of the three divisions of the community had a sheriff and a judge. Saturday was court day, when the sheriff presented cases. Serious penalties could be imposed on guilty offenders. Among them were forfeiture of crops, expulsion from the Bend, guard-house confinement, hard labor on the home farm. A limit of $1,000 was placed on fines. The superintendent of freedmen at the post wielded ultimate authority and jurisdiction over the system. He could fine and punish sheriffs and judges who were remiss in their duties. Most of the cases involved minor civil offenses and were judged with compassion and liberality or were dismissed for lack of evidence. Nonparticipating Bureau officers were satisfied that the system worked well. One officer reported that the freed people took the elections seriously and chose the best men among them. Besides the economic successes of the companies of freedmen cultivators, then, the success of the judicial experiment was indeed a favorable sign of the potential independence and viability of freedmen's communities.[21]

Between the success of Davis Bend and the failure of Roanoke Island there were numerous and various examples of freedmen regulating their own communities. The American Freedmen's Union Commission, assessing the results of emancipation in 1867, made its favorable judgment on the Davis Bend freedmen the basis of comparison. Its report stated that the same method had been followed on a smaller scale in many other localities. During the two years before the Freedmen's Bureau took over complete responsibility from the various and separate predecessor officers in 1865, freedmen's villages were frequently guarded and policed by details of men as at Corinth. This was done at White River and at President's Island and in several other camps in Eaton's jurisdiction. Early in 1863 his subalterns reported freedmen guards in the camps at Cairo, Illinois, Grand Junction, Holly Springs and Memphis, Tennessee, and Bolivar, Mississippi. In some of them freedmen shared the responsibility with army personnel. The strong hand of paternalistic white supremacy is obvious. Its presence tends to diminish the freedmen's independent role and weakens the judgment of their capabilities.[22]

Yet it would be unfair to make any judgment based solely on experiences limited in time and by the exigencies of war that made these exercises in paternalism experimental and tentative. Paradoxically, freedmen's self-development was both inhibited and encouraged. The contraband camps were inhabited by a kind of refugee dependent black population, of women, children, the infirm, and the aged; most of them awaited the return of their men at the end of war. In several instances skilled men also participated significantly in these first freedmen's communities. The able-bodied went off to fight for a permanent emancipation and to eradicate the notion of contraband status. It is all the more impressive then that the inhabitants of contraband villages achieved measures of self-sufficiency and quasi-independence.

As the freed people found employment outside the army, they moved away from the camps and villages attached to them. Some of them advanced to a higher stage of independent community building. In a number of cases, the initiative was taken by men with leadership qualities or already in leading positions as ministers, preachers, and exhorters or former overseers and leading men of plantation slave communities. Let us leave such men to the next chapter, where we consider the matter of leadership.

An emergent feature of that higher stage was a variety of internal community organizational structures. Admittedly, the data for them are in need of corroboration and elaboration. The skimpiness of the evidence may reflect the protective secrecy freedmen maintained, as they had done during slavery. Even the sympathetic General Saxton testified in 1863 that there was no independent organization among Sea Island freed people not imposed by whites.[23] Yet at the same time Robert Smalls gave contrary and better evidence that was corroborated independently in Prince Rivers's leadership experience. Saxton reported in 1865, however, that freedmen in some of the islands had established "civil government, with constitutions and laws for the regulation of their internal affairs." Moreover, they had departmentalized administration of "schools, churches, building roads, and other improvements."[24] On a tour of the islands and the mainland coastal regions in 1865 Trowbridge was impressed with the tens of thousands of freed people settled on independent farms, "in self-governing communities from which all white intruders were excluded."[25] One of them was apparently Mitchelville, which had grown to a village of 3,000 persons by the end of 1864. When a delegation of visiting black church leaders arrived at Hilton Head Island in August 1865, they were introduced to Reverend Abram Murchison, the newly elected mayor of the village. He was a Baptist minister, formerly a Georgia slave, whose speech revealed he had had no formal schooling. Murchison told the head of the delegation, well-educated Bishop Alexander W. Wayman of the AME Church, about his election and the majority he had received. Later, Wayman wrote in his autobiography, "He thought he was a *de facto* mayor." De jure or de facto, Murchison apparently had the support of the villagers and perceived himself as their leader, the "mar of this town."[26] Had Wayman witnessed a meeting two weeks earlier in another area where freedmen were practicing self-government, he might have connected it with his Mitchelville experience and valued the latter more. About 500 to 600 adults from about twelve to fifteen plantations in the country near Savannah, between the Great and Little Ogechee rivers, gathered to decide on a course of action to improve their conditions. Residents of each plantation caucused by themselves and elected three representatives to join with others and petition for tools, seeds, and animals. The Northern newspaperman who reported the meeting found as much wisdom there as among those who ran the "political machinery" of northern villages and towns. He was inspired by these "venerable old patriarchs of the plantations" to reflect on the iniquity of denying the ballot to blacks.[27]

    A similar penchant for running their own affairs in concert was revealed when planters returned to claim lands on Edisto Island under President Johnson's restoration policy. Freedmen firmly resisted the claims and the physical effort to press them. They used as authority their belief in their general right to the lands as well as the specific one under General Sher-

man's Order No. 15. Some form of decision-making body must have been
functioning among them. The mediator of this planter-freedman standoff,
Colonel H. E. Tremain, reported that adult male freedmen conducted
regular weekly meetings on the island.[28] Moreover, a general-interest
meeting on the island was headed by a general committee. In 1865 at
Contraband, the settlement of 3,000 freedmen up river from Chattanooga, affairs were administered by a president and council whom the
black citizens elected.[29] Under the Bureau's supervision, the council acted as a court hearing trials of minor offenses and sentencing the guilty.

Among the island freedmen governments that Saxton and Trowbridge
mentioned, the most dramatic example probably is the establishment of
black rule on St. Catherine's Island by the Reverend Tunis G. Campbell.
Born in New Jersey, he was a minister of the Zion Methodist Episcopal
Church. He arrived in Beaufort, South Carolina, in the second year of
the war, and according to his testimony General Saxton in 1864 had
made him governor of St. Catherine's, Sapelo, Ossabaw, and other islands.
This was Campbell's interpretation of his appointment as the Freedmen's
Bureau agent there. In addition, Campbell claimed his orders included
jurisdiction over mainland territory to a depth of thirty miles. His authority could be upheld if necessary by a force of 13 soldiers, but backing
them were 275 black men on the islands. Among whites after the war
Campbell was considered the "autocrat of the island." The judge of the
superior court of Georgia told a congressional committee in 1871 that
Campbell had created a black government and that one of its laws excluded white men from the islands. This government at St. Catherine's held
the island "against the lawful owners" after the war, probably to prevent
the return of former Confederate planters, as in the case of Edisto Island
and others. Eventually, troops were called and Campbell was ousted. And
the "house of representatives" and "senate" of the islands were forced to
remove to the mainland while the island was restored "to the possession
of its owners," according to the judge's ruling. But he also stated that
Campbell's actions protected the freedmen's civil rights. In its two years
the St. Catherine's community (Sapelo and St. Catherine islands) supported two schools, for 250 pupils, taught by Campbell's wife, son, and adopted son. Land had been parceled out among the islands' (629) residents.
Northern capitalists leased land on which 147 freedmen earned wages,
and on Sapelo others farmed for a two-thirds share of the crop.[30]

Another such community was established in February 1865 on Skid-
away Island, after the arrival in nearby Savannah of thousands of inland

freed people. The colony consisted of more than a thousand people. Three hundred and twenty-six of them were in families headed by ninety-six men and three women who held titles to 2,875 acres under General Sherman's order. These had comprised eight large plantations, almost all of whose acres were soon restored to the former owners. But in June 1865 the island was under cultivation, and several hundred acres of corn and vegetables and a small lot of cotton were in an advanced stage. Reverend Ulysses L. Houston, pastor of Savannah's Third African Baptist Church, led the colony. He had been among the black leaders, with Garrison Frazier, who conferred with Secretary Stanton and General Sherman on January 13, when they had spoken up for land and the opportunity to settle in their own communities. They apparently now took advantage of the opportunity. "Fraser" was reported to be governor of the island in June, but in July Houston was reported to be the "black governor." Houston had indicated even before the colonists set foot on the island that they had devised a plan for organizing life in the community. "We shall build our cabins, and organize our town government for the maintenance of order and the settlement of all difficulties," Houston said. The people did elect a governor, a sheriff, and three inspectors. The community "selected their lots, laid out a village." A Boston reporter saw the movement as a reenactment of the Plymouth colony, "the Mayflower on the islands of the South Atlantic coast."[31]

After his ouster from St. Catherine's, Campbell and some of his community settled on a 1,250-acre plantation that he had purchased in McIntosh County. Here he not only led the colony's day-to-day activities but also became a political leader and in the wake of the Reconstruction Acts was elected to the Georgia legislature. Among the poor rice farmers he was regarded as a king, and among whites as a notorious troublemaker and corrupt manipulator. One of the first actions of the colony in March 1867 was to form the Belleville Farmers Association to improve the status of farmers and laborers. Campbell was president, and there was some nepotism in that his son, Tunis, Jr., was the vice president and his adopted son, Edward E. Howard, was correspondent and record keeper. The association drew up rules for its government. A sheriff and constables were named. Other officers included a fence viewer, a road master, a market inspector, a janitor of buildings, and a hog and cattle reive. In each case the officer was charged with duties promoting cleanliness, order, security, health, and prosperity. In applying to the Freedmen's Bureau in April for rations for 113 colonists, Campbell indicated that many

had "never wielded the hoe; nor plough; but have resolved to learn."
And they resolved to make a good crop nevertheless. At the end of 1867,
twenty-five farmers had raised 9,706 pounds of cotton, which earned
them $552. They owed the government a balance of $526 for rations
originally valued at $1,050. This was a poor yield, which Campbell at-
tributed to the cotton worm and unfavorable weather.[32] But poor as the
colony appears to have been, the sense of community was evident in the
charter for self-regulation.

Not all the establishments of community were undertaken with equan-
imity such as those of Houston and Campbell. There may have been many
such as the Edisto islanders, who were moved to act cohesively and mili-
tantly to legitimize community. Although the Reconstruction Acts seemed to promise greater opportunity for freedmen self-expression and communal opportunity, it was not easily forthcoming. In some cases the Edist
model was followed and surpassed. One such effort was in the abortive
attempt by Bullock County, Alabama, freedmen to set up a "Negro government." Under the leadership of George Shorter, near Perote, Loyal
Leagues were organized to support an uprising against civil authorities.
The freedmen were reported to have drawn up a code of laws. They appear to have operated by night to enforce their laws and to bring resistant or reluctant blacks to trial before courts that they organized. The
objective of the uprising was to have been "extermination of the whites,
and the taking possession of the country." Troops were called in to suppress the movement and succeeded in arresting and jailing fifteen of the
black insurrectionists. Shorter was tried and sentenced to six months in
jail. It remained a mystery, however, as to how he escaped from jail on
or about December 20, 1867. The insurgent mood aimed at "taking possession of the country" may have been more important and widespread
than even Shorter's mild sentence suggests.[33] In nearby Tallapoosa Count
in February 1868, freedmen gathered to hear speeches advocating ratification of the new state constitution. One of its firm supporters was Alfre
Gray, a former slave. In the course of his militant speech he called for
integrated schools and linked them to the freed people's rights to the
land. Voices in the audience loudly affirmed his assertions. But Gray
was no firebrand urging immediate confiscation. He advised waiting
"until Congress gives it [land] to us."[34] A delegate to the Tennessee
Colored Citizens State Convention stated the matter bluntly: "What is
needed for the colored people is land, which they own. . . ."[35]

This need fortified the reconstruction of the freedmen's families. The two requisites—family and land—intersected in fashioning the freedmen's community. In the process the role of "primordial sentiments" was made vivid. They involved the powerful binding force of kinship and culture and centuries of bondage on the land. When the extraordinarily sensitive New England teacher Elizabeth Botume first came to Beaufort, South Carolina, in 1864, she was struck by the strength of those sentiments among Combahee River area freedmen. Separated by war from their homes, they were refugees in a contraband village, housed in cabins erected by the Army Quartermaster Corps. Botume found them to be tidy and decent despite the freed people's other difficulties. They had chosen a leader from their own ranks to supervise their little community. The younger men had joined a regiment under Colonel James Montgomery and had been sent off to Florida on a raid. The women and children and old folks left behind by these husbands and fathers, sons and lovers, were the community that Botume met. The strength of their ties to one another was made manifest in their family relationships, African names, distinctive black English language, and religion. The exuberant black children in her school taught the warm-hearted teacher much about family relationships that books did not. For one thing, she learned family nomenclature, that "bubber" meant brother, "titty" sister, "nanna" a mother, and "mother" a grandmother. The Combahee children applied "father" to all male leaders "in church and society." All the terms were so widely used as to give Botume the impression that she was in the midst of "one immense family."[36] The depth and force of this pattern of kinship has been exhaustively investigated and freshly interpreted by Herbert G. Gutman. But it is sufficient for our purposes to note the suggestion of a community sustaining itself in great part on kinship, an extended family extended to a plantation, a camp, a village. In her visits to the children's homes, the New England woman entered more than one in which three generations resided, and one that sheltered five. A black child guiding her tour introduced Botume to family members with a generous supply of African names. She had already discovered the persistence of such titles among the children in her schoolroom. Cudjos and Sambos were mingled with Pompeys, Rhinas, Rosas, and Floras, as well as day names; and some were named for months of the year. In the home visits she met Venus, John, Cudjo, Mingo, Gumbo, Aunt Dinah, and Dido as well as Shadrach, Phyllis, Flora, and Billy. These residents of the village they called "Mon'gomery's Hill" clung stubbornly

to one another despite the difficulties that forced them to move to the
coast. Their strong sense of identity was expressed in the proud statement
"We's *Combee,* ma'am." Although their group consciousness harked back
to slavery, when they had referred to themselves as "massa's niggers,"
they also had expressed themselves eloquently by acting together in fleeing him.[37]

The power of kinship was later demonstrated by another group of Sou‐
Carolina freedmen. Across the state in the Abbeville district, groups of
families settled on land they purchased from the South Carolina Land
Commission and organized their villages. Among these pioneers there
were seven brothers, the Moragnes, who acquired tracts that descendants
a hundred years later occupy. Twelve other family names of original settlers also are found in Promised Land near Greenwood, South Carolina.
One-fourth of the Abbeville land made available by the commission, 2,74‐
acres, was taken up by the Moragnes and seven families named Williams.
In his classic study of Reconstruction era South Carolina blacks, Joel
Williamson concluded that freedom enriched rather than dissolved their
clannishness. "The freedman," he wrote, "not only recognized the claims‐
of sons, daughters, and wives but he also valued his ties with cousins, uncles and aunts, with ancestors back through the generations, and with his‐
children's children ad infinitum." It is significant to add that another spu‐
to the Abbeville community may have been political. Klansmen had beaten Eli and Wade Moragne with a wagon whip shortly before they settled‐
on the former Marshall tract. They were thus cruelly punished because
they were believed to have been active in politics, "the leading Radicals
in the neighborhood." Klan violence against freedmen voters and political activists in Abbeville had been especially ferocious. The Moragne
incident accounts for the Abbeville blacks naming their acquisition
Promised Land.[38]

Local Black Leadership: 5
Moses As Model

> ... de Klu Klux come out. Dey claim dey gwine kill
> everybody what am Republican. My daddy charge
> with bein' a leader amongst de niggers. He make
> speech and instruct de niggers how to vote for Grant's
> first election. De Klu Klux want to whip him and he
> have to sleep in a hollow log every night. —Lorenzo
> Ezell, in Yetman, ed., *Voices from Slavery,* p. 115.

Free black communities in the United States never lacked leadership.
Eighteenth-century New England blacks took advantage of a slavery more
liberalized than that in the Southern colonies to press their claims to "natural rights." Their actions were bold and represented black community
aspirations. The few men who petitioned and won their freedom in Massachusetts courts from 1773 to 1779 were in this sense leaders. For that
matter, so were the 5,000 blacks who served in the army of the Contin-
ental Congress.[1] Yet the historical record leaves them in relative anony-
mity and obscurity. The record clears up with the appearance of Absalom
Jones and Richard Allen in the leadership of Philadelphia's postrevolu-
tionary black community. Thereafter in the nineteenth century there is
no dearth of evidence of free black community leaders. The names among
them were Henry Highland Garnet, Frederick Douglass, Martin R. Delany,
James Forten, David Ruggles, David Walker, Sarah P. and Charles Lenox
Remond, John Mercer Langston, and John S. Rock. Among slaves Nat
Turner dazzles the observer's eye but leaves visible two other major leaders of slave revolt conspiracies, Denmark Vesey and Gabrial Prosser; and
two women, Harriet Tubman and Sojourner Truth. Otherwise history is
virtually mute about slave leadership.

However, an articulate set of spokesmen during slavery may be inferred from the black men in Union uniforms during the Civil War. Colonel
T. W. Higginson preserved impressions of his most perceptive and eloquent

black soldiers, who aid our appreciation of their leadership. Corporal
Robert Sutton, Sergeant Prince Rivers, Corporal Prince Lambkin, and
Corporal Thomas Long had come from plantation fields and shops. They
distinguished themselves by their courage under fire on the battleground,
in daring raids up the St. Mary's and St. John's rivers. They also roused
their comrades to armed struggle for emancipation. Rivers and Robert
Smalls—the latter creating a sensation by his deft delivery of a Confederate vessel into Union hands on May 13, 1862—had been leaders in their
slave communities and appear to have continued their roles into the war
and beyond it into postwar political activity.[2] As the next pages will
show, theirs were not isolated actions; hundreds of former slaves continued or rose to lead communities in various roles.

"The chief witness in Reconstruction, the emancipated slave himself,
has been almost barred from court," W. E. B. Du Bois wrote in his classic study of black Reconstruction.[3] Yet even his master work regarded
leaders as being principally those who were well educated and accultur-
ated to middle-class American ideas and objectives. Nevertheless, Du Bois'
complaint could not until recently be denied. Heeding his strictures,
scholars have been attentive of late to black local leadership in the Southern post-Civil War upcountry, village, and plantation settlement as well as
in cities. The research has disclosed a working-class leadership of freedmen's communities.

Ironically, a positive vision of local black leadership and of the communities for whom it spoke emerges from one of the most depressing
documents of American history, thirteen volumes of testimony in the
1871 congressional investigation of Ku Klux Klan violence against blacks
and whites. Testifying to outrageous treatment of themselves and others
in their settlements, black artisans, laborers, sharecroppers, and farmers
spoke in their own right. Although they related experiences of horren-
dous gravity, they also indirectly revealed the people's efforts to gain
schools and land, to provide for the welfare of their families, and in general to improve the quality of their lives.[4]

The Klan hearings reflected monumental political strife beginning in
1865 with President Johnson's decision to dilute the victory of Union
arms and the revolutionary defeat of the Confederacy and the slave system. Long an enemy of the power of slaveowning aristocrats and a popular spokesman of nonslaveholding Southern whites, Johnson, as governor of Tennessee, had remained loyal and kept much of the state loyal

to the Union through the war. Shortly after Lincoln's assassination, and while Congress was not in session, Johnson assumed the responsibility and authority for Reconstruction and readmission of Southern states. He opposed slavery and was quite ready to settle the conflict on the abolition of the system and stop there. Radical Republicans such as Thaddeus Stevens and Charles Sumner saw great danger to the Union and to the system of "free labor" for which they had fought if the President persisted, as he did during the summer of 1865, in pardoning former Confederates and restoring them and the Southern states into the Union without penalty. The key to the Radicals' success in the struggle against the President and former Confederates, who represented a program of restoration of the old labor system in slightly altered form, was the mass of 4 million black freedmen and of a few hundred thousand Southern Unionist whites. Their enfranchisement and the disenfranchisement of recalcitrant whites were soon realized by early 1866 to be the instrument by which the overthrow of slavery and the expansion of a free-enterprise system could be guaranteed.

Provisional state governments in the South under President Johnson's aegis struck the first blow in 1865 and 1866 in an essentially counter-revolutionary strategy by enacting severely proscriptive black codes. These state laws imposed a system of peonage upon the South. Moreover, they came into effect and were utilized to blunt the freedmen's drive for equal political rights and their assertiveness in demanding land and decent conditions of labor. The codes also temporarily blunted the Freedmen's Bureau's efforts to aid the freedmen. However weak the Bureau may appear in retrospect, the former Confederates and landowners understood clearly that their power rested on the conquest of Southern black and white labor and the obstruction of any external aid they might receive from federal agencies such as the Bureau, or even from the philanthropic work of sympathetic Northerners. President Johnson aided in this obstruction of a Radical Republican program by vetoing two key measures in 1866 designed to enlarge the freedom and influence of freed people: the Civil Rights Act and the Freedmen's Bureau bill.

Congress, following the Radicals' lead, sensed danger to the Union and to an emerging national capitalist system. So-called moderates joined the Radicals in overriding the vetoes and enacting the bills, certain that unless a firmer guarantee, such as a constitutional amendment, were provided, a renascent planter and Southern Democratic power in Congress would in a short time reverse the outcome of the military struggle. Northern Republicans were not firmly committed to racial equality or to greater equity for workers. Tactically, they found it necessary to propose the Fourteenth Amendment, which made a great advance in conferring citizenship on blacks. In making it national, Congress removed the matter from the discriminatory Southern provisional state governments and the black codes they had enacted. But suffrage for blacks was only indirectly provided in the amendment, which paired off a state's discrimination against citizens' voting rights for reasons other than crime or participation in the rebellion, on the one hand, with reduction of that state's Congressional delegation, on the other. Radicals denounced the weak, backdoor approach but could not summon sufficient numbers to carry a stronger measure. Even this weak amendment was rejected by the Southern states during the remainder of 1866, with President Johnson actively leading the campaign against ratification.

Thus early in 1867 Congress remained in continuous session while it passed a Reconstruction act on March 2, with three subsequent clarifying acts in March and July and in March 1868 to give the federal government control over the recalcitrant former Confederate states. Congress provided for the establishment of five military districts over ten Southern states because, according to the act, those states did not legally exist. The army was authorized temporarily to supplant the illegal provisional states that had been recognized by President Johnson. The military commanders were made responsible for initiating the process of election of new state governments based on the enfranchisement of blacks and the disfranchisement of those former Confederates disqualified in the Fourteenth Amendment. First, registrars of elections were found among the loyal black and white population; then registration of voters was conducted during much of 1867. They went to the polls to elect delegates to state constitutional conventions that met in 1867 and 1868 to frame new state charters. Finally, qualified voters elected state officers and state and federal legislators. They also were required to approve the Fourteenth Amendment as a condition of representation in Congress. This was the political context of the emergence of local black leaders as divulged by the Klan hearings.

Social scientists have found it difficult to define precisely the concept of leadership, and of black leadership in particular. The most sensible guide to understanding Reconstruction era local black leadership is to regard the men who will be named in this chapter as leaders because of the roles they played or, more precisely, because of the influence they exerted upon others to attain community goals.[5]

In this chapter leadership is demonstrated by a variety of specific organized social and political activities among the freedmen. Evidence of such leadership is inferred or directly taken from accounts of individuals attacked by the Klan for political reasons. Leaders were also to be found among black men marching to the polls or to a political rally accompanied by fife and drum; or among black men maintaining an armed guard over both black and white persons or conducting schools and benevolent associations such as the one to be described later in Meridian, Mississippi. The black captains of the South Carolina militia companies and the many presidents of Union League and Loyal League clubs provide more direct evidence of black leadership.[6] Finally, members of state constitutional conventions, state legislatures, and clergymen were obviously leaders. Table 1 names some leaders, most of whom have heretofore never appeared in Reconstruction historiography.

Forty-six men emerge as leaders from this study of the hearings. The largest group was that of the sixteen members of the state legislatures; nine in Georgia, two each in Alabama, South Carolina, and Florida, and one in Mississippi. The next largest group, six men, had reputations as "leaders among colored people" in their Mississippi and Florida neighborhoods (Table 2). The third group consisted of five South Carolina militia company officers appointed in 1870 by Governor Robert K. Scott. Four men in the fourth group were identified as presidents of Union League or Loyal League clubs (two in Alabama, one each in Mississippi and South Carolina). Despite the apparent passivity of some black leaders, white upper-class witnesses nevertheless found others to be threatening. They expressed their shock because some former slaves acted in what was termed "inflammatory" ways. For example, George Houston, a black tailor in Sumter County, was accused of making violent speeches and of threatening to destroy one of the towns in the county. In his defense, however, Houston asserted that he had opposed "colored men being shot down like dogs, when I knew that the officers of the county could stop it." He had told this to the sheriff and to a public meeting. Under later committee questioning one white witness admitted that Houston's reputation as a troublemaker began only after he entered politics and was elected to the state legislature in 1868. Similarly, James B. Steadman, a lawyer in Unionville, South Carolina, complained of "in-

TABLE 1
Local Black Leaders During Reconstruction

Name	Age	Occupation	Leadership Function
ALABAMA			
Alston, James H.	Not clear	Musician and shoemaker	1. Union League leader, 300-500 members. 2. Register of election, 1868. 3. Representative of Macon County in lower house, Alabama legislature.
Burke, Richard	"Old man"	Domestic servant	1. Elected in 1869 to lower house, Alabama legislature. Representative of Sumter County. 2. Rallied black men to stand and fight in riot at Livingston, Alabama, August 13, 1870. 3. Teacher of a school with 22 pupils.
Houston, George		Tailor	1. July 1868, register of elections. 2. 1868 elected lower house, Alabama legislature. Representative, Sumter County. 3. Demands outrages cease against black people. 4. Member, Union League.
Long, Burton		Farmer	1. Candidate for legislature, Alabama (robbed of election).
Turner, Prior		"Industrious, hardworking," living on plantation	1. Prominent Republican among black men. 2. Loyal League leader.
Williams, George		Wheelwright	1. Militant speech at Huntsville courthouse yard in 1868 (called a "negro orator" by white men).
Geary, Andrew			1. Class leader in the Methodist church, Tuskegee.

TABLE 1 (continued)

Name	Age	Occupation	Leadership Function
FLORIDA			
Fortune, Emanuel	39	1. Carpenter ("common laborer") 2. Formerly a shoemaker (his main trade)	1. In constitutional convention, 1868. 2. Member legislature, to 1870.
Meacham, Robert	36	1. "Drove a carriage once" 2. "Superintended around my old boss—my father." (He was a doctor.) 3. Domestic servant 4. Clergyman	1. State senator since 1867. 2. Register, U.S. Land Office. 3. First position was register under Reconstruction acts under Gen. John Pope. 4. Had also been superintendent of schools, Jefferson County.
Reed, Henry	37	Carpenter and farmer	1. "True republican, a leading man, and tried to influence men to the best of my ability."
Rogers, Calvin			1. Elected constable in Jackson County. 2. Stump-speaker. 3. Leader of men regarding working contracts. 4. "Prominent" among "their race."
Granbury, Oscar			1. (Close friend of Rogers), "a leading colored man." 2. "A very daring man, and had a splendid education."
GEORGIA			
Allen, Thomas M.	38	Pastor—Baptist church, Marietta; ex-shoemaker, farmer	1. Active in Georgia constitutional convention. 2. Elected to Georgia legislature in 1868. 3. Organizer of Grant Ranger clubs. 4. Union League member (secret).

T A B L E 1 (continued)

Name	Age	Occupation	Leadership Function
Barnes, Eli	36	Mechanic—wagon shop	Elected to legislature 1868.
Colby, Abram	52	Barber (before war), hauling wood, etc.	Elected (1868 and 1870) to Georgia legislature.
Flemister, George	27	Shoemaker	1. Tried to raise armed guard for black prisoner in jail at Madison; insited that the mayor guard the man. 2. Member Union League "sick committee."
Floyd, Monday	68	House carpenter	Representative in lower house Georgia legislature, 1868, 1870.
Harrison, W. H.	28	Schoolteacher—1867; since then split rails, picked cotton, pulled fodder and worked on Western and Atlantic Railroad; body servant while a slave	1. Constitutional convention, 1867 and 1868. 2. Elected to legislature 1868. 3. Member of Georgia State Central Committee, Republican party, since 1869.
Hendricks, Charles	42	Carpenter	One of three on committee to superintend election, December 11, 1870, in Norcross, Georgia.
Moore, Romulus	53	Blacksmith during war; since war, part-time blacksmith, and part of the time "I helped to reconstruct the state." Keeps public house in Atlanta for black people—"but nobody is turned away"	1. Registrar of elections. 2. Constitutional convention. 3. Representative lower house, Georgia legislature. 4. Sent to Louisiana to look for lands for black people.
Richardson, Alfred	34	1. House carpenter 2. (Partner in brother's grocery store)	1. Elected to legislature in 1868.

TABLE 1 (Continued)

Name	Age	Occupation	Leadership Function
Turner, Henry M.	37	Clergyman and politician; missionary agent and presiding elder of district AME church; Freedmen's Bureau employee in Georgia	1. Presiding elder in the African Methodist Episcopal church. 2. Elected to legislature, December 20-22, 1870 (ejected November 3, 1871). 3. Leading part in Republican politics.
Turner, Abram			Member of legislature.
MISSISSIPPI			
Cooper, Peter	27	Shoemaker and teacher	1. Teacher in black school. 2. Drew up a petition.
———, Jerry			"Had much influence with colored people." Rallied them to vote Republican.
Dupree, Jack			1. President of Union League Club. 2. Prominent in politics. 3. Led voters to election in Aberdeen. 4. "Boisterous," "noisy" but trusted as president of club. 5. A sort of teacher among black people.
Graham, Andy		Worked on section no. 53, Mobile and Ohio Railroad	"Regarded as leader among colored men."
Jack, Bully			"Sort of a leading man in the neighborhood." "Formed himself into a court—and held negro courts about." "Blacks against him/and enemies among white people."
Malone, Dick		Blacksmith; in charge of a squad of men working some man's plantation	1. Talked with black men and proposed arming themselves to counter Klan attacks. 2. "Prominent among the colored people."

TABLE 1 (continued)

Name	Age	Occupation	Leadership Function
(Dennis) (Clopton), William (Meridian riot)			1. On committee to see governor in Jackson regarding "condition of affairs" (raids from Alabama). 2. Speech for arming blacks, removing city officers, "or burn the town down."
Kizer, John W.			1. Member county board of supervisors. 2. Served on a committee to see governor.
Lee, Isaac (Meridian riot)		Brick mill worker	Alleged to have made threats against whites.
Moore, J. Aaron (Meridian riot)		Clergyman; in 1901, a blacksmith in Jackson, Mississippi	1. Representative in legislature from Lauderdale County. 2. Named by white postmaster as one of three leading black men in Meridian (Clopton, Moore, Tyler).
Radford, Isaac (Meridian riot)		Teacher, Lauderdale County	Served on committee to see governor. Went with Moore to see sheriff, March 4, 1871.
Tyler, Warren (Meridian riot)		Teacher	1. Teacher. 2. Named by white postmaster as one of three leading black men. 3. Leader of meeting, March 4, 1871—authorized by sheriff to get black men for a guard.
Williams, Joseph		Officeholder	1. "Obnoxious" to whites and blacks. 2. Drilling a company of black men. 3. Member, county board of supervisors. 4. Influential and prominent among black people.
SOUTH CAROLINA			
Bates, John			1. Heads black militia demonstration of 700-1,000 men. 2. Inflammatory speaker.

TABLE 1 (continued)

Name	Age	Occupation	Leadership Function
Hill, Rev. Elias	50 (52)	1. Preacher (10 years) 2. Teacher	1. President of Union League Club. 2. Baptist preacher. 3. Schoolteacher.
Johnson, Henry	31	Bricklayer and plasterer	1. Elected to first session of legislature, 1868. 2. Census taker. 3. Active campaigner, July-October 1870. 4. President of Loyal League in town. 5. Enrolling officer of militia company. 6. Was a trial justice for two years.
Johnson, Jack	45	Stone mason and farmer	Riding about counseling black people to vote Republican.
Johnson, Willis	30	Laborer	Distributed ballots on Election Day, and brought voters to polls, 1870.
Nuckles, Samuel	57	1. Blacksmith 2. (Drayman in Columbia)	1. Member of convention, 1868. 2. Member of house of representatives of South Carolina.
Wilkes, Jim			1. Captain militia company (in clash at Chester) (fights defensive battle).
Williams, Jim (Jim Rainey)	Not clear	1. Carriage driver 2. Farmer	1. Captain of militia company. 2. Urged white neighbors to vote Republican.
Wright, Alfred	44	1. Blacksmith 2. Farmer	1. Lieutenant in militia company. 2. Delegate to Union County convention.

TABLE 2

Leadership Roles of Local Blacks

	Ala.	Fla.	Ga.	Miss.	S.C.	Total
Union League or Loyal League officer	2	0	0	1	1	4
Member of legislature	2	2	9	1	2	16
Member of county board of supervisors	0	0	0	1	0	1
Candidate (not elected)	1	0	0	0	0	1
"Impromptu" leadership	1	0	1	0	0	2
"Church class-leader"	1	0	0	0	0	1
Elections superintendent	0	0	1	0	0	1
Schoolteacher	0	0	0	1	0	1
Alleged to have threatened whites	0	0	0	1	0	1
Influential campaigner	0	0	0	1	2	3
Reputation as leader among black people	0	2	0	4	0	6
Militia company officer	0	0	0	0	5	5
Constable (elected)	0	1	0	0	0	1
Member, committee of protest to governor	0	0	0	3	0	3
Total	7	5	11	13	10	46

NOTE: Although some men performed more than one leadership role, only what seemed the most prominent role was chosen as the basis for entry in this table.

flammatory harangues delivered in public by colored orators," including a former family servant, Abram Duggan. Steadman claimed to have been present at such speeches.[7] Some whites thus portrayed emancipated black in the worst possible way. Such men refused to admit that former slaves could conduct their own political affairs, or deluded themselves into believing them to be more irresponsible and dangerous than they really were.

In order to focus on local communities and their possible indigenous leadership, northern blacks who were victims of Klan attacks were eliminated from this chapter. Almost all local leaders mentioned in the hearings had been slaves. Only three of them had been free before 1865. This bears heavily against the Stanley M. Elkins thesis of slave infantilization. The emergence of these men from a recent slave status into leadership indicates that they were far less depressed and psychically damaged than Elkins hypothesized. These self-confident men suggest that Elkins was mistaken in believing that men in confinement are incapable of developing mature, independent or semi-independent personalities.

The most striking feature of the group of forty-six was the artisan status of about two-fifths of its members. Moreover, some share croppers and some landowning farmers among the forty-six combined farming with various trades. For example, nineteen of them worked as blacksmiths, carpenters, stonemasons, shoemakers, tailors, barbers, and mechanics. However, not all of them were pursuing these at the time they gave their testimony. Some had done so as slaves and continued to do so as freedmen. Others had been forced to change their occupations when they were evicted from their homes. There were as well five laborers: a brick-mill worker, two railroad section hands, a plantation laborer, and a drayman who had been a blacksmith in his hometown. Four clergymen and four teachers filled out the list of occupations (Table 3). Some of these individuals, such as W. H. Harrison, Romulus Moore, and Samuel Nuckles, had had more than one occupation. Harrison, for instance, was a twenty-eight-year-old former slave from Sparta, Georgia; a schoolteacher in 1867, he then became a farmer and part-time railroad worker; by 1871 he owned a thirteen-acre cotton farm. Moore, born a slave, but free since 1858, was a blacksmith and pastor of a Baptist church. Nuckles, of Union, South Carolina, a former "hard down" slave, as he described himself, had a blacksmith shop there but was forced to leave and became a drayman in Columbia. Thus in Table 3, thirty-four persons are shown to have had forty-three occupations.[8] Unhappily, occupational data are lacking for thirteen of the forty-six.

Despite the limitations and gaps in the data, we can derive some suggestions from it as to their overall status. Evidence shows that nineteen of the forty-six were former slaves, two of whom were freed before 1858. Three were born free. Seventeen owned property, ranging from a mule and basic farm implements to shops, farms, and houses. Eighteen were married and of these thirteen had families. Twelve men could read and write, some having taught themselves or having been taught during slavery in disobedience to slave codes. Three men could read only "a little."

TABLE 3

Occupations of Local Black Leaders

	Ala.	Fla.	Ga.	Miss.	S.C.	Total
Blacksmith	0	0	1	1	2	4
Barber	0	0	1	0	0	1
Bricklayer and plasterer	0	0	0	0	1	1
Carpenter	0	1	3	0	0	4'
Mechanic	0	0	1	0	0	1
Shoemaker	1	1	2	1	0	5
Stonemason	0	0	0	0	1	1
Tailor	1	0	0	0	0	1
Wheelwright	1	0	0	0	0	1
Laborer						
Plantation	1	0	0	0	0	1
Factory	1	0	0	1	0	2
Railroad	0	0	1	1	0	2
Drayman	0	0	0	0	1	1
Servant	1	1	1	0	0	3
Teacher	0	0	1	2	1	4
Clergyman/preacher	0	0	2	1	1	4
Farmer						
Renter	1	0	0	0	2	3
Owner	0	0	2	0	0	2
County officeholder	0	0	0	1	0	1
Public housekeeper	0	0	1	0	0	1
No evidence	1	2	1	5	3	12

NOTE: Although there are forty-three occupations listed, they were filled by thirty-four persons, some of whom simultaneously held more than one job.

Four were unable to read or write at all. Of the ten whose religion could be determined, four were Baptists, three were Methodists, two were African Methodist Episcopalians, and one was a member of an unspecified

TABLE 4

Ages of Local Black Leaders

Age	Ala.	Fla.	Ga.	Miss.	S.C.	Total
20-29	0	0	2	1	0	3
30-39	0	3	4	0	2	9
40-49	0	0	1	0	2	3
50-59	0	0	2	0	2	4
60-69	0	0	1	0	0	1
"Old man"	1	0	0	0	0	1
No evidence	6	2	1	12	4	25
Total	7	5	11	13	10	46

church. Twenty-eight of the forty-six were born and raised, or had lived for more than ten years within twenty miles of the places where they assumed the functions of leadership.[9]

The beginnings of a pattern of local leadership can be constructed, even from such limited evidence. Former slaves, most of them in the artisan or laborer class, with little or no schooling, but in contrast more literate than most freedmen, held seats in state legislatures after 1868, organized and led militia companies, or were prominent leading men among the black people in the upcountry areas of five southern states. Many were under forty years of age, implying a mature and energetic leadership group (Table 4).[10] They were the principal victims of Klan retaliation against black political equality and what most whites perceived to be threats of social equality. Finally, they rejected paternalism.

That blacksmiths, carpenters, shoemakers, tailors, and other artisans were leaders among poor black people should not come as a surprise. Slave artisans by the nature of their skills and talents enjoyed higher status than field hands. Despite the efforts of slaveowners to isolate artisans from laborers, the relationship may have been much closer than planters, overseers, or historians realized. Their relatively greater mobility, on plantations and in urban settings, was a necessary condition of their occupations and a spur to leadership potential. For brief periods, moreover, the artisan slave who hired out entered into quasi-freedom. Indeed, he en-

Figure 3.
"THE FIRST VOTE." By A. R. Ward, *Harper's Weekly,* November 9,
1867. Vivid symbols of freedmen's community leadership—the artisan
with stonecutter's hammer and chisel, the well-dressed middle-class
man, and the non-commissioned army officer—are shown in a polling
place, soon after implementation of the Reconstruction Acts of 1867,
in Richmond, Virginia.

countered a varied world of associations and persons, of customs and ideas not to be found on the plantation; hence, opportunities for learning were opened up to him and some of these must have included the practical subject of collective action. Thus, a former slave carpenter, Denmark Vesey, had set an example in Charleston of what hiring out, artisan status, and mobility could mean in developing leadership among slaves. During Reconstruction, black artisans reenacted that experience to some degree when they became leaders in the fight against white terror and when they asserted their recently obtained political rights.

In this role they differed little from British and French artisans in the late eighteenth and nineteenth centuries. Edward P. Thompson's *The Making of the English Working Class* clearly established such a role in English cities and manufacturing towns. The staymaker and essayist Tom Paine was their ideologue; the London cobbler Thomas Hardy was one of countless indigenous (but anonymous) leaders.[11] A more relevant parallel to freedmen artisan leadership is suggested by Eric Hobsbawm and George Rudé, who have described the roles played by village artisans in the so-called Captain Swing uprisings of English agricultural laborers in 1830.[12] It would be too facile to suggest that the want of wages and work in Swing country and the consequent rebellion might have served as a prototype for the want of land and the resulting mass black political activity in the postbellum South. Nevertheless, the similar relationships between village and urban artisans and farm and plantation laborers enlarge our understanding of the nineteenth-century leadership role of the black American craftsman.

Far from being the objects of manipulation by Northern whites as charged by Southern paternalists, these black men made clear by their behavior that they were their own men who made up their own minds. George Houston best expressed their thoughts when he said, "No, I don't trust all of them [Northern white men]. I pick them wherever I try them, and see that they are right, and then I am there. If he is a southern man, and he is right, I am there. That's my doctrine." He refused "to stick to a man that . . . tries to get me to be used as a tool, why he will find my edge is going to break off; and if it breaks off once, he never can grind it any more."[13]

Above all else the Klan hearings demonstrated that black people wanted stability in order to live in peace ("to live like humans"), to have land and schools, independence and self-respect.[14] These hopes motivated collective activity such as the formation of Union League and Loyal League clubs, and black electoral activity such as putting oneself up as a candidate for office, voting, and conducting mass meetings. On several occasions black people marched in military fashion to the polls, with drums beating and fifes piping. While such behavior alarmed whites who saw it as threatening their supremacy, or as being contemptuous of their paternalistic entreaties, blacks were not to be dissuaded. Blacks trusted their old masters in business matters but not in things political. They preferred to support the Republican party which they identified with their emancipation, suffrage, and educational opportunities.[15]

Violence against black people moved them to attempt to survive either by lying out at night away from their cabins, or, in desperation, migrating elsewhere in groups, trying to purchase land, and establishing new settlements. Alfred Richardson, Romulus Moore, and Alfred Wright led or participated in such actions. Another form of defense was to eschew the Republican party or any Loyal League activity. For instance, Benjamin Leonard, a Bluffport, Alabama, mechanic and gunsmith, was forced to take such a step and give up his participation in a local election campaign. Whites called Leonard "a turbulent character . . . disposed to stir up strife." Thereupon he openly severed his connection with Radical Republicanism. "I did it in order to secure my peace," he told the committee. Others responded to violence, fear, and insecurity by joining the Democrat party and ostensibly working for it. Some used this as a camouflage while secretly they continued to support Republicans.[16] Those who persisted in aiding the Democrats, whether through fear or opportunism, received little sympathy from Radical blacks.[17]

The realization that they possessed rights inspired some black men to celebrate, exercise, protect, and, at times, fight for them. This also helps to explain the mass enrollments in Union League, Loyal League, and Grant Ranger clubs; as well as the parading of armed and unarmed blacks, and the singing of the popular song *John Brown* at many of their demonstrations.[18] Furthermore, it was that realization that lay beneath the political proclamations made by men who have already or who will appear in this chapter: James Alston, Richard Burke, George Houston, and George Williams in Alabama; William Dennis (Clopton), Warren Tyler, and J. Aaron Moore in Mississippi; Abram Duggan in South Carolina. It also motivated the 150 armed black men who rallied in 1870 to protect the Reverend Henry M. Turner in Georgia against white terrorist threats; and the 1,000 armed men who assembled in fifteen minutes to guard a Florida

state senator, Robert Meacham. It inspired as well South Carolina militia
captain Jim Williams to refuse to relinquish the arms of his company until he had certain clear guarantees. The details of the events in which these
men were involved have been retold by Allen Trelease in *White Terror:
The Ku Klux Klan Conspiracy and Southern Reconstruction.* It is sufficient to focus here on their leadership roles in relation to the freedmen's
struggle for their rights.

The 1870 Atlanta municipal election underscored for blacks the importance of suffrage and the right to act as freemen. In this conjunction
it is of interest to note that during the election a man was arrested at the
polls and charged with voting illegally. The account by Andrew D. Rockafellow, a white carpetbagger, does not specify whether the man was a
Republican or Democrat, white or black. In any event, a riot followed.
The significant part of Rockafellow's story was that "the colored men
and some of the whites" came to rescue the man from the police. "I saw
them coming down there with axes, picks, and shovels. . . . I suppose
they ran with whatever they happened to be working with. Some had
planes and hatchets." Laborers concerned about another man's rights
had stopped work but had not put down their tools. They carried them
along, possibly for use as weapons.[19] Why? Obviously to keep one man
out of the hands of the police; but the story invites further exploration
of the motivations of the workers and of their political awareness.

Few freedmen could read and it is doubtful that most of those who
were literate had read the war amendments or the Reconstruction Acts.
But some among them must have understood and appreciated in some
way the value of those measures. Henry Lipscomb, a Spartanburg, South
Carolina, farmer, gives evidence of this when he declared that black people were not afraid of Klan terror "at the start." Intent upon exercising
their political rights "they went up and voted, every one of them, and
some swam the river in order to, and some waded. . . ."[20]

Additional evidence of such *understanding* is to be found in the behavior of other local blacks. A few sketches of their pertinent activity indicate how little is yet known about such persons. However, the following brief narratives of local black leaders clearly furnish the framework
for fuller portrayals.

James H. Alston, a cobbler in Tuskegee, Alabama, organized a Union
League club in 1867 and then a Republican club, which had between 300
to 500 members and whose presidency he won in a contest with white

candidates. The following year he was elected to the state's lower house. Alston said he refused a $300 bribe Democrats offered to him in order to capitalize on his influence in the community. This refusal brought on a violent attack against him. He explained his situation: "I was threatened every day, but I rode around and got them all, and insured them as my constituents with my authority; from my assurance to them that I had acted for them where they placed me as my constituents, I had them right with me to do whatever I wanted done in the county." His constituents held him in such high regard that 200 to 300 people crowded the streets around his house in Tuskegee the better to protect him after he was shot in May 1870, a punishment for his too political role. A white lawyer testified that Alston had sent runners over the entire county summoning the blacks.[21]

Richard Burke of Gainesville, Alabama, a former slave, was by 1870 a Baptist preacher and the representative in the state legislature for Sumter County. He had a reputation for being a peaceful man. Nevertheless, in August 1870, he was shot to death in a riot in the town of Livingston. The shooting occurred at a political rally when some white men attempted to break up the meeting and in the course of the ensuing fracas opened fire on the assembled blacks, some of whom fled because they were unarmed. Burke met them at the edge of town and denounced them as "cowardly sons-of-bitches; You go back and shoot out your last load of ammunition, and then club your guns and fight to the last." This was the Nat Turner side of the peaceable former slave.[22]

George Houston, like Alston, refused to renounce his radicalism and especially his Union League membership because he felt that the organization served "to teach our ignorant colored men." But some wealthy white men of the county saw the Union League in a different light: Houston was not the benign, crippled village tailor they remembered from slavery days; he had become an inflammatory orator.[23] Like Burke, Houston had become a rebel.

Little is divulged in the Klan hearings about George Williams, but he too distinguished himself in a single militant act. Two whites testified that at a Huntsville, Alabama, meeting in 1868 Williams led other blacks to deny "a local gentleman" access to a platform where he could speak to the public because he was not a Republican and opposed the Loyal League. The meeting adjourned in great excitement; and afterwards the gentleman offered to speak to anyone willing to listen in the courthouse yard. Williams and two or three other black men heckled him. William Richardson, a white lawyer, declared that Williams "pointed from the north end of this courthouse building to the buildings around the town, and said that if the people of the South did not accord them their rights as citizens, remember that it was through their labor and toil that all these buildings were constructed, and that they could destroy them; that was the idea in substance."[24] What is significant here, if this report was not exaggerated, was the insistence on the rights of black men as free citizens and the idea that black working people had built the town and could destroy it, revealing both a profound sense of identity and alienation.

Dennis, Tyler, and Moore were singled out in 1871, and with good reason, as a triumvirate of leading Meridian blacks. These three men were as angry as Alston, Houston, and Williams over Klan outrages committed during the winter of 1870-1871. Frustrated by the failure of the government of Mississippi and the mayor of Meridian to guarantee them protection, a large number of blacks met at the courthouse on March 4, 1871 to hear Tyler, Dennis, and Moore speak. The three warned that if the attacks did not stop, and if the authorities continued to ignore them, blacks would take measures to protect themselves. After the meeting, the people organized themselves in military order and "with fife and drum marched around the streets of Meridian." Some wore swords, but observers did not remember seeing anyone carrying firearms. While testifying before a state legislative committee investigating these events, Reverend Moore said that the men came out of the courthouse in a line "marching and beating drums, *as usual*" (emphasis added). A white witness said he had heard Dennis threaten to reduce the city to ashes if whites did not quell Klan attacks. Tyler was reported to have said that "he had been advised to leave here, and the next man, white or black, that advised him to leave, he would slap him in the mouth; this is the black man's country; . . . they had built the houses, the railroads, and cleared off the forests. When all this was done the white man was figuring them to hell."[25]

Williams's and Tyler's angry outbursts contained a conception of right based on the idea of the value of black labor. Blacks had built "the houses, the railroads, and had cleared off the forests" and, therefore, ought to share in the community's wealth. Hence they would destroy property if its owners did not assure them of better social and political arrangements. Their revolutionary talk was frequently carried out by other blacks in acts of incendiarism, for example, in barn burnings. White incendiarism, on the other hand, destroyed schools and churches, which were potentially low in producing economic values but high in social ones. Insofar as they refused to accept a breach in the social order, whites in the Ku Klux Klan struck back at all black attempts to alter the economic, social, and political values and relationships. Apparently, the silent Southern white leadership agreed with this violent reaction.

Moore followed much the same lines as Williams, Tyler, and Houston. He said that he had made a conciliatory speech at the March 4 meeting, but a white witness insisted that Moore had asserted that unless steps were taken to protect the colored people, "the city might be burnt up . . . for if ever there was a Sodom and Gomorrah in the world, Meridian certainly was."[26]

So fiery a formula attributed to Alabama and Mississippi black men appears to have more than isolated significance. It suggests a chiliastic thrust. Perhaps it sprang from a hope that a world of peace and security could emerge from the ashes of their sinful city. If all else failed, if a superhuman effort to endure oppression failed, if white men refused to live in peace and equality with black men, despite all accommodations by blacks, then, perhaps, the way to a new world was through fire. Even exodus, one of the oldest forms of resistance and negation, would not satisfy some black leaders. Moore's speech was more than mere malediction or a cry of helpless despair: it was a declaration of right, a prediction that an indignant God would no longer permit the wrongdoings of whites. While Williams invoked a secularist labor theory of value, Moore used a biblical metaphor to sanction a cleansing dispensation of justice.

"Billy Clopton," as Dennis was better known, emerged as a stormy and militant person, a firm advocate of immediatism. On the Saturday evening following the courthouse meeting, a fire of undetermined origin destroyed the store and house owned by the Republican mayor, William Sturgis. When it threatened to spread, it was reported that Clopton urged the black firemen (the traditional de facto fire department) to let it alone, at least to let the fire go on beyond the store, because it was a white man's fire. He was reported to have called upon some black men to go and get their guns. "Why the h——ll don't you go and get your arms; something to shoot with? What in h——ll are you standing here for? I have no secrets to keep; what I have to say I say openly and aboveboard." Clopton took Jack Lee, a black man, by the hand and admonished him: "You d——mn paper collar hotel boys are not doing your duty; why don't you go home and get your guns." Other witnesses reported the ringing of a church bell in the town's black section as a signal for black men to go and guard Clopton. Armed black men responded to the summons. A white man wanted him arrested for allegedly shooting at him. Clopton called him a damned liar. Tempers rose. One white witness heard some black people call Clopton and Tyler very bad persons, but another witness testified that the "negroes cocked their guns and said they would stand by General Clopton." He was arrested, however, together with Tyler, that evening.[27]

"Usual" or "frequent" parading as it was termed by observers also was a means by which blacks expressed their solidarity in Livingston, Alabama. There they frequently came to town in marching order, with music and guns. As they paraded through the streets, they would shoot off their guns, the town's mayor declared. Not only were they defiant in manner, they menaced white citizens as well, he asserted, even though he could not cite one instance of actual violence. Their belligerent attitude turned out to be little more than vague threats that they would burn down the town if Klan whippings, beatings, shootings, and other such harassments continued. Nevertheless, the parades seemed as assertive and defensive as the Meridian demonstrations, and at least as defensive as those armed black plantation people in the swamp of Sumter County who declared: "We are here to protect ourselves, our wives, and children."[28]

Next to preserving and protecting lives, black people appeared most eager to establish themselves on the land. A thing that was very difficult to accomplish. Asked what his people would do if they were permitted to live "peaceably with their families and attend to their business," Abram Colby told a congressman that they would choose to take up farming; they would not live in cities. He estimated that three or four thousand Atlanta blacks were actually refugees from the countryside who preferred farms "if they could be allowed to stay there." Reverend Henry M. Turner gave essentially the same answer. He declared farming to be his people's first preference "because they have been educated and trained to that," but he left the door open to "any kind of labor whatsoever." Turner reminded the congressional committee that among his people were men skilled in almost every occupation that whites followed. He mentioned carpenters, smiths, watch- and clockmakers.[29]

The overwhelming desire of black people to own and cultivate land was underscored by their enthusiastic reaction in 1868 to the rumor that large plantations would be confiscated and their lands redistributed. The intensity of their expectations was revealed by their widespread purchase of boundary markers for $1 to $5 apiece from white men who encouraged them to stake out any forty-acre tracts they might wish to claim. Those stakes would then become bona fide title to the land. A white witness denied that black people ever could have conceived of the idea of getting or taking anything, especially land, from their former owners.[30] Another concluded that no white man would have believed such a fanciful tale. But, he added, the blacks "were very ignorant, or they would not have believed such things, but they did believe it, and I have no doubt, implicitly." That they did so suggests that land acquisition was a real issue in the political campaigns of 1868 in Georgia and Alabama.

Another example of the yearning for land is provided by the case of Lucy McMillan, a former slave, forty-six years old, and a widow with two daughters. She supported herself by farming and lived in a one-room log cabin near Spartanburg. One night, in 1870, the Klan burned the house to the ground because, as Mrs. McMillan asserted, "I was bragging and boasting that I wanted the land." She had gone to a meeting "to hear speaking," as she put it, and apparently came back to her settlement to report what she had heard. Above all, she seems to have communicated too well her desire to own land. Some of her neighbors became alarmed at such bold thoughts. "They all said I was making laws," she testified, "or going to have the land, and the Ku-Klux were going to beat me for bragging that I would have land." The Klan did that and more. Lucy McMillan was forced to abandon even the bit of land she tilled and flee to safety in Spartanburg. There she could find work only as a washerwoman for white people.[31] Her land hunger remained unsatisfied.

Black people faced great difficulties even when they wanted to lease land. Abram Colby said that they were systematically barred from renting in Greene County, Georgia, where sometime in 1870 white men had agreed among themselves not to sell or rent land to blacks. Hence they were obliged to work as hired hands under white men, or "they should not be allowed to live in the county."[32] Sometimes, however, they were allowed to buy small parcels on the edge of town.

The general situation for most black rural laborers was peonage. Lacking ready money because they were rarely paid in cash, they quickly fell into debt when they had to buy provisions from their employers. At the end of the year, when the reckoning was made, "almost always the colored man was brought into debt." Thus the cycle repeated itself, for he was forced to indenture himself to his employer to pay off what he owed.[33]

It may have been in response to such a situation that black men in Starkville (Oktibbeha County), Mississippi, organized a cooperative store, or as they termed it "freedman's exchange."[34] It had about a hundred black stockholders (holding shares valued at $5 to $20) who hired a manager, a Scot named McLachlan. After he was driven away by Klan persecution, a freedman, Tom Woody, took over the management. The cooperative also seems to have been an evening meeting place for the local people, suggesting both community consciousness and action.

Such activity could be found elsewhere in the South. For example, in Meridian, the Methodist church of J. Aaron Moore was the weekly meeting place for a benevolent society "whose objects were to take care of the sick and bury the dead." Lowndes County, Mississippi, had a Union aid society that joyously celebrated the Emancipation Proclamation every January. The town of Livingston, Alabama, had a black friendly society that brought together both races in a Fourth of July celebration—with barbecue, speeches, and flag presentation.[35] Freedmen in Pike and Upson counties, Georgia, organized equal rights associations. Their officers were a mechanic, a shoemaker, farmers, and ministers. Their objects were "to get up schools, attend to the poor and the sick, bury the dead, and cultivate good feeling between the freedmen and their former masters." One officer, William Guilford, had an unspecified shop at Barnesville and was president of the Upson County equal rights association. Its objects, he testified in a trial, were to "establish schools, bury the dead, and hire lawyers."[36] Such community concerns were elevated by Tennessee freedmen who established a state organization, which gathered in at least one annual meeting at Nashville. At the 1866 Tennessee Colored Citizens State Convention, delegation after delegation from the counties reported on the few schools organized and the fervent desire for more. And not least of their expressed concerns pertained to the land.[37]

The mutual-aid societies may have originated in Africa or grown out of the slave experience in America or been the result of black contact with European immigrant artisan traditions. What is important is that their outward sociability and conviviality strongly suggest a sense of community. Their celebrations of national as well as so-called racial holidays resemble those "rituals of mutuality" that Thompson and others found in the emerging English working class.[38] They also went beyond the usual practical functions of ministering to the sick and maintaining burial funds.

Black social advancement was painful whenever and wherever it oc-curred. In Mississippi, for instance, the building of schools proceeded rapid-ly; but the black determination to overcome the status and stigma of sla-very was looked upon with special rancor by the Klan. Its retaliation was brutal and its victims included both black and white schoolteachers. Three such leading black teachers were Elias Hill in York County, South Caro-lina, and Warren Tyler and Isaac Radford of Meridian. It is difficult to say that teaching alone was the leadership function that made them the ob-jects of such violent attacks, for they were politically active as well.[39]

Two black leaders in Georgia, Colby and Harrison, demonstrated in different ways how important schooling was to Reconstruction black people. Colby was illiterate, but he had sent his son William to school. When, in 1868, he was elected to the legislature, his son, then twenty-one years old, became his secretary. Harrison had attended night schools after emancipation. In 1871 he complained that he could not complete a home-study course because his nights were preoccupied with "looking out for disguised men."[40]

On the other hand, Reverend Thomas M. Allen was disappointed by his people's rapid loss of interest in education. "They come in at first by the thousands," he said, "and then it is a kind of drag. They do not know the value of education." But he was quick to deny that this sen-timent applied to all blacks and was proud of the fact that some black youths were graduating "from the university here in Atlanta."[41] The generalization, he asserted, applied only to the most ignorant of his peo-ple. Asked where that ignorance prevailed in Georgia, he observed:

> Generally on large plantations, where people never see anything; where they have been kept down like cattle and horses, bought and sold. A great many of them have been raised on a plantation and have never seen anything of the world. I heard Mr. [H. M.] Turner say in a speech that if they got into the middle of a plantation they seemed to think that they were right in the middle of the world.[42]

And there's the rub. What really was that world? What did Allen know about it and possibly forget about it? Was his and Turner's picture of ig-norance too depressing and, hence, unwarranted?

In an attempt to find a key to the black world during Reconstruction, this chapter has identified some local leaders—leaders, it should be noted, whose names are not mentioned in present-day literature of the era.[43] No doubt there is evidence still to be discovered and ironies still to be pondered. Perhaps, the one irony that ought to be remembered as we reflect on the black community and its culture is the case of Abram Colby. His people had fled to safety in the city; yet the three or four thousand blacks in Atlanta, he asserted, valued safety in the city less than farming their own land. They wished ardently to realize the vision about the kind of world that they could call their own.

Illiterate and gullible as they appeared when buying false boundary stakes as tickets to that new world, they were discerning enough to recognize those members of their own community who might be able to lead them. Men such as James Alston, Richard Burke, George W. Houston, Romulus Moore, Abram Colby, and Samuel Nuckles were elected to state legislatures. They rallied with arms to protect "General" Billy Clopton and Reverend Henry M. Turner. They joined militia companies and marched with Jim Wilkes and Jim Williams in South Carolina: In one case they stood with Wilkes and fought a pitched battle to defend their rights; in another they marched with Williams in order to obtain guarantees from the government before relinquishing their arms. Although he does not appear in the Klan hearings, Charles Caldwell of Clinton, Mississippi, was a notable, almost typical freedman leader. For a brief period before his murder in 1875, he also led a regiment of black soldiers on a daring march through hazardous white territory.[44]

It would be romantic to suppose that all this activity proved successful or that these individual men and women were not without their negative characteristics. Not all blacks were politically conscious militant leaders. They may indeed have had deplorable personal shortcomings, as Southern paternalists and other advocates of white supremacy maintained. Barn and gin-house burning, parading with arms through the superficially quiet villages and towns, and loud shooting in the evenings were not conducive to changing the ways of or winning friends among the white folks who clung tenaciously to the notion that blacks were innately inferior or dangerously rebellious. Such raucous behavior proved offensive and unnerving. Mass turnouts with arms at elections seemed a bizarre and excessive way to perform a basically dispassionate function of the democratic process. Yet had white men not made the polling place the point of provocation, indeed, the point of disruption of the democratic process, blacks would not have had to resort to similar tactics. Warnings that towns would be burned, even when preceded by the too often ignored conditional clause—"if these disturbances don't stop"—may have alienated wavering white men who might have been prepared to work with blacks. Attacks on black Democrats by stoning, heckling, denunciation, or ducking in a pond may also have been more punishment than their alleged crimes warranted. On the other hand, black men who yielded to white attacks and recanted or who accepted bribes served as poor models of civic courage.

Moreover, it would be deceptive to ignore or minimize the Klan terror. Twenty thousand murders in the South between the beginning of Reconstruction and October 1871 cannot be forgotten. They cannot be brushed aside, for they go far to bedevil all assertions of accommodationism. What might be called negative black behavior seems insignificant when compared with the Klan's regulation of black people and the acquiescence of leaders of Southern white society in its actions. Planters, lawyers, and doctors denied the very existence of the Klan or discounted its crimes.[45]

This is not to say that all whites supported suppression. The hearings reveal that some white artisans collaborated with blacks. The village blacksmith in Marengo County, Alabama, who organized a Loyal League was one of these. Another was Daniel Price, who was accused of being the evil genius behind Houston and 2,000 marching black people in Sumter County, and later on was also suspected of being behind Clopton, Tyler, and the black militants of Meridian. Price was anathema to respectable upper-class Southern whites, some of whom described him as a cruel and calculating opportunist who exploited blacks. Since little was known of him, people could speculate about his background. George Houston found Price "the only white man in the county that took a real interest in the [radical party], as I thought ought to have been done."[46]

The Klan hearings disclosed a leadership and a community of feeling, thought, and action among rural blacks. Skilled black workmen, like their counterparts a generation earlier in English rural villages, were the backbone of community leadership. An examination of both General John Schofield's appraisal of Virginia black politicians and the Freedmen's Bureau officers' reports on leading Virginia black men in 1867, quite apart from the Klan hearings, confirm this discovery. So do a white businessmen's blacklist of "unworthy" blacks in Columbus, Mississippi, in 1874, and a recent study of North Carolina black legislators from 1868 to 1872.[47] These leading men in the countryside had their counterparts in at least two Southern cities, Savannah and New Orleans. Of 201 black politicians in the latter place, almost all had been free men of color be-

TABLE 5

Percentage of Artisans Among Black Leaders

Name of Study	Men with Known Occupations	Number of Artisans	Percent
1. Klan hearings (1871)	34	19	56
2. Virginia, Freedmen's Bureau (1867)	99	33	33.3
3. Virginia, Gen. Schofield (1867)	21	9	43
4. North Carolina, Balabanoff (1868-72)	11	5	45
5. Mississippi, Nordhoff (1874)	48	23	48
Total	213	89	41

fore the war, differing in this status from their country cousins. (See
Table 5.) Occupations are known for 151 of these men, and 85 of them,
or 56.3 percent, were skilled workmen. Many may have been members
of that city's Société des Secours Mutuels des Artisans. Carpenters, shoemakers, tailors, masons, plasterers, bricklayers, and cigarmakers were a
significant part of the free black population and of the political leadership.[48] Where the study of New Orleans black leadership focused on political roles, an examination of Savannah's black community revealed a
richly complex fabric of social leadership in which artisans were prominent. Of the 922 officers of 193 clubs and societies between 1865 and
1880, an overwhelming majority were skilled workmen and workwomen.
They furnished the basis of an effective leadership.[49] Among them were
clergymen-artisans such as the Reverend Ulysses L. Houston and Reverend James M. Simms. Both men had been slave artisans and had hired
out their time in order to buy their freedom. Houston was a butcher and
probably a tanner. Simms was a carpenter. Both men also were elected
to the Georgia legislature. Simms organized Union Leagues and the Republican party in Savannah in 1867. He was an ordained minister and
served as deacon and clerk of the First African Baptist Church from 1858
to 1863. Houston was pastor of the First Bryan Baptist Church, treasurer
of the Educational Association of the Colored People of the City of Savannah, and leader of the black communal settlement on Skiddaway Is-

land. Houston was, in addition, one among the twenty black clergymen who met in January 1865 with General W. T. Sherman and Secretary of War Edwin M. Stanton. Their colleagues in that most important conference included barbers, pilots, sailors, and some who had been overseers on rice and cotton plantations. Their spokesman, the venerable Garrison Frazier, was a carpenter.[50] Although most of Savannah's black leadership had been slaves and those in New Orleans freemen, they shared artisan status. They tend to confirm the finding of a substantial and active working-class leadership during Reconstruction.

In the Reconstruction era, black artisans provided a substantial and active community leaderhsip. This was not lost upon disfranchised and defeated planters and others of the Southern white upper classes. They recognized the potential of that black working-class leadership and successfully fought to behead it. At least, the brutality of Klan terrorism substantially damaged the effectiveness of those highly conscious, articulate, and assertive black community leaders.

Moses seems to have been the model for some of these men. Like him, they attempted to lead a sorely tried people to a promised land. That Savannah black churchmen shared a fixed conception of their future in a New Canaan of black folk is expressed by Ulysses Houston's organization of the exodus to Skiddaway Island. Virginia freedmen artisans also furnished such community leadership and patriarchy: Henry Pryor, a carpenter, built and led Zion Town near Richmond; Israel Cross, a former slave, farmed and preached and bought land at Holy Neck in his native Nansemond County where he established a freedmen's community and built homes, a church, and a school; and Gentleman Jim Tynes, a carpenter, farmer, and preacher, led a similar enterprise in 1865 at Smithfield, Isle of Wight County. During the forty years of Cross's leadership in prospering Holy Neck he continually urged his people to "buy some land, build a home, and get some education."[51] This was the perpetual theme of such men all over rural Virginia in the aftermath of the war: Buy land (and by cooperative methods). What they appear to have meant was: Build your own communities. They expressed the hopes of freedmen from Virginia to Texas.

Shall We Have Land?   6

The freedmen had got the impression that the abandoned lands of their old owners were to be divided amongst
them. Their impressions arose from the talk they had
heard around them by the white and colored soldiers.
—Elizabeth Hyde Botume, *First Days Among the Contrabands,* p. 170.

[Landowners] steadily refuse to sell or lease lands to
black men. Colored mechanics of this city [Vicksburg,
Mississippi] who have made several thousand dollars
during the last two years, find it impossible to buy even
land enough to put up a house on, yet white men can
purchase any amount of land. —Samuel Thomas, Colonel, Assistant Commissioner B.R.F. and A.L. for Mississippi and N.E. Louisiana, July 1865.

The mass of black humanity that marched relentlessly toward Savannah
with Sherman's army expected freedom. The men, women, and children
in it appear to have set their sights only on that horizon in 1864. But
when the general heard the Savannah black elders state their desires, he
and Secretary Stanton, and through them the nation, knew in January
1865 that the freed people expected land, beyond their freedom. The
Congress acted quickly in March to enact the Freedmen's Bureau bill
and provide in it a compromise offer to lease abandoned lands to freedmen and "loyal (white) refugees." This was far less than the expected
confirmation by Congress of a grant that Sherman had made of almost a
half-million acres of land to freedmen in Georgia, South Carolina, and
Florida, and upon which 40,000 freed people had rapidly settled. Nevertheless, the seed had been planted, and freedmen within and beyond the
coastal preserve of Sherman's Special Field Order No. 15 cultivated the
idea that they would receive their former masters' lands. Like a hardy
perennial, the expectation bloomed in the last months of 1865, was seemingly crushed to earth in January 1866, only to flower again in the clos-

ing days of 1866. Reports of expected divisions of plantations, allotments of forty acres and a mule, persisted down through the end of the century. A promise had been made during Sherman's wartime action, and the freedmen had accepted it as irrevocable. And even when it was clear within months that the government "welshed" and proceeded to restore hundreds of thousands of acres to former enemies of the United States, freedmen tenaciously believed that the promise would somehow be redeemed.[1]

That sense of expectancy swept like a hot wind across the former Confederacy through the summer and fall of 1865. Remembering the dying days of slavery for him in Alabama, Simon Phillips told an interviewer in the 1930s how it was. He had belonged to Bryant Watkins, a wealthy planter and owner of 300 slaves near Greensboro, Alabama. Phillips recalled that his old master had to dissuade a group of freedmen from putting down stakes to divide up the land. The old man's recollection is a rare piece of testimony from a former slave. It neatly fits the picture rendered by Freedmen's Bureau agents in Alabama reporting to superior officers from October through December 1865: The freedmen expect the division and distribution of the plantations among them before Christmas. In Texas an officer of the Bureau found freedmen east of the Trinity River who late in 1865 did not know they were free until he told them they were. Yet even they had heard vague rumors that they were to be freed on Christmas and that on New Year's Day they would receive half of the property in a "grand division."[3] In North Carolina another Bureau official found hopes so firmly fixed in freedmen's minds that he and his staff found it "not easy to eradicate them."[4] At Lumberton a Bureau agent thought freedmen had "extravagant ideas in relation to confiscated lands." The local Bureau agent reported they were waiting "to see what will be done for them, if anything, the first of January 1866."[5] At Warrenton, 150 freed couples were married by an Episcopal minister on August 25 and 26, two days before the visit of a Bureau officer. They appear to have thus solemnized their relations in order to have a prerequisite for an expected division of lands to heads of families. Even if a few were really prompted to the wedding ceremony by "mischievous soldiers" who told them they must be married before receiving land, the expectation of land was nevertheless great. On August 27, 2,500 freedmen packed the Warrenton public square to hear a speech by a Bureau agent, in anticipation of "new laws" announcing their impending bounty. Like Old World peasants awaiting words of justice from a distant and wise mo-

narch, Warrenton's freedmen "looked neither to the State nor to their
old masters but to the 'Northern Government' to assist them."[6] The sol-
emnity with which they anticipated their just reward was matched if
not exceeded by a group of Mississippi freedmen. Among them the story
had been told that the Freedmen's-Bureau had received a "Great Document," sealed with four seals. These would be broken on January 1, 1866,
revealing "final orders" from an omnipotent Northern government. When
a Quaker missionary toured a number of towns in that state, in November 1865, he was repeatedly confronted with the massive demonstrations
that freedmen expected "something great was going to take place about
Christmas." At Meridian, 500 black people must have sat painfully through
a meeting at which the Reverend Mr. John Henry Douglas assailed their
"foolish ideas" about land. He repeated the performance at Aberdeen
and a meeting of more than 2,500 freedmen in Macon.[7] At about the
same time, Captain Stuart Barnes of the Bureau in Petersburg, Virginia,
told a meeting of freedmen who crowded into the largest African church
in town that the lands of their former masters would not be divided
among them.[8]

Journalists as well as missionaries attested to the powerful air of expectation that hung over the South. The New York *Tribune*'s Whitelaw
Reid reported it from Lynchburg, Virginia, and from several other points
as he traveled farther South.[9] John Dennett of *The Nation* learned from
a Kingtree, South Carolina, freedman that he would not work cotton
crops and was "waitin til Jenewerry" to see whether he would get land.
At Edgefield, Dennett was present at a meeting of 2,000 freed people
who had come to town to hear a speech by a general of the army. A local landlord told the reporter, "If the general don't tell them cuffees
they're to have a share o' our land and hosses and everything else, you'll
see a hell of a row today. . . . they don't expect nothin' else but they're
to have half." Traveling on southward, Dennett was anxiously asked by
a Baton Rouge, Louisiana, freedman if it was "probable that Negroes
would get land of their own, by gift or by purchase."[10]

Despite the repeated efforts by General Howard and other officials
to dissuade the freedmen from their "extravagant" and "foolish" expectations and "false impressions," they persisted. Freed people in South
Carolina, Georgia, and Florida continued to hope in December 1865 for
the gift of lands from the government or the right to purchase them. The
bitter reality for them was that President Johnson had forced General

Howard to restore lands to former rebels as early as June 1865. The process had gone on apace, and by November and December, the general's messages to freedmen were true—there were no confiscated or abandoned acres to give them. The well-intentioned Howard, at the head of the Freedmen's Bureau, had been finessed and overpowered by Johnson in his alliance with former planters and slaveowners.[11] Even in the face of the bitter news they received in January 1866, when they were forced to go to work for others at wages or in sharecropping, freedmen refused to relinquish the dream. In February 1868 a story representing the general and persistent land hunger came out of Madison, Georgia. There 200 freedmen remained idle, waiting for the Georgia Reconstruction convention to divide the land. It was not to be done; yet they clung to the idea.[12] On the Santee River, Captain Charles Pinckney asserted, carpetbaggers had promised forty acres and a mule. He was sure that "at Adams Run negros came to the polls bringing halters for mules which they expected to carry home."[13] Five years after emancipation and after the frustration of Sherman's intentions in Special Field Order No. 15, South Carolina freedmen retained a "chief anxiety"—"to get possession of land."[14] In Alabama, it would appear, hopes had been aroused anew after March 1867 when Thaddeus Stevens introduced a confiscation measure in Congress. Although defeated, Stevens's bill and news of it probably came to the attention of freed people, according to the Southern historian Walter L. Fleming. He asserted that a symbol of that land expectation—painted sticks to stake out land divisions—was still evident in 1873 and as late as 1900.[15]

The powerful longing for land, whether expressed as a desire for subsistence garden plots or twenty, forty, or more acres on which to raise market crops, was a normal one. Olmsted in his antebellum southern sojourn found one slave who expressed even then that what he wanted was freed and a bit of land of his own. Although the direct link cannot be made between the advocacy of collective land acquisition in the black national conventions of the 1840s and the slaves, it is conceivable that through existing modes of communication between free and slave blacks such idea may have been transmitted and received. For one thing, we cannot entirely ignore the possible effect of the appearance in the *Anglo-African Magazine* early in the Civil War of a call for confiscation, division, and redistribution of former plantations to freed people. The editors in New York were explicit and unequivocal in asserting the land need of the enslaved people in the Southern states, whether those states had remained loyal or were in rebellion.[16] But at this time behind the lines of the Confederacy the enslaved were making their first moves toward self-emancipation. They did not at this point assert the demand for land.

In the next two years their experiences in a free labor system evoked the natural desire for land and community. On the one hand its expression appears to have been a positive assertion of their self-concept and on the other a negative judgment on the wage-paying or so-called free labor system that they had encountered in the Sea Islands, the Mississippi Valley, and New Orleans. In these places the government's actions and policies whetted the freedmen's appetites for their own economic and social management. In addition, when U.S. soldiers came in contact with freed people, some of them appear to have touched a sympathetic chord in the freedmen by their agitation of the land question. These two components of the freedmen's experience probably were the catalysts that hastened the transformation of desire into expectation.

The government lacked the clear, simple, and direct goal that freedmen shared with free Afro-Americans and abolitionists. But in its fumbling way, Washington, through congressional and executive policy making, and the army, through necessity, aided in shaping the conditions under which freedmen could sieze the opportunity to contribute their share in the emergent revolution. The 4 million Afro-Americans in the South were a critical force, for they were the base of Southern society, and as they turned their weight from bondage to freedom, they produced fatal cracks in a moribund social order. The government delivered decisive force from outside Southern society to overthrow it. The two interests converged especially in confiscating the material base of slavery—slaves and land.

The soldier was one of the sharp instruments that helped to shape the emergent freedmen's community and to play a part in pressuring the government for an equitable land policy. Even after discounting probably exaggerated accounts by Southern whites of insurrectionary designs among black soldiers and black communities, the troops did contribute to the freedmen's assertiveness with respect to land. Early in 1863 Union soldiers near Jackson, Mississippi, freeing the slaves on a plantation, gave them arms. The freed people were reported to have divided the plantation among themselves together with its cotton and farm implements. Unfortunately, they were not to realize their ambition, for they were captured by Confederate soldiers and removed to Jackson.[17] Similar in-

cidents of self-proclaimed liberation and expropriation were reported in
Alabama, North Carolina, and Virginia. In Albemarle County in the latter state freedmen said that they had been given the impression by Yankee soldiers and other persons that they would benefit from a land division in the summer of 1865.[18] In Mississippi during that year the Meridian *Clarion* expressed editorial concern over the black expectation of
lands. Senator L. Q. C. Lamar said that whites came into Vicksburg in
fear of black men who were demanding land by Christmas "or they would
take them by force."[19] Such fears were found among Alabama whites
who alleged that black soldiers and Freedmen's Bureau agents told freedmen to arm themselves for the coming struggle for property. In one county $3,000 worth of new Spencer rifles allegedly were found in black ca-
bins. Fleming suggested that the hysteria was misplaced and that the guns
were merely held by the freedmen as a mark of freedom.[20] He might
have added that a gun was necessary to hunt for a food supply in the
woods and fields of the Alabama countryside. When Governor William
Marvin of Florida tried to dissuade freedmen at a mass meeting in Mari-
anna from expecting land distribution, he was told that soldiers had informed them of the coming division.[21] *The Nation's* correspondent discovered in his travels that a "few mischief makers" in federal regiments
persuaded freedmen to refuse to work, because "they are the rightful
owners of the land." When President Johnson dispatched Carl Schurz and
General Grant to report on conditions in the South, he received from
them confirmation of the widespread soldier agitation of freedmen.[22]

If some whites perceived the role of troops as mischiefmakers and insurrectionists, they doubtless expressed their own sense of impending rec-
tification of past inequities. What they did not say but what they may
have understood was the leadership role of soldiers, and particularly of
black soldiers, in freedmen communities. One such army man was Jacob
Richardson of the 49th U.S. Colored Infantry. He presided over the June,
1865, mass meeting of freedmen in Vicksburg that drafted appeals for
the right to vote and the rejection of Mississippi's reentry into the Union
until their suffrage condition should be met.[23] Landowners near Huntsville, Alabama, combined to refuse to rent land to blacks in the fall of
1865; soon afterward, a company of black soldiers was stationed there
and their presence was believed to have modified the whites' attitudes.[24]
Near Doctorville, Georgia, the captain of the 12th Maine Volunteer Regiment feared that black soldiers "unsettled labor" and were harmful to
the freed people in the vicinity.[25]

Perhaps it was fear of such assertiveness for civil and economic freedom that prompted property owners to "expect" insurrection and, worse,
murder and pillage. Responding to such fears, the army in some places
moved to clip the power of black troops. In western Tennessee two white
regiments were dispatched to "offset possible danger caused by the presence of colored troops." In Louisiana Major General Edward R. S. Canby acted on General Grant's direction to bar black soldiers from purchasing their arms as they were being discharged from the service. This vio-
lated a standard practice of the army. But in South Carolina, General
Quincy Adams Gillmore was reluctant to muster out freedmen from the
Southern states and more significantly those "few bad soldiers who were
formerly slaves in the neighborhood."[26] The general merely confirmed
the close bonds between men in uniform and the people in their neighborhoods and communities. Their concerns appear to have been identical: a reconstruction of society to recognize and honor their rights.

Even when they appear to have formed wandering bands and behave-
ed as outlaws in classical primitive rebel fashion, some freedmen soldiers
articulated their program of reconstruction. As one alarmed white North
Carolina citizen paraphrased these black soldiers, "They said their object
and business was to examine papers, secure arms, get *forage,* drive Negroes
off the farms, and rectify the country, generally.' "[27]

The claims of impending black conspiracy and insurrection proved
false. There was a total absence of any sign of action of blacks rising up
against whites in January 1866 or at any time thereafter. The New Orleans *Tribune,* bitter over the apparent camouflage for continuing planter social control, pointed out that the alleged "danger" had passed but
that a real danger remained. Especially incensed over General Canby's order, the newspaper asked "Shall our brethren be permitted to return to
their homes without means of defense—and shall the colored patriot be
deprived of his arms and delivered up without means of protection into
the hands of the rebel militia?"[28]

Black soldiers should have been expected to react in a near mutinous
fashion when they learned of the restoration of lands to former slaveowners and Confederate rebels. But they continued nevertheless to hold out
hope, as their civilian kin did, for an opportunity to purchase land and
to begin new lives once they had been discharged. Thus whole regiments
built up pools of funds to purchase land. Thomas W. Conway reported
from Louisiana early in 1865 that twenty black regiments were prepared
to buy all the available confiscated and abandoned land in the state. That

would have totaled 62,528 acres. One regiment alone had raised $50,000
in order to purchase five of the largest plantations on the Mississippi River. "This interest in the soil is general with these soldiers," Conway wrote.
They looked forward to owning small farms on their discharge, and companies and squads applied to Conway for land. Some tried to demonstrate
their capacity for success by stating that they had wives who were willing
to work. Others cited their families as eager and equipped to make their
purchase pay off. Conway reported that these *groups* of soldiers had saved
from $200 to $500 for the purpose.[29] Another regiment, the 13th U.S.
Colored Infantry, stationed in 1865 at Nashville, organized a Kansas Home
stead Colonization Association. The aim of the 500 enlisted men and
their officers who formed the association was to "take homesteads together, in the same county in Kansas, where we can have homes." The
plan was not realized. Another regiment, near Jacksonville, Florida, at
about the same time, was the object of its chaplain's scheme to buy 8,000
acres, subdivide them, and resell plots to the men. They had banked
$40,000 to $50,000, of which Chaplain Moore proposed to use $16,000
for the plan. He obtained use of a U.S. transport vessel, the *Hattie,* to
bring colonists who settled on plots of from one to five acres. When the
soldiers of the 34th U.S. Colored Troops decided to use their money in
the bank themselves, the chaplain sold out, leaving the colonists without
titles and the land surveyor without his fees.[30]

About a year and a half later, a group of 260 freed men and women
in Adams County, Mississippi, formed an association to purchase a 10,000
acre plantation. Their statement of purpose indicated that they were pled-
ging bounty money expected from the U.S. government. A sampling of
the names on their petition in 1867 suggests that many of them were formerly in the 6th U.S. Colored Heavy Artillery Regiment. They were discharged in 1866 at Natchez.[31] Some sense of community, as well as individual advancement, was expressed in their actions. That inspiration
may have sprung from their common lot as slaves born in the nearby
Mississippi countryside and the upper Louisiana parishes. It probably
was reinforced by common exposure to the hazards of war and in the
same military units.

That spirit of cohesiveness had already been displayed by black soldiers in northern Louisiana in October 1865. When hysteria gripped white
in the area over supposed black insurrections, they petitioned Governor
Madison Wells to take preventive measures. It may have been merely the

self-organization in civilian life of disbanded black regiments that aroused the white citizens. A New York *Herald* correspondent reported, "It is said that these regiments retain their organization, notwithstanding their disbandment." Obviously, there was much smoke here, but the real fire of the black soldier's sense of community produced sufficient heat to be felt widely.[32]

In addition to these concerns, the soldiers' sense of family responsibility was clearly demonstrated in letters to relatives. Gulf area black soldiers sent thousands of such communications through the New Orleans office of the army's Bureau of Labor. They enclosed money in their letters that in the aggregate constituted a "large sum," according to the officer in charge. Other ways were found to demonstrate a soldier's ties to his people, if not to direct kin, then to others whose misfortune was their loss of kin. Thus a regiment stationed near Helena, Arkansas, wound up its term of army duty by making a major contribution of money and labor to construct a black orphans' asylum. Ten companies in the regiment raised more than $2,000 by donations and another $73 by a concert that they gave on January 4 and 5, 1866. Their regimental officers and staff also contributed $55. The money purchased land, lumber, building materials, and cows. The soldiers deeded their purchase of thirty acres to the Indiana Yearly Meeting of Friends for the Asylum. Besides, they marched to the building site week after week, encamped there, and cleared forty acres, dug ditches for drainage, split rails, and made fences. And then they erected the buildings, did much grading, and made cisterns and wells. This was their labor of love.[33]

Similar labors have already been noted by soldiers supporting schools. Their striving to learn to read and write, their struggle to acquire land, and their support of their families strongly suggest strengths unimaginable to believers in slave infantilization or the rigid concept of paternalistic mastership over them. These soldiers may have been reared in the ways of those Significant Personalities who ruled from the Big House. They failed utterly to be dominated permanently by the masters' values and imperatives. When they could, these Afro-Americans asserted their own. The sense of community and of responsibility, which masters presumably had denied them, emerged vividly. If anything appears to have collapsed, it was not the freedmen's positive self-concept but the masters'. Those inculcations of the masters that slaves allegedly internalized appear to have been ephemeral and were subordinated by freedmen. The former slaves-turned-soldiers and then civilians developed and asserted their own values and imperatives. These freed men and women acted out of an understanding that they must transform the world into which they were born so that they and their children could have a better one. This was their passion.

If that ardent longing was to be realized, freedmen decided, then they must have the lands of their former masters. This too was their *passion.* That was precisely the word used in independent testimony in January 1866 by Colonel Charles H. Howard after a tour of inspection through South Carolina and Georgia and by John W. Alvord upon return from an investigation throughout the Southern states. [34] Laura Towne had observed three years earlier on the Sea Islands "for the possession of land the most intense desire." [35] At that time the Georgia-born former slave Harry McMillan told the American Freedmen's Inquiry Commission: "The people here would rather have the land than work for wages." He urged that men who "have the faculty of supporting their families" be singled out to be given land. [36] From Mississippi in 1865 Colonel Samuel Thomas reported that in every part of the state freedmen longed to have their own homes. Seventy years later a 104-year-old former Crawford County, Georgia, slave residing in Depression-era Arkansas remembered the desire. "An de slaves taken out of dey bondage, some of de very few white folks give dem niggers what dey liked de best a small piece of land for to work." [37] Most got nothing. When Congress investigated the Klan in 1871, a white Alabaman testified that some freedmen stole horses, mules, bedclothes, bedding, and provisions. As if this expropriation of the former masters was not heinous enough, then the staking out of land, "and mules and everything picked out," capped this catalog of crimes. These freedmen thought "they were the big dogs of the ring." Some, the Alabama witness stated, "think they had a right" to the cotton, corn, mules, and pigs they had taken. [38] But Tunis Campbell before the same congressional committee in Georgia testified to the desire for land; "the great cry of our people is for land." [39] A subdued version of that cry emerged from an Arkansas freedman who approached General Sanborn at Fort Smith: [40]

> Freedman: "Sir, I want you to help me in a personal matter."
> General: "Where is your family?"
> F.: "On Red River."

G.:   "Have you not everything you want?"
F.:   "No, sir."
G.:   "You are free!"
F.:   "Yes, sir, you set me free, but you left me there."
G.:   "What do you want?"
F.:   "I want some land; I am helpless; you do nothing for me but
        give me freedom."
G.:   "Is not that enough?"
F.:   "It is enough for the present; but I cannot help myself unless
        I get some land; then I can take care of myself and family;
        otherwise I cannot do it."

Edgefield district, South Carolina, laborers under contract with a planter
displayed a "restless disposition to wander" in July 1865, even after they
had planted a bounteous crop. It only remained for them to harvest it;
yet one night every freedman disappeared, leaving the whole crop to the
planter. Stories of land given to freedmen on the islands near Charleston
had reached them, and they appeared to have "set out to get their share."
Like thousands of other freedmen, they pursued their desire.[41]
   The majority were only to be frustrated by legislative and private pro-
hibitions against acquisition of their share of acres. Even when they were
prepared to pay, freedmen were barred by combinations of planters. When
Thomasville, Georgia, freedmen wished to rent land in 1865, they were
told that no black man would be able to have land by lease. They made
their way around the obstacle by finding a white man who rented a plantation for them. They contracted to pay him a share of the crop above a
specified amount.[42] At Amherst County, Virginia, farmers united and
resolved to refuse to rent lands to black men.[43] Mississippi planters, however, went further and apparently persuaded the legislature of the provisional state government in 1865 and 1867 to prohibit the ownership
or leasing of lands by freed blacks.[44] And in South Carolina, as Lucy
McMillan had testified, a black woman who thought "out loud" about
owning land could have her house burned down by the Klan.[45] The New
Orleans *Tribune* clearly labeled the planter "the stumbling block" and
the "great obstacle to peace, to regular labor, to public security, to union
and harmony." The editor called for new ways to get the land out of
their hands and into the hands of "a new class of man."[46]

There was the nub of the matter—the struggle over the land in the summer and fall of 1865 was an agrarian class conflict. The planters resisting expropriation used the machinery of state. In the provisional state governments under President Johnson's protective leniency, planters not only prohibited black landownership but enacted extreme measures of social control that virtually restored slavery. The black codes struck directly at freedmen striving to escape their subordination and to obtain their communities. It was class and race legislation. But planters escalated the struggle on the political plane by pressing President Johnson to curb the redistribution of lands to freedmen. Simultaneously, they demanded that the results of the war be set aside by their insistent demand for restoration of their lands. The President responded with alacrity during the second half of 1865 and until his impeachment. At the same time it should be realized that former Confederate planters hoped to prevent their displacement as a ruling class by the so-called carpetbagger or Northern entrepreneur and planter. This much may be conceded to their paternalistic self-conscious assertion of hegemony. Some were willing to adopt capitalist modes and capitalist values; and some did have to relinquish their antebellum capitalistic identities. However, their heaviest blow against threats to their domination fell on the freed black people, their allies in the Freedmen's Bureau, the teachers of the Southern countryside, and those favorably disposed to them in the state and federal governments.

The freedmen were the principal victims of both the planters' revenge and their account books. The aged and infirm freed people were now a more visible burden on the costs of production; some planters totally eliminated the expense by evicting them. They similarly cut off productive laborers after crops were laid by and thus hoped to eliminate the wages bill or the croppers' share of the later market earnings. Freedmen's Bureau records are swollen with freedmen's complaints of such planter behavior (see Appendixes III and IV). The Bureau's assistant commissioner for North Carolina, Colonel Eliphalet Whittlesey, for example, reported that his officers had been busy during the last quarter of 1865 in attempting to settle "claims for labor." In Warren County alone 150 such claims were filed, freedmen complaining of ill treatment or denial of wages or shares of the crop. Whittlesey found an old story repeated thousands of times: no definite agreement between planter and laborer, and no wages promised. A freedmen would complain, "Massa said stay till the crop is made and he would do what is right." Massa refused to do what was right according to the freedmen.[47] From 1865 to 1867, when complaint books were maintained by the Bureau agents in Albemarle County, Virginia, they recorded 500 entries involving labor questions between planters and black laborers or disputes over contracts. One agent found planters taking advantage of freedmen in making contracts. "I find others, who," he wrote, "having completed the harvest, wish to rid themselves of such laborers as work by the year. To this end they provoke them to a breach of their contract." But such farmers were not numerous in the district, he said. Among the complaints he was obliged to investigate was that of Joshua Perry. This black freedman was head of a family including his wife and six children, "six working hands" who had been working for the planter against whom he brought charges. They had labored for him since Lee's surrender and had received no pay except a little corn and molasses. Another complaint concerned "an old colored man . . . (whom) you have driven away from your premises, . . . has a contract with you . . . and cannot be broken." On the other hand numerous letters of Bureau agents to freedmen reflected their wide discontent; "While protecting you in every right that pertains to you as Freedman, we will compel you to respect contracts when they are just and equitable and made voluntarily." While many contracts may have been equitably and willingly drawn up, apparently they could not settle the freedmen's discontents, nor the planters' either. An Albemarle County resident noted that farmers fixed wages at $5 per month for a male first-class laborer, $3 for a female first-class laborer, with food furnished but no clothing. In addition planters permitted some of the privileges of slavery, "gardens, fowls, etc." In other Virginia counties planters' meetings fixed wages at $5 per month. Complaints were made of the freedmen that they formed erroneous ideas about their freedom. "They are insolent, sullen and disobedient," and their behavior led their employers to whip or beat them or to discharge them.[48] This was not an uncommon practice; and it crossed state lines. In the Lumberton, North Carolina, Freedmen's Bureau office, freedmen made numerous complaints against employers during the summer of 1866. Their contracts for a share of the crops were being violated by planters who were driving some of them off after the crop had been laid by.[49] Bureau agent George R. Ballou, who was responsible for four Georgia counties (Stewart, Quitman, Randolph, Early), registered similar charges in 1868. He was forced to investigate "criminal acts" of freedmen that apparently had arisen in response to "fraud and outrage" by whites; a fel-

low agent responsible for Lee, Terrell, and Calhoun counties reported
similar conflicts involving outrages, arbitrary discharges of laborers, and
a lack of security among the freedmen. Ballou described the separate anguish of farmers and laborers imposed by an inequitable system:

> For example, a freedman labors faithfully for 10 months; has per-
> haps, in his desire to accumulate something for himself, deprived
> himself and family of many necessaries. (I have known instances
> of their going without food even), and after the crops are made
> and nearly gathered the freedman is driven away with his family,
> upon some slight pretext (or none at all), and loses all; he be-
> comes discouraged, disheartened, and to a certain extent, des-
> perate; he has no tribunal to which he may appeal for justice,
> and his only resort, to prevent actual starvation, is to steal and to
> kill the stock of the planter who defrauds him.[50]

"Jenewerry" 1866 came and went, and there was no division of the
lands. A year later, freedmen faced the same dismal disappointment. The
soldiers had by now come home and settled down to farming for others
for wages or as tenant sharecroppers. Some of them purchased land. Despite the Johnsonian restoration, freedmen continued to hope for a confiscation policy, at least for an opportunity to make use of the 1866 Southern Homestead Act. This legislation fell short of a vigorous confiscation
policy. It remained a last best hope to be expected from Washington, a
shadow of early Civil War proposals.

Driven by the abolitionists, Radical Republicans and free Afro-Americans, the government early in the war began the process of undermining
the economic and social foundations of slavery.[51] In the first Confiscation Act of August 1861 Congress authorized the seizure of property
used in fighting against the United States. During the same summer session, Congress enacted a direct tax on real estate and apportioned the tax
among the states. This was implemented in June 1862 with a measure
creating tax commissioners who would collect the delinquent taxes in
the occupied areas of Confederate states. After calculating and determin-
in the tax liability, the commissioners were authorized to seize and sell
the lands of the delinquent at public auction. This activity was placed
under the Treasury Department, and it thus obtained, for example, 187
plantations in South Carolina. However, Salmon P. Chase, the Secretary

of the Treasury, agreed to a proposed experiment in working the plantations with "contraband" labor, that is the labor of the former slaves who
refused to flee with their masters from the Sea Islands to the safety of the
mainland. Just as General Benjamin Butler at Fortress Monroe in 1861 had
employed such labor about his camps and paid wages, so the Sea Island
authorities would pay wages to cultivators of the lands and sell the cotton raised to pay delinquent taxes. Later, when he was transferred to
New Orleans, Butler occupied abandoned sugar plantations. He established a wage system as he employed freed blacks who were sent out from
refugee camps. Subsistence plots were allotted the freed people at Port
Royal while they labored in cotton fields superintended by Northern
capitalists. By mid-1862, some freedmen had risen to the status of agricultural wage earners, while others had become service occupation wage
workers.

The Second Confiscation Act, of July 17, 1862, pushed further along
the road of revolution by authorizing the seizure of rebels' property whether or not directly used in the war. This was followed by the Confiscation
Act of 1863, which empowered the Secretary of the Treasury to take
control of abandoned land in the Confederate states. Radical Republican
George Julian of Indiana introduced a bill in Congress early in 1864 that
would have brought confiscated and abandoned Southern estates under
the Homestead Act of 1862. As public land, it would have been thrown
open to settlers to occupy forty- and eighty-acre tracts. Limited to U.S.
Army soldiers, freedmen, and loyal whites in the South, the bill would
have made ownership complete after settlers lived five years on their
homesteads and cultivated them. But the bill never passed the Senate,
although rising sentiment toward such confiscation was apparent in the
House vote in favor of the measure. With the 1863 confiscation law the
government had assembled a considerable legal basis for acquiring millions of acres as Union armies reestablished U.S. jurisdiction. The Treasury Department's agents rapidly implemented plans to lease abandoned and confiscated plantations as they acquired them. The land thus put
under cultivation or where crops already had been planted before abandonment yielded harvests that fattened Treasury deposits and lessees'
profits and gave wage-earning opportunities to thousands of freedmen.

The 1863 law, for example, put 80,000 acres of farmland and 142
city lots in Mississippi under the Treasury's jurisdiction by 1865. Most
of them were transferred to the Freedmen's Bureau in 1865. In leasing

plantations the government set field laborers' wages. When Secretary Chase learned of the exploitation of freedmen by planters in the lower Mississippi Valley, he ordered an upward revision of wages from $7-$8 to $25 per month for prime male workers, $20 for second-class men, and $14-$18 for women. Lessees were a bit more subjected to controls than they had been by Treasury agents. In some locations small numbers of black lessees only underscored the domination of well-heeled operators from the North or former planters who had returned to their old plantations. Nevertheless, these black farmers successfully planted and marketed their cotton crops and suggested that freedom might mean opportunities to become independent producers. Generally, however, Treasury agents or tax commissioners stood in their way by favoring capitalists and quick-profit seekers over them. The army, in the person of General Lorenzo Thomas, in the Mississippi Valley, also barred freedmen progress by reversing the wage increases. Thomas met with Treasury agents in March 1864 and appears to have won the power to reduce wage scales to from $3.50 to $10 per month plus clothing and rations. Even when the clothing allotment could be commuted to cash of about $3, freedmen could earn a top wage of $13 a month and women $10. This was half the scale decreed by the Treasury Secretary. But despite the dismal rivalry between the Treasury and the army to control the lands and the freedmen in the Vicksburg, Natchez, Helena sectors, General Grant established a purported "Negro paradise" at Davis Bend, Mississippi. Black lessees on an individual basis proved to be efficient and knowledgeable cultivators and reaped profits with their cotton. Their success was all the more impressive for their having planted late and still having overcome the disastrous effects of the army worm. This experience was the prologue to the experiment in 1865 of a relatively self-sufficient Afro-American freedmen's community at the Bend. As such, it became a significant step in the government's unwitting, perhaps reluctant, advance toward social revolution.

The army-Treasury rivalry had already been acted out on another stage by the time Grant and other officers made their decisions about Davis Bend. That was in the South Carolina Sea Islands, where General Rufus Saxton tried to head off tax commissioner sales of lands in 1863. He exerted considerable energy in urging freedmen to preempt lands on the islands. Indeed, he had urged division of the lands into subsistence lots for the freedmen and their families as early as February 1862. He had suc-

ceeded in postponing the land sales of early 1863 until March. Of the
16,479 acres put up for sale, freedmen cooperatively purchased 2,000.
Saxton seems to have fought a successful holding action while freedmen
improved their chances to save toward the purchase of some of the 60,000
acres not sold in March and scheduled for sale early in 1864. Saxton and
the Reverend Mansfield French seized on a loophole in President Lincoln's
instructions of September 1863 for the next land sales to argue that freedmen would be unable to obtain lands against the expected bids of speculators and more wealthy competitors. Under the President's instructions
about 16,000 of the 60,000 acres to be sold would be reserved for black
heads of families at $1.25 per acre. Saxton continued to urge blacks to
preempt homesteads and perfect their titles later. But he also calculated
that Lincoln's instructions would in practice provide half of the freedmen
with two acres each. He feared that speculators would gain the advantage,
and he believed them to be "persons who had no interests in common with
the negro except the profit to be derived from their labor on the lowest
possible terms." Saxton and French appealed to the Treasury Secretary
and the President, who responded with new orders in December 1863
that effectively barred speculators from obtaining land in the Sea Islands.

According to the new orders, then, all lands except those reserved for
military and educational purposes were opened to preemption at $1.25
per acre. A down payment of two-fifths of the price could be made and
the remainder when the deed was received. Purchases could be made only by loyal persons twenty-one years of age and over and who had been
living in the department (Georgia, South Carolina, and Florida) for six
months since the occupation by federal forces or who were living there
in December 1863. Most significant was the provision that such persons
could preempt twenty- or forty-acre tracts. Saxton hastened to urge the
freedmen to lose no time in selecting lots and filing claims with the tax
commissioners. Nearly all the lands were thus duly claimed, and the required payment was deposited. But two of the three commissioners balked and refused to receive the claims. They went instead to Washington
to try to win reversal of the December instructions. They succeeded only
in taking back to South Carolina a suspension. Saxton insisted that the
original instructions had never been revoked. Nevertheless, the damage
had been done. The sales took place as the commissioners had planned,
in February 1864. The historian of the Sea Island "experiment," Willie
Lee Rose, observed that the December 1863 instructions contained "the

genesis of the famous postwar expectation of the freed slaves that the government would provide them with forty acres of land." It should be noted that these were proposals not for a "gift" but for distributions for which freedmen would pay with the fruits of their own labor. The suspension outraged the freed people. Farms that they had preempted at Saxton's urging and on his instructions from the government had been sold out from under them. Freed people on St. Helena declared that they would not work for the purchaser; and those at Redwood Point also refused to work and to permit the return of their preemption payment. But on Wassa Island freed people pooled their funds and successfully outbid speculators to purchase lands on which they lived and worked. In general, however, freed people were left with little but anger and frustration and the need to go to work for others, probably under the onerous conditions Saxton had noted. A promise had been broken, and the hopes of freedmen callously upset. Almost unconsciously, the government had been forced to make contrabands of slaves, then to recognize their need for self-determination, and, finally, to convert them into wage workers, "free" men in a "free" society.

During the war, the government occupied millions of acres, of which 800,000 acres were abandoned by former owners. These acres were turned over to the Freedmen's Bureau in the spring of 1865. Coming so soon after Sherman's order, this congressional action appeared a natural step toward the goal of land confiscation and redistribution. But this hope foundered on the President's obduracy and the Republicans' weaknesses.

Former Confederate landowners gained inestimable support from President Johnson's policies during the summer and fall of 1865. Particular strategic advantages were won in the struggle for land by his reversals of established policies. When General Howard attempted during the summer to advance the Sherman land grant policy to freedmen, the President forced him to reverse himself and withdrew his orders. The Bureau of Refugees, Freedmen and Abandoned Lands was in reality forced to become a bureau for the frustration of freedmen's desires and rights to land. The celebrated Christian General Howard was placed in a most humiliating and unenviable position. In June he began to carry out his responsibility under Special Field Order No. 15 and the Freedmen's Bureau Act of March 3, 1865. General Rufus Saxton had been busy since January rapidly settling about 40,000 persons on the reserved coastal strip. But he was hard-pressed during the summer of 1865 to prevent evictions of freed

people, in view of the President's pardoning power, which restored rights
and property to former rebels. Meanwhile, planters besieged Howard in
Washington with requests for restoration of lands as they hastened to
take a required oath of loyalty to the United States.

In preparation for his task, Howard asked Attorney General James
Speed for an opinion on his responsibilities with respect to the 800,000
acres of abandoned lands placed in his jurisdiction by the Freedmen's
Bureau Act of March 3, 1865. Speed replied that Howard had the
obligation to use the lands for the benefit of refugees and freedmen
and that he was required to assign forty acres of land to every male in
those two categories. Even on a request to reread the act, Speed held
firm in his opinion. Howard was thus empowered to proceed with the
distribution of plots of land in addition to those parceled out under
Sherman's orders.[52]

But freedmen's titles to the lands remained under a cloud. General
Sherman's Special Field Order No. 16 had made final title for freedmen
conditional on presidential confirmation.[53] Congress had failed to grant
permanent titles in the March 3, 1865, act and Speed had not written an
opinion on the title issue. The loophole thus created enabled pardoned
landowners to push their claims for restoration and eviction of freedmen
lessees and residents. Saxton hastened to implement the policy as he
understood it, which corresponded with Speed's interpretation. Having
witnessed the colonization of the Sea Islands and the rapidly established
freedmen's communities, Saxton was eager to advance the temporary land-
granting clauses of the Freedmen's Bureau Act to permanent entitlements.
After a disappointing meeting with Howard in Washington late in June
1865, Saxton nevertheless went ahead with the issuance of his Circular 1,
which announced in July that freedmen would receive forty-acre farms on
the abandoned lands under the Bureau's jurisdiction in Georgia, Florida,
and South Carolina. Eleven days later, Howard issued his Circular 13,
which implemented the Freedmen's Bureau Act according to Speed's
opinion. The general announced the actual distribution of forty-acre
plots to freedmen. He ordered assistant commissioners in the Southern
states to select the lands and set them apart for rental or sale to refugees
and freedmen "with as little delay as possible" and report to him on the
completion of the orders. At best, some 20,000 freedmen would benefit, but the promise to the former slaves was about to be redeemed. Saxton immediately complied by awarding lands on Edisto Island to resi-

dent freedmen farmers.[54] Thomas S. Conway, the Irish-born assistant
commissioner in New Orleans, also complied enthusiastically. He issued
instructions that included procedures for applying for the forty-acre parcels, and they were published in the New Orleans *Tribune* and received
early response.

This was the most advanced step the government took toward reconstructing Southern society to benefit freed people. But it was halted before it could take effect. President Johnson intervened to order the army
commander in Saxton's district to prevent any land distribution under
Circular 13. He also impressed Howard with his displeasure over the circular. By September the commissioner was revising his orders and attempting to work out a compromise that would honor both restoration and
redistribution. Clearly, he could not ride both policies without a fall. And
by mid-September, under presidential pressure, Howard issued Circular
15, which rescinded the earlier orders and effectively killed the forty-
acre plan. Powerful Southern landholders succeeded in having Saxton
fired. But he refused, as late as January 1866, to compromise or yield
on the implementation of Sherman's order. In a telegram to Howard,
five days after notice of his dismissal, Saxton wired: "I find no limits to
the time the possessory titles under Gen. Sherman's order were to run.
So far as I am informed the titles are alike. Some informal titles were
given. Large numbers of freedmen who are entitled to possessory titles
have not received them yet through no fault of theirs." It was no wonder that freedmen held several rallies in his honor in his last days in Charleston.[55] In retrospect the measure appears to have been Johnson's rebuke
and challenge to Congressman Thaddeus Stevens of Pennsylvania and to
all confiscation and redistribution plans.

Only a week earlier, the Radical Republican leader, campaigning in
Lancaster, had made the speech that would long be associated with his
name. Stevens proposed to take 394 million acres of land away from
about 70,000 of the larger landowners. Each adult freedman would receive 40 acres. The remaining 354,000 acres would be divided into "suitable" farms and put up for sale to the highest bidders. Southern poor
whites and others who had chafed under the land monopoly held by the
larger plantations owners and slaveowners would also have an opportunity
to redress their grievances. Income from such sales would finance pen-
sions to "deserving veterans" and widows and orphans of soldiers; and
a surplus would pay the national debt. But this was too heady a formula

for most Northern capitalists and their spokesmen. The New York *Tribune* and *The Nation* regarded the Stevens proposal as short of madness. Congress never seriously considered approving it during the session that convened in December 1865.[56]

Stevens persisted, however, in proposing some measure of land division. When the second Freedmen's Bureau bill was before the Congress early in 1866, Stevens tried to strengthen it by providing for far-reaching guardianship for white and black victims of the war and the social upheaval in the South. He advocated the rental to loyal white refugees and black freedmen of 3 million acres of good public land in Alabama, Arkansas, Florida, Louisiana, and Mississippi. The rent would be ten cents an acre; and later an applicant could purchase the land at a price not more than $2 an acre. Freedmen occupying land under Sherman land grants would have their titles confirmed. If a former owner could prove his title, freedmen would be provided with other land. Congress balked at this too. When the Freedmen's Bureau bill finally passed in July 1866 over an earlier presidential veto, it established and confirmed titles to the lands sold to black heads of families in the Sea Islands under President Lincoln's December 1863 orders. And 38,000 acres of land held for tax delinquencies were to be sold at $1.50 per acre to freedmen holding land under Sherman's order. The remaining land held by the tax commissioners was to be sold in the same manner to freedmen forced to move because of land restorations to former owners. Section 9 of the act authorized six-year leases on twenty acres each to freedmen holding land in the coastal reserve; at the end of that period they could buy the land at $1.50 an acre. A provision that freedmen should be permitted to harvest their crops before the land was restored to former owners tended to slow down the eviction of the black occupants. In sum, the freedmen were refused permanent title to the lands they occupied and on which they had constructed schools, churches, homes, and organized villages and communities. Thaddeus Stevens made this point in the 1866 debate on the bill, reporting that restorations in Tennessee amounted to $22 million worth of property and that 16,000 freed people were evicted on the Virginia pensinsula between Fortress Monroe and Williamsburg. All this was in addition to the turmoil created by restoration of Georgia and South Carolina coastal lands. But one other measure, passed in June 1866, hopefully would soften the effects of restoration and at the same time check the counterattack of the former slaveowners.[57]

Indiana's Radical Republican representative, George Washington Julian, was the prime mover of the Southern Homestead Bill, which was enacted on June 21, 1866. Freedmen would have a first opportunity during the first six months of the legislation to apply for 80-acre tracts to be held only for two years; after that period, 160 acres could be claimed. And after January 1, 1867, whites, whether loyal or not, became eligible for homesteads in the 44 million acres set aside from public lands in Arkansas, Alabama, Florida, Louisiana, and Mississippi.[58] The implementation of the act was frustrated by the sluggish General Land Office and by the freedmen's inability to realize any advantage in the six-month head start because of their contractual obligations to work and by their general inability to pay for transportation to distant land offices, even if they had been open in time to service applicants. Above all, planter hostility and freedman impoverishment doomed the act to failure. Insofar as federal legislation was concerned, the Southern Homestead Act was a sorry last gesture. By the end of 1869, 4,000 freedmen had made entries in the five Southern states covered by the act.[59] Three thousand of them were in Florida. By that time the Freedmen's Bureau had long since ceased its distribution of rations and had curtailed its role as an intermediary between freedman and planter. Except for the support rendered the freedmen's cause by allies in the Loyal Leagues and the Republican party, the people were self-supporting but oppressed. Their quest for homesteads and farms had not been fulfilled; the federal government's promise had been broken, and the freedman was left on his own, as he had been through much of the Reconstruction era, to rebuild a community on land of his own.

As pardoned Confederates returned to inspect and claim their former domains, during the summer of 1865, they challenged and aroused the freed people. Those in turn who had been occupying the soil regarded themselves as its natural and rightful cultivators and possessors. Although not all freedmen in all places in the South responded with ire to the new turn, many in the Sea Islands, on the Virginia peninsula, and in the lower Mississippi Valley did. Their resistant behavior that summer probably brought the United States to the brink of its first open class conflict, on a vast geographical field. "The General Strike," according to W. E. B. Du Bois, designated the refusal of freedmen to vacate lands they had sown and were tilling, to contract for labor lest they lose a claim on permanent homesteads, and their general exercise of their freedom to move about or remain at rest in time and space.[60] It may be fair to suggest that on the Sea Islands at least, a potential rural proletarian revolt was in the making. Inasmuch as the agrarian laboring class was Afro-American, the protest was more complex, involving communal and cultural components as well. Experiences as slaves had taught freed people that survival was achieved through communal solidarity, and their brief encounter with freedom had shown them how to remake a community. And so when the movers and shakers of the larger world outside their own world decreed and enacted their expropriation, freedmen expressed their rage in forcefully demonstrative ways. But they also declared a rationale for their resistance, which, as we shall see, elevated their contentions above the level of blind retaliation.

After President Johnson had forced General Howard to renege on the Freedmen's Bureau offer to distribute lands to freedmen, the general set out on a humiliating journey among the disappointed people to explain why they must not expect lands and that they must instead contract to work and accommodate their bosses and masters. This was the meaning of Circular 15.[61] When he delivered his message to freedmen in a meeting at Fayetteville, North Carolina, one responded by saying, "Dat no Yank; dat just some reb dey dressed up in blue clothes and brought up here to lie to us."[62] When he attempted to explain the new land policy to a packed New Orleans theater audience, saying that "we" must "put down our pins and hold on to what we have and be sure we have got it before we try to push ahead any further," he was met with cries of "No!"[63] At the outset of the dismal voyage the general spoke to Edisto Island freed people. Their pained refusal to accept his message was distilled in one man's shout from the gallery: "Why, General Howard, why do you take away our lands? You take them from us who are true, always true to the Government! You give them to our all-time enemies! That is not right!"[64]

Edisto islanders have much to tell us about land and community. Life on the island that summer was marked by continuous arrivals and departures. A census of Edisto and nearby islands (Jehossee, Fenwicks, Baileys, and Little Edisto) in August 1865 reported 1,000 families and showed an aggregate population of 5,300 persons. During that time, 367 certificates had been issued for forty-acre allotments. Between August and the end of the year the total net population decreased. It has been estimated that over 500 arrived and more than 1,000 departed. By December 1865

most of the inhabitants of the island were mainlanders. But whether they
were "salt water" or "fresh water" freedmen, a division that sometimes
produced friction between the two groups, they unanimously refused to
go to work for former owners "on any terms whatsoever." That stubbornness prompted planters to appeal to the President and General Howard.
Among other results of their appeal was Howard's visit to the island. Following his effort to persuade the freedmen to work for the planters, they
organized a committee to consider the matter, placing utter faith in the
general to be just. As he and other officers discovered, this island community was well organized. One of its customs was a regular Saturday
public meeting. A prominent feature of those weekly gatherings was the
reading aloud of the *South Carolina Leader,* a black newspaper, and others,
in order to keep abreast of what was going on among other blacks elsewhere. On the island as in nearby Savannah, one officer testified, "They
have shown that they can organize, and have formed organizations already for their own protection and advancement. If it should become
necessary for them to be unanimous in feeling and action, they will be
unanimous."[65]

In their deliberations over General Howard's recommendations the
committee called a public meeting to hear any views freedmen had to
present. Speakers indicated that "They wished to *own lands.*" If the government could not furnish land for them to purchase on Edisto, then
they were prepared to purchase elsewhere, but they must have land for
their homes and for their families. And they appeared unanimous in op-
posing the annual contract system. When Colonel H. E. Tremain attempted to mediate bargaining between planters and freedmen, he found that
both sides were adamant. But he found the freedmen willing to concede
a point and contract for labor if the planters would sell them only one
acre. The planters stubbornly refused this condition and would consider
only contracts or leases.

Freedmen, however, approached Captain Ketchum privately after a
meeting and told him that the freedmen had such complete faith in the
government that they would even move away if the government thought
that was the wisest course. He attested to their dignity, sobriety, and the
businesslike conduct of their affairs. The committee of freedmen that
met with the planters was led by two men who had never been slaves,
Henry Bram and F. C. Desvanny. Other members of the group were F.
Sampson, Ishmael Moultrie, R. Tolbert, and Ned Murray. The latter mem-

bers formerly resided on the mainland or on adjacent islands. Bram was spokesman and articulated the freed people's desire for landownership. He suggested that under the general Homestead Law of 1862, they would be willing to migrate to Florida. He appears to have been well informed, if we may judge by his suggestions. Little information about the man is available, but he and his comrades suggest a sophisticated community leadership. They displayed acumen in bargaining with the planters, declaring that almost all of the people had money and were prepared to buy at a reasonable price small family plots of land of from one to five acres. The planters asked what was a reasonable price. The committee suggested that tax valuation be the basis for determining a price. Planters rejected this, arguing that the tax estimate was for tax purposes, not for a sale. But Ketchum reminded them that many of them had been granted amnesty by President Johnson by arguing the reverse, that tax valuations showed their estates to be worth less than the $20,000 that would have disqualified them from a pardon. But the argument fell on deaf ears.[66]

The freedmen then appealed directly to the President:

Wee the freedmen of South Carolina wish to address you with a few lines conserning the sad feelings that is now resting upon our minds wee pray that god may guive you helth & good spirets that when you receive theas few notasis that you may receive them as the father did the prodical son wee have for the last four years ben studing with justis and the best of our ability what step wee should take to become a people: wee have lernt to respect all Just Causes that ever came from the union.

Mag genrl howard has paid the freedmen of South Carolinah a visit & caled a meating on Edisto Island South Carlinah in the Centrel part of the island at the priskple Church thair hee beutifly addressed the freedmen of this island after his adress a grate many of the peple understanding what was said they got aroused & awoke to perfict sense to stody for them Selves what part of this law would rest against us, wee said in rafarence to what he said that nothing did apier at that time to bee very opressing upon us but the one thing that is wee freedmen should work for wages for our former oners or eny other man president Johnson of u st [United States] I do say . . . man that hav stud upon the feal of battle & have shot there master & sons now Going to ask ether one for bread or for

shelter or Comfortable for his wife & children sunch a thing the u st
should not aught to expect a man [to do] . . . the King of south
Carolina [i.e., one of the former slaveholders] ask the Privalage to
have the stage that he might a Dress the ordenence [audience] of
the freedman . . . [the] old master [claimed] such a fealing to
Comply with the best order & also what was the best for the freedmen. . . . [We said to him] Here is Plenty Whidow & Fatherles that
have serve you as slave now losen a home . . . give Each one of them
a acres & a one-half to a family as you has the labers & the Profet
of there Yearly [early] Youth. . . [when] the Questin was asked
him by General Howard, what would it sell your lan for a acres his
anser that I would not take a hundred $100 of a acres that is a part
of his union fealing so then we therefore lose fate [faith] in this
southern Gentelman. . . . [They beesech] the wise presidon that
sets on his seat [to give them] a chance to Recover out of this
trubble. . . these 3 Committee has Pleg the Trouth to you dis day,
October 25, 1865.[67]

But this heartfelt and eloquent statement failed to budge President Johnson. Land on the island was restored to former owners. The freedmen determined "to work for no rebels." On Edisto they refused to enter contracts with their former owners. As a result, plantations were put up for
rent, and the army cooperated by imposing a rigid control over movement to the island and by providing a guard for former owners who attemp
ted to induce freedmen to contract with them.

Obviously, as James Allen has pointed out, the mood of the freed people turned bitter and produced risk for owners without military protection. When Governor Aiken of South Carolina, accompanied by a military guard, visited his rice plantations on nearby Jehossee Island his offers
too met refusal. One of the army officers was asked by the freedmen to
"see de gubbermint, and ax him if he wouldn't sell de land, and leff um
to pay sum udder time, an ef we dont pay in two year, den he may take
um back."[68]

Freedmen thus stood by their offers to purchase and became adamant
in resisting restoration policies and policies that would reduce them from
farmers to farm laborers. Freedmen on Fenwick, Wadmelaw, Ossabaw,
and St. Catherine's islands refused to contract.[69] Eighty men, women,
and children from the latter two islands rowed to Savannah, leaving behind their crops and household goods rather than contracting with old

masters.[70] Fenwick, Wadmelaw, and Edisto islanders armed themselves
and prepared to fight for their lands. Charles Howard reported that 900
people on Sapelo Island planned to leave if the former owner returned.[71]
When planters came to Edisto to claim their lands, they were met by an
angry group of freedmen, who told them: "You had better go back to
Charleston, and go to work there, and if you can do nothing else, you
can pick oysters and earn your living as the loyal people have done—by
the sweat of their brows."[72]

At another plantation on the coast, a planter who returned found that
the freed people had divided it up and had planted their crops. He summoned them to meet with him, whereupon he informed them that the
land was his but that they could have the crops then in the ground. But
one of them told the planter: "We gwi wuk! We gwi wuk all right. De
Union generals dee done tell us tuh com back f'om follin' arter de army
an' dig greenbacks under de sod. We gwi wuk fuh ourselves. We ain't gwi
wuk fuh no white man! . . . We ain't gwine nowhere. We gwi wuk right
here on dis land where we wuz born and whar belongs to us." A freedman in uniform stepped out of his cabin, gun in hand. Bringing it down
with a crash he declared, "Yes, I gwi wuk right here. I'd like to see any
man put me outer dis house."[73] Freedmen on other coastal plantations
demanded possession of them. They pulled up bridges to prevent former
masters from returning, barricaded themselves, and shot at approaching
owners.

In Georgetown County, freedmen exhibited militancy on March 31,
1866. A freedman by the name of Abram on the Keithfield plantation
quit work and summoned others from the fields. Arming themselves
with axes, hoes, hatchets, and poles, they drove a black agent of the owner off the land and sent him scurrying for a boat. Sampson, one of the
aroused freedmen, threw a hatchet at the agent that barely missed his
head, and struck the water near the boat. The manager returned later
with two U.S. soldiers and the black agent. As soon as they entered the
settlement street, they were met with a fierce onslaught. The people had
armed themselves with "axes, hoes, sticks and bricks." They pelted the
outsiders with these weapons and took a gun away from one of the soldiers. The party was forced to flee, the manager jumping into the river
and swimming to the other side.[74] In other places, even when some laborers had signed contracts, they repudiated them, as in the case of a
group of freed men and women at Chicora Wood. Freedmen set fire to
the Pringle house in the same neighborhood and threatened to burn a

$50,000 steam rice mill. In fact, the Joseph Manigault plantation workers had dismantled his rice mill, barns, mill machinery, and boilers and transported them to Savannah for sale.[75] Apprehension must have been widespread, for the freedmen's anger at restoration also took the form of attacks on property in several locations. Whites in the Colleton district, which included the islands of Ashepoo, Edisto, James, John, and Wadmelaw, were alarmed by the appropriation of crops, the slaughter of livestock, and the cutting of timber, which freedmen were charged with bringing to Charleston for sale.[76] William Morel complained that two workers on his plantation should be removed to prevent them from burning or pulling down houses.[77] Farther north, in Mecklenburg County, Virginia, freedmen were charged with killing sheep, poultry, and hogs and with destroying cornfields.[78] A letter to all Freedmen's Bureau superintendents in the state was sent out from headquarters in Richmond, ordering them to protect the fencing, wood, and timber on the farms in the district. The order had been prompted by complaints of freedmen "learning that they are to be dispossessed" when their leases expire and the land returned to former owners. They destroyed the wooded property.[79]

Freedmen on James Island had been approached three times by planters to contract for labor, and they had rebuffed the former owners. three times.[80] On the first visit the planters were met by forty armed black men who rushed down to the boat landing and drove them away, threatening to kill them if they returned to disturb the freedmen and women in their homes. Captain Ketchum accompanied the planter on the second visit, and only his papers showing him to be a government officer saved the party. They had been met by the guns leveled at them and not released from capture until Ketchum's papers had been read by one of the freedmen. The planters again left the island without a contracted labor force; indeed, the freedmen pressed Ketchum to say who were the real owners of the land, these loyal black men who had been settled there by the government or these rebels who had fought the government. Ketchum said, "That is uncertain."

On the third visit, John Trowbridge accompanied the group of planters, and we rely on his account of it. The members of the party separated, each to search out his own former estate. When they first set out, they found the freed people's houses shut and the island community of 2,200 people a silent and an unwilling host. The men were nowhere in sight, simply avoiding the visitors because they apparently had been ordered not to resist the visit. Among the few people Trowbridge met and questioned were two aged men; even they were supporting themselves on forty-acre plots. They did not wish to work for the planters. One of them, who had raised peas, corn, and potatoes and purchased his own clothes, said, "Gov'ment don't help me none." The other patriarch rejected contracting with planters by saying, "What little we do will be service to weself." A group of women working in a field replied, "Gov'ment drap we here. Can't go 'till Gov'ment take we off." A little later, Trowbridge met a party of men and women working in the fields. Interviewing them, he learned from one of the men, "No, I don't want to contract, I'll eat up my peas and corn fus'." When the visitor suggested that the freedmen should consider the planters' offer, he was met with, "If I contract, what good does my forty acres do me?" When he pressed the argument for wages as more certain than the questionable titles to their forty-acre tracts, the women stormed against the argument, making him feel like an enemy. But he did observe "the religious attachment of these people to their homes," and was relieved that he had not persuaded any of them to relinquish their homesteads. Among the freedmen the mood was one of bitterness that frequently expressed itself as independence. On one of the two visits when armed freedmen appeared at the landing, they were asked for the white surgeons of the military post. The freedmen replied that "they were their own surgeons now."

When a black Bureau officer told freed people that the Whaley plantation where they resided in January 1866 must be restored, they answered bitterly, "Christ had been betrayed by one of his own color." At the same time, freedmen on another large plantation armed themselves to prevent their eviction by force. A personal appeal from General Robert K. Scott, the Bureau's chief in South Carolina, persuaded them to make yearlong contracts. Twice, in September and in mid-October, General Bennett was reported to have taken action to suppress disturbances. In the first action he disarmed all persons on the Cooper and Ashley river plantations; in the second he sent a force to "quell a disturbance" in Ashepoo.[81]

Outside of the Sea Islands and coastal reserve, other freedmen demonstrated their fierce opposition to making contracts and to eviction. Instead, they pressed their claim to landownership. Duplin County, North Carolina, freedmen in the fall of 1865 were openly declaring their intention to have lands "even if they had to shed blood to obtain them." In December, speakers at a Greensboro, Alabama, public meeting of freedmen declared they "would have 'lands or blood.' " On January 1, Louisiana Red River country freedmen were reported to have risen up in arms and attempted but failed to murder an overseer. Arrests were made on several plantations, and quantities of secreted arms were taken by the militia. A newspaper reported laconically, "Previously, the freedmen in that section had refused to work." Freed men and women on the Cherry Hill plantation of Thomas C. Arnold in Bryan County, Georgia, in December not only refused to make a contract for 1866 "upon any terms," but they refused to leave the place and threatened to resist with violence any effort to evict them. Moreover, they threatened those other freedmen Arnold had persuaded to contract and come to work for him.[82]

Georgia and South Carolina field laborers perplexed planters by refusing to leave lands where they lived and worked. Planters viewed the refusal simply enough: Freedmen who refused to contract must leave. Freed men looked upon their old masters/new employers in a more complex way. In some cases, when the masters had abandoned land during the war, leaving slaves to work the crops, the latter did so and then claimed a total interest in their sale and its proceeds. Thus in June 1865 an army officer complained that William Singleton, former slave of John Robert of Robertville, South Carolina, refused to contract for a half-share of the crop and threw Singleton off the plantation. Singleton and another freedmen protested that Robert could have no share at all and that, moreover, the army officer had no authority to intervene on the runaway planter's behalf. Singleton went to General Saxton to settle the jurisdictional and moral questions. He received Saxton's support and returned to the plantation to broadcast news of it. Captain A. P. Ketchum of Saxton's staff informed the army officer that Robert must first take an amnesty oath before his application for restoration of his lands could be considered; that the freedmen had a right to all of the crop; and that the officer, whose reputation for physically abusing black soldiers under his command was widely known, had no jurisdiction in the matter. The Freedmen's Bureau was responsible for freedmen's affairs and contracts. In Chatham County, Georgia, 146 freed people remained on the W. H. Gibbons rice lands through 1866 and, in December, refused to leave. One hundred and four of them occupied tracts on Gibbons's Argyle Island "Shaftsberry" plantation. But this was no isolated activity. General Davis Tillson in November 1865 acknowledged "numerous instances . . . where the freedmen not only refuse to labor on the plantation, but refuse to leave it." His own visit to Sapelo and St. Catherine's islands early in 1866 confirmed this impression Some freed people on Cumberland Island in May 1867 defied the woman who owned the plantation where they worked. She sought their eviction because they had insulted her and told her "I had better wait until I had land to drive them off." Despite this defiance, other freed people had contracted with her.[83]

Aaron Bradley was charged with agitating freed people to disobey Freedmen's Bureau orders by refusing to leave abandoned lands. He was tried by a military commission in Savannah in December 1865 for using seditious language in a public meeting. But even this alleged firebrand had cautiously urged that freedmen should make the best possible contracts. Furthermore, according to a train of defense witnesses including Ulysses L. Houston, who had been present at Bradley's speeches, he had advised freedmen that they should continue to work and remain on the lands where they were located and "not to leave them for any rebels." They should stay until ordered off by the government. Summing up in his defense, Bradley provided an acute and a striking legal argument for freedmen's resistance to restoration policies. Bradley defended himself on the basis of the First Amendment guarantee of free speech, but first he established a legal ground for citizenship in order to appeal to that article of the Bill of Rights. He claimed general black citizenship by virtue of emancipation, and military service under conscription laws, and drew upon Supreme Court Justice Benjamin Curtis's opinion in the 1857 *Dred Scott* case. Moreover, he struck at the legality of the Southern states and argued that they actually had territorial status until Congress decided their condition in the Union. He cited as a precedent the formation and recognition of West Virginia early in the war.[84]

Freed people's resistance and protest were essentially defensive. But they also went on the offensive in several places by seizing land or by squatting on the plantations where they had been slaves. Plantation seizures were recorded as early as 1862. In Plaquemines Parish, Louisiana, slaves on one plantation drove the overseer away and took possession of the place. On a neighboring sugar plantation, slaves erected a gallows in the slave quarters as a portent of their seizure of the plantation and the hanging of their master. Near Tigerville, slaves stayed behind when their master fled, organized themselves into a "rude labor phalanx," and elected a leader. They went to work cultivating the sugar and maintained the plantation as their own. But the tempo of land expropriation increased in 1865. "Mrs. Weston's Negroes" in the first week in March 1865 divided the land of her Georgetown County, South Carolina, plantation. A Screven

County, Georgia, farmer complained in November that although he had agreed with his laborers to share the crop in exchange for their labor, they soon designated a portion of the land under cultivation as theirs and another as the employer's. Then they devoted all of their time and labor to cultivating their portion and neglected their agreement to share the entire crop equally. Similar complaints were filed a year later with the Freedmen's Bureau in Savannah by the firm of Flye, Middleton, and Magi which operated a plantation on Ossabaw Island. Are the freed people to be allowed, the complaint asked, "to select such houses as they may choc to occupy, and to appropriate to their own use such land as they may choose to cultivate, without any reference to the proprietor or lessee?" Freedmen on the Santee River were reported in 1866 to have apportioned land of an abandoned plantation among themselves. Three years later, 300 blacks on Ogeechee River rice lands were reported to have driven out white plantation owners and seized their properties but were subduec by federal troops. A year later, near Louisville, Georgia, a freedman named Cujo Fye organized clubs resembling later civil rights protective organizations. One of their aims, according to a Southern historian, was "ultimately to gain control of land." Planters in Russell County, Alabama, complained in 1867 that black people were taking over some of the plantations.[85]

A fundamental concept of right informed the freed people's action and thought about the land question. There was always among freed people a "bourgeois" concept of private property paid for in cash or credit. The oft-expressed desire to purchase or to rent with an option to buy (or hire-purchase or land contract) could have been realized in classical marketplace exchanges, with money as the medium. Congressmen and members of the American Freedmen's Inquiry Commission did not fail to pre the question: "Have the negroes generally correct ideas as to the element of property; do they know what is meant by property?" When a Freedmen's Bureau officer replied, "Yes, sir," a congressional investigator in February 1866 pressed him, "Do they distinguish conscientiously the principle of *meum* and *tuum*?" The officer again answered in the affirma tive. But he explained that the freedmen had the idea that they had "a certain right to the property of their former masters, that they have earn ed it." They believed that any amount of it that they could "lay their hands on" belonged to them. Explaining further, the officer stated that freed people thought they had a right to the grain and the livestock they had raised and taken care of. But the New Orleans *Tribune* urged suppo for a citywide freedmen's aid association in order to raise funds so that groups of freed people could *purchase* the lands they worked on in 1865. An officer of the association asserted the freed people did not want gifts of aid; instead, they pledged the coming crop in payment. Other freedmen pressed more disturbing principles, as one in Albemarle County, Virginia, demonstrated. In an altercation in which the freedmen appear to have balked at working terms, the employer appealed to the army commander in the eastern part of the county. An officer came to investigate and heard the "head man" of the freedmen, as their spokesman, declare that he wanted to know "what kind of freedom this was? Were the freedmen not to have land given to them?" The officer's inspiring response was to point to a nearby graveyard and say, "The only land you will get or any of you will be 6 x 3 feet in that lot, and if you do not behave yourselves properly you will get your share very quickly." But others from the Union side supported the freedmen's right to the land of their masters. The *Freedmen's Advocate* urged a postbellum version of a powerful political principle of the 1850s: "Free colored laborers, free soil, and free Northern men, working in sympathy. . . ." But one sensitive correspondent of the Unionist *Free South* (Beaufort, South Carolina) veered away from this agrarian capitalist view toward one that was to be enunciated repeatedly by freedmen. "J. A. S." wrote: "The negro owns every foot of these lands, by a thousand valid titles, by right of eminent domain and of personal requisition. He alone had fulfilled the divine condition of all ownership or occupancy of the earth, by cultivating, subduing, and replenishing it." Even as a question of wages, freedmen had prior claim to compensation that had been denied for 200 years. Material and arithmetical reasons were easy enough to calculate and compile. But these missed the main right; bondage and its effects had created "an accumulative immensity of right which all the parchment title deeds of the world would not give."[86]

Bayley Wyatt, a Yorktown, Virginia, freedman, articulated the concept of right that sanctioned possession of the land. Wyatt responded one evening in 1866 to a notice by Freedmen's Bureau officers that he and thousands of other former slaves and their families must vacate restored lands. Wyatt recalled the anguished days of slavery when "we made bricks widout straw under old Pharo." He reminded his listeners at the public meeting in which he spoke of the days of separation—"you all members the home house and de wife house," and of that aching void a slave husband felt when he went to the "wife house," only to discover

that his loved one had been sold down south. He would fold his arms
then and say "O Lord, how long." Like Wyatt and his neighbors, other
slaves had fled from their masters in Virginia's interior. To be driven off
the land now and to return to their home counties was a special cruelty,
Wyatt said. They had left the rebels and had gone over to the Yankees.
Now they would be "as a dose of pizen" in the eyes of those former Confederates. There was obvious justification in Wyatt's disillusionment with
Northern officers who would place the freed people in such jeopardy.
Wyatt did not ask for alms, nor for gifts of land. He explained his and
other freedmen's self-determination: ". . . we sacrificed all we had and
come to de Yankees. Some of us had some money to buy our freedom,
and some of us had a house, and some of us had cattle with which we
hoped sometimes to buy ourselves." But they listened to the promises
of the Yankees and now were to be evicted by those Northerners to accommodate the former masters.

> We now, as a people desires to be elevated, and we desires to do
> all we can to be educated, and we hope our friends will aid us all
> dey can. . . .
> I may state to all our friends, and to all our enemies, that we
> has a right to the land where we are located. For why? I tell you.
> Our wives, our children, our husbands, has been sold over and
> over again to purchase the lands we now locate upon; for that rea-
> son we have a divine right to the land.

And in a final lesson in political economy learned in the fields of slavery and in the fields of freedom, Wyatt declared:

> And den didn't we clear the lands and raise de crops of corn, ob
> cotton, ob tobacco, ob rice, ob sugar, ob eberything? And den didn't
> den large cities in de North grow up on de cotton and de sugars and
> de rice dat we made? Yes! I appeal to de South and to de North if
> I hasn't spoken de words of truth.
> I say dey have grown rich and my people is poor.[87]

If emancipation had revitalized community leaders like Wyatt, federa
eviction policies tended to sap their hopes and their energies. Rather tha
suffer defeat silently, Wyatt and others protested. They were powerless
to mount successful armed contests, but their rebellious spirits were aro

They overthrew notions of their docility and dependency and attempted to express their sense of betrayal and loss and their hopes for land in political activities.

In conjunction with the campaign during 1865 to petition for suffrage, freedmen's conventions also called for land. The Norfolk, Virginia, Afro-Americans who met in June inserted into their address to the people of the United States a call for the organized purchasing of land. New Orleans and Louisiana black men had made similar declarations early in the year. And toward the end of the year, Florida freedmen in convention petitioned for suffrage, education, and land. On the other hand, a black convention in Augusta, Georgia, took a conservative line and refused to support a land confiscation policy. It did pass a resolution, however, affirming the freedmen's coastal lands and urged that they not be taken away without an act of Congress. Generally, black legislators subordinated the land and confiscation questions to suffrage and school campaigns.[88]

A far more militant stance was taken by Virginia freedmen during the summer of 1866. One historian asserted that most of the blacks "ardently supported" confiscation of lands of former Confederate plantation owners. South Carolina freedmen who went to the polls in the 1867 election carried the ballots home with them believing they could use them as land warrants. When the Republican state convention met in Richmond, Virginia, in April 1867, the dominant opinion of the black delegates was for confiscation. Constituting the majority, they represented forty-nine counties. Blacks applauded when a white delegate announced that if the Congress failed to give freed blacks lands, they should use violence to seize it. But white Republicans debated the issue and succeeded in referring the resolution on confiscation. This did not dissuade freedmen from giving enthusiastic support to radical and confiscatory proposals during the April and May registration to vote.[89] Confiscation measures failed adoption or enactment throughout the former Confederate states. Congress, too, frustrated the desires of freedmen, and the President, of course, closed the question by his early restoration policy. South Carolina alone among the former rebellious states under the spur of its black legislators created a land commission to solve the problem. But its function was to purchase land and resell it to freed people, not to confiscate and redistribute it. In this benign manner some 70,000 persons, or approximately 14,000 black families, participated in the state's Reconstruction land program.[90] The great promise had not been kept. In the end the freed people were thrust on their own resources and their own efforts to acquire a patrimony.

An American Black Village Movement

There are a number of colored men here, each cultivating 50 and 100 acres each. . . . The 56th USCT Regiment is here and gives all the protection needed. We have a colored church with a large congregation, school are few but more will be established. I have one with 40 scholars. —Letter from a teacher in Arkansas, *The Colored Tennessean* (Nashville), August or September 1865.

Announcing the Southern Homestead Act: ". . . Improve the land. . . .It requires hard work in many cases; and many families should, if possible, go together so as to help each other, and have schools and churches together." —*Loyal Georgian* (Augusta), October 13, 1866.

A good way is to club together and buy a piece of land and divide it up into lots. —*The Free Man's Press,* Austin, Texas, August 1, 1868.

Freedmen adopted several methods to acquire land. One was rental, whe they found willing landlords. Another was purchase by individuals or a single family. The collective or cooperative purchase or leasing of lands by groups of families and other linked individuals was a third means. Finally, immigration, whether to Kansas or to Africa, was proposed and practiced by some during the post-Reconstruction era. The precedents for the last two modes had been established in the Canadian black settle ments at Buxton, Wilberforce, Elgin, and other communities in souther Ontario between Windsor and London and Toronto.[1] Even more strikin ly analogous were the Jamaican and Guyanese postemancipation village movements, which predated the Emancipation Proclamation and the

Thirteenth Amendment by a generation. Beginning late in 1839 and reaching a peak of participation in 1851, for example, free black Guyanese sugar plantation laborers, eager to own land, pooled funds to purchase abandoned cotton plantations. They established independent villages under democratic organization and communal principles. Land was divided in equal lots and distributed among families of settlers who built their own homes and raised their own sugar cane. An elected headman presided over communal maintenance as well as the operation of the sugar factory, marketing of sugar, and drainage and irrigation of the lands. The Guyanese black village movement embraced 46,368 persons by June 1851, more than half of the preemancipation slave population.[2] Similar patterns of purchase and settlement by free laborers on plantations where they resided and worked were later attempted in Reconstruction Louisiana and Mississippi.

Self-assertive cooperative activity is a subject that has escaped serious treatment in Reconstruction historiography. Consequently, the state-by-state studies and the revisionist responses leave students with the impression of sporadic, weak, and fruitless efforts at cooperative land acquisition. However, if the land question is considered from the point of view of the freedmen, over time and space, and as much more than an economic question alone, there emerges a vigorous pattern of community building by this mode. The cooperative effort in the countryside was not a success story. Far too few of the efforts noted in this chapter were ever realized or made lasting. But that should not obscure the freed people's self-assertive and conscious effort to re-create a world of their own.

The most powerful motivation for taking up ten, twenty, forty and more acres was a profound attachment to place. Such a place or community meant to the freedman a network of human relationships. Family concerns governed them. Freed people made this explicit on several occasions and implicit in the pattern of their land purchase efforts. Let us first consider the South Carolina Sea Islands.

As early as March 1863 freed people on the Edgerly and adjoining Red House plantations on Port Royal Island purchased the first of the two, which comprised 800 acres. They had raised about $500 from their earnings as cotton cultivators on government-held lands. In addition, they received an advance from the Reverend Solomon Peck and obtained the place for $710. Peck conducted the transaction for the freed people at their request and later was repaid when the freed people received what the government owed them for their labor. The land was surveyed and divided among them. Ten or twelve houses were completed by the fall of 1863, "with sashes whitewashed inside and out" in striking contrast to the "dark dirty huts" most of the dozen and more families "had burrowed in" during slavery. As owners they labored diligently, most of the laborers being women and children, as the men were away in the army They successfully raised a variety of food crops for their own consumption and for sale, and 1,200 pounds of ginned cotton. Usually, they worke the land with a hoe; sometimes they used a mule. Marking their distance from slavery, they had no superintendent or overseer but designated one of their own to be a foreman. He (or she?) had "oversight only of what was owned in common. They worked their crops separately."[3]

When late in 1863 President Lincoln on General Rufus Saxton's urging instructed the U.S. direct tax commissioners for South Carolina to permit black heads of families to preempt and purchase government lands at $1.25 an acre, freed people quickly responded. They claimed 2,776 acres and deposited $3,464.25 with A. P. Ketchum, registrar under General Saxton. Ketchum, an alumnus of West Point (with an abolitionist family background), had been joined by an army chaplain and a Methodist missionary, the Reverend Mansfield French, in encouraging freedmen to mak preemptions. They went further and persuaded the President and Treasur Secretary, Salmon P. Chase, to authorize the preemptions.[4]

In all, by January 1864 Sea Island freedmen had filed preemption clai for 6,000 acres. Two of them, on Port Royal Island, in January 1864, called for division of the Julius Chaplain place into 16 plots of 20 acres each (320 acres for 16 claimants) and the J. F. Chaplain place ("Oakland" into 18 plots (320 acres for 18 claimants) of the same size. The applicant filed diagrams of the proposed division (see Figures 4 and 5). Noteworthy in the J. F. Chaplain claims are the three adjoining 20-acre plots of Ben Stevens, Ben Stevens, Jr., and Robert Stevens; and the separate plots of Joseph Green and Joseph Green, Jr. We might guess that there were two black men who had served as significant models to their sons, who seeme willing to bear their fathers' names and live close by. On the Julius Chaplain place, three adjoining plots are shown as claimed by Si., Isaac and Robert Washington. Other preemption claims suggesting a desire to preserve familiar homesteads were made on the H. Sams' plantation on Dathaw Island; nine men listed as "head of family" or "1st S.C. Reg. Vo applied for plots of from 20 to 80 acres, totaling 500. On Ladies Island twelve claims on the McKee plantation were filed by "Kit Green and others." Harry and Kit Green apparently succeeded in raising profitable cotton crops. They were cited by Reverend Mansfield French, who, arguing for distribution of lands to freedmen rather than to capitalists, said, "These men are not exceptions. It is only their experiments that form the exceptions." French cited not only their capability but also their readiness to become self-supporting immediately. Instead of establishing a bureau for the freedmen in the government, he asserted, "It is the avaricious spirit, the love of gain in the North, that needs the bureau of restraint." Freedmen were saying, as French reported, " 'We's bin shut up long 'nuff, we want no go in bureau nor any oder place, just want's to be let alone. Gib us de land and we will take care ob de gobernment and ourselves.' "[5]

Two of the three tax commissioners had prevailed, however, in the reversal of Chase's orders. Public sale by auction was to go ahead as planned before the preemption orders. Freedmen were expected by much wealthier buyers to be no competition and no bar to their own purchases. Thus, early in 1864, two plantations that freedmen had preempted were sold away from them. They refused to take back their preemption money and refused to work for the new purchasers. A white teacher had observed that the freed people felt "that they have a sort of right to live upon their own plantations." One of them explained that leaving their places would be as bad as slavery. They resolved, therefore, to attempt to bid against Northern white purchasers. They pooled their funds in order to do so, thus posing an unexpected threat to the outsiders. The freedmen purchased a tract of 280 acres on Wassa Island for $2,100 and another of 190 acres, called Bolus Point, for $1,250. They tried to buy several other large tracts but could not outbid the Northerners. For Bluff Farm they had bid $2,000, but a white man took it for $3,025. Freedmen, with a bid of $2,200, almost took the Ashdale house tract, but it sold for $2,550. On Dathaw Island black people bid $3,100 on a tract of 300 acres "where they resided." A white man bought it for $3,500.[6]

With the road to preemption and purchase blocked, freedmen took the next opening, leasing lands at $2 per acre for one year from January 1, 1864. When A. P. Ketchum reported to General Saxton in April, he wrote that three leases totaling $900 had been granted by the tax commissioners to the William Perryclear place, the Ann and Rose Perryclear places, and on Otaheite. These were the plantations on which the lease applicants

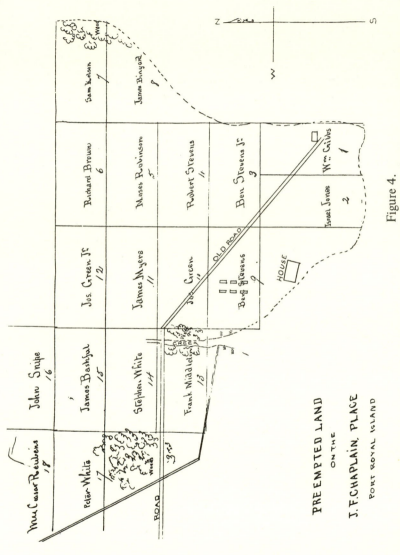

Figure 4.
Freedmen's plans for division of lands

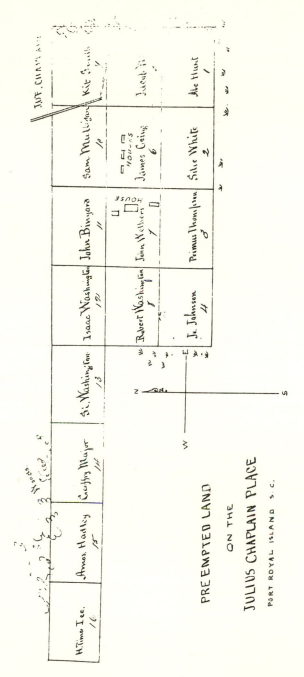

Figure 5.
Freedmen's plans for division of lands

"and the people they represented" had chosen and preempted land under Lincoln's December 30, 1863, instructions, land that they had readied for planting. Ketchum observed that if strangers had acquired the three leaseholds just mentioned when the land had been in such an advanced state of cultivation, "it would have been a painful experience for the negroes."[7] A month later, a Philadelphia newspaper published a letter from an elder of a black people's church in the islands addressed to a former female teacher there:

> *Do,* my missus, tell Linkum dat we wants land—dis bery land dat
> is rich wid de sweat ob we face and de blood ob we back. We born
> here; we parents' graves here; we donne oder country; dis yere
> our home. De Nort folks hab home, antee? What a pity dat dey
> don't love der home like we love we home, for den dey would
> neber come here for buy all way from we.[8]

The concept of a home, a place where one could be free and independent with one's family, was intimately connected with the cooperative effort to buy or lease land. Many white observers recorded that longing: Whitelaw Reid and Admiral Dahlgren, whom Reid quoted, the South Carolina U.S. direct tax commissioners, and especially A. D. Smith, the commissioner from Wisconsin, and Colonel Thomas Wentworth Higginson among others. The delegation of black leaders of Savannah meeting with General W. T. Sherman at the end of his march to the sea made it plain that the delegates wished to obtain land of their own in order to build their community. A freedman in Louisiana explained how he hoped to use his savings of $400 or $500: "All I wants is to git to own fo' or five acres ob land, dat I can build me a little house on and call my home." As early as January 1, 1863, the direct tax commissioners for South Carolina noted that

> Another prominent feature of their [freedmen's] character is their
> strong desire to obtain permanent and free homes in the region of
> the country where they were born and reared. . . . they . . . feel
> most keenly the longings of that inhabitative instinct which is so
> marked in their social and individual character and habits.

Therefore, the commissioners recommended division and sale of lands in small parcels "with the privilege of pre-emption." A few months later when the American Freedmen's Inquiry Commission took direct testimony from white and black persons, it was told by Colonel Higginson that he saw great value in the government "announcing a bounty in land for those colored men entering its military service." Higginson elaborated: "They take pride in the possession of the land; it would be a part of their domestic feeling, which is strong;—it is a great thing with them to feel that their families are provided for." When pressed by his interviewers, Higginson replied positively that the freedman's feeling for his family was "very strong." Smith testified to the same body that freedmen "did not want to go away; they were attached to their homes." They needed freedom and protection from reenslavement. "But in order to get that encouragement and hope they must have the family organized, and a homestead must be given them—*they must have land, land.* . . . it was necessary to get a permanent title from the Government."[9]

The government later responded affirmatively with Sherman's order. Freedmen settled rapidly on the coastal tracts but not without careful thought about their rights. For a people who allegedly acted with abandon and with little concern for their future, the freedmen demonstrated some contradictory behavior. A Boston reporter recorded impressions about them in April 1865, in the midst of that seemingly reckless race to their acres, that renders incredible notions of their incapacity or their dependence upon their old masters. The occasion was a meeting in the old slave market in Savannah. Lieutenant Ketchum and Reverend French addressed the freed people and answered questions about their status as landowners. The reporter confessed his underestimation of these recently freed slaves and observed their "unexpected" shrewdness. Most significantly, he left a record of their sense of self-worth in their concerns for their tenure and for a family homestead that could stand clear of encumbrances through future generations. "They wanted to know what title they would have to their land—what assurance they could have that it would be theirs after they had improved it," the reporter wrote.[10]

That powerful drive to maintain the *continuity* of their community was not only evident in the South Carolina Sea Islands but was perhaps even more emphatically expressed in the 1865 Louisiana land applications. When Thomas Conway, Freedmen's Bureau assistant commissioner for

Louisiana, announced in September 1865 that 58,000 acres of land on 68 abandoned plantations were available to freedmen, they responded immediately. In all, 267 applications were recorded. Of these, 73 cooperative groups applied for 16,482 acres. These groups comprised 584 men, 458 women, and 644 children. By itself, this would seem to be a significant indication of the community and family concerns that motivated the freed people. Actually, the pattern that emerges is one of *groups* of families asking for the lands on or near which they already resided. The first entry in Conway's register of applications was by a Frank Glover of New Orleans for the Upper Whitehead plantation of 3,000 acres in St. John the Baptist Parish. The fifty men, twenty-five women, and twenty children offered assets of "$2500 money, 2000 bbl corn, 47 mules, plows, etc." David Curly, who resided on the St. Bridgette's plantation in Terrebonne Parish asked for its 250 acres in the name of fifteen men, twelve women, and five children. Their assets were "70 barrels of corn, 7 mules, 2 horses, some hay, 2 plows, harnesses, etc., $500 money." Grandison Hunter on September 1, the earliest of the applicants, asked for three Terrebonne Parish plantations in the names of the 102 *families* residing on them. Thirty-six families (forty men, thirty-three women, and seventy-five children) desired to lease "the whole of the Woodlawn plantation." Their recorded means were $3,000-$5,000 and thirty mules and horses. Their hope was large, for the plantation measured 3,000 acres. Forty-four families (forty-four men, thirty-seven women, and forty-seven children) desired to lease the William Bisland plantation, where they resided, and their means were "$2000 capital." The size of the place was not noted in these records. Twenty-two families (twenty-four men, twenty women, and forty children) on the third of Hunter's applications asked for the whole Rauche plantation (800 acres), and their means were "$1200-$1500 capital." Twenty-seven days later they reapplied. The application was made by Stephen Dickson and twenty-seven others. The number of men increased to twenty-eight, of women to thirty, and of children to fifty. Similarly, "Frank Glover and others" resident on the Upper Whitehead plantation on September 20 entered a revised application asking for only 1,000 acres. Now the request was made on behalf of fifty men, thirty-nine women, and sixty-one children.[11]

It is noteworthy that in the two revised applications the numbers of women and children increased at a greater rate than the number of men.

This suggests that in the two or three weeks between applications, families had gathered together to get ready to occupy the land. Other applications with similar male-female-child ratios support the idea of probable nuclear-family groups in communities, determined in part by location. For example, Willis Ross and thirty-nine other freedmen of New Orleans applied for 2,000 acres on the Pierre Rost plantation in St. Charles Parish. They did so in behalf of forty men, forty women, and fifty children. Miles Summerville in New Orleans applied, on behalf of twenty-five men, twenty-five women, and thirty children, for the rental of "250 acres of good land in Terrebonne Parish." J. W. Huston and twenty others (in all, twenty-one, along with nineteen women, and twenty-eight children) in La Fourche Parish wanted to lease 325 acres of the Johnson place in that parish. Nelson Watts in New Orleans, for sixty-nine men, sixty-one women, and thirty-two children, applied for a lease on the Bowden plantation in Ascension Parish. Ned Little and others applied for 300 acres on the Mount Thomas place in Ascension. The families represented were made up of fifty-seven men, sixty-three women, and fifty-nine children. Only one of the group applications showed a disproportionate number of women: the "M. Young & 33 others" (thirty-three men, fifty-six women, forty-two children) request for 1,944 of the Ashland plantation's 2,500 acres in Terrebone Parish. A possible explanation is that there may have been unwed female relatives or wives of absent men. Whatever their situation, these women apparently were being offered homes at least, places to live and work, close to either friends or relatives. If the women were "strangers," then the group arrangement takes on even more importance, for it suggests that the applicants cared for them and that the women were welcome in the community.[12]

These changing land applications appear to be a phase of the essential Afro-American experience in the emancipation era—the process of creating and re-creating community. The augmentation of nuclear families with women and children suggests an aspect of Ashanti kinship and social organization. Even foreign slave women, in the West African society from which many American slaves' ancestors came, attained the status of a lineage within a village organization that was bound together by kinship. Although it may be difficult to draw parallels between the African village and Reconstruction plantation settlement, the principle of mutual aid, of the poor aiding the poor, is evident in both. That mutuality appears to be a prototype of behavior by black extended-family networks prevalent in the century following emancipation, as demonstrated in Carol B. Stack's *All Our Kin: Strategies for Survival in the Black Community* and in Shiflett's study of Louisa County, Virginia, black families.

The cooperative method of acquiring or working land on lease may be due in part to the resolutions of the 1864 Syracuse Convention of Colored Men and in part to the encouragement of General O. O. Howard. His circular of May 30, 1865, from Washington and Conway's Circular 10 from New Orleans, encouraged the collective approach. However, in Louisiana, the initiative was taken by the black community as early as January 1865, when several organizations came into existence. One, the Convention of Colored Men, on January 9 at New Orleans, provided a general organization of the Louisiana black and mulatto population. Significantly, the country parish delegations, including Terrebonne, La Fourche, Assumption, and others, proved to be more radical than the Crescent City delegations. Prominent in the convention was one of its vice presidents, G. Hunter (probably Grandison Hunter), representing Terrebonne, where he would later petition for plantation leaseholds.[13]

The Farming Association was another organization that was important in preparing the way for freedmen's assertiveness. A prospectus issued on February 1, 1865, was addressed to "those who have no income and are at present unemployed, and who are desirous of making an honest living." It was a proposal for organized self-help: "Let us with our families associate together for the purpose of farming. . . . let as many families as can agree together work the land for three or five years. Let the manager be one chosen from among the associates, who is capable and who enjoys their confidence." The participants were to commit themselves for a year; shirkers from "a just proportion of work" were to be punished by deductions in their share of the crop; idlers who would not work were to be expelled from the association and reported to the authorities as vagrants. "The share of each person in the proceeds of the crops," the prospectus stated, "shall be in proportion of the labor performed." The association was to be a partnership. Copies of the plan were available at the Third African Church, in New Orleans. By February 23, three freedmen's farming associations were reported to have been formed, with memberships of 70, 100, and 130 persons respectively. The last of the associations worked a plantation formerly owned by Confederate General "Dick" Taylor. The freedmen in these groups elected "first, second, and third managers" and were preparing the land for the next crop. One serious obstacle to success was the lack of cash and equipment and stock of their own. State laws forbade formation of "associations for agricultural purposes." Therefore, black and white men organized the Freedmen's Aid Association, a benevolent association that would be able to raise funds. The extent of its work cannot be determined from the available evidence. However, it did assist the cooperative that raised cotton and sugar cane on the Whitehead plantation in St. Charles Parish, at least a month before Frank Glover made application for the people living there.[14]

Cooperative, joint-stock company, or partnership arrangements to purchase land were made in other former slave states. Only two weeks before the first of the Louisiana applications were being filed, a group of freedmen in Kinston, Lenoir County, North Carolina, formed a "society to purchase homes by joint stock, and for other purposes. . . ." They resolved to raise $10,000 for homesteads by January 1, 1868. Two hundred and fifty men, "the best and most reliable freedmen in Lenoir County," would comprise the society. They would be assessed $48 a year payable in monthly installments of $4 each. In the country around Mobile, Alabama, journalist Whitelaw Reid reported that freed people were "already talking of clubbing together and working plantations." He was pessimistic about their capability to succeed, an observation not warranted by the exemplary success of freedmen who had operated plantations at Davis Bend, Mississippi, during the war. In the spring of 1866 a reporter for the *New York Times* filing his story from Lynchburg, Virginia, found some freedmen entering partnerships with poor white men in the area "for the purpose of raising tobacco and other products . . .they have in some instances done very well."[15] Three hundred freedmen in the contraband camps around Fortress Monroe in 1866 raised $30,000 to purchase a large estate near Hampton. Unfortunately, there are no reports of the success or failure of this effort. A similar fleeting reference to large-scale purchase concerns a group of Vicksburg, Mississippi, blacks attempting in 1864 to acquire a 1,000-acre tract. The *American Missionary* magazine enthusiastically reported on 160 freedmen in Georgia who during the spring of 1865 formed a joint stock company, elected a superintendent, and raised bountiful crops of rice, corn, beans, and other smaller crops. When land was put up for sale in Liberty County, Georgia, following the war, freedmen there united in colonies and purchased land at Woodville, Ogeechee, and Belmont. By 1874 they owned 6,390 acres. Edisto Island people in a mass meeting in 1870 addressed an appeal to South Carolina Governor Robert K. Scott to purchase a 900-acre plantation on the island. In January 1871 a Beaufort County delegation requested the governor to use his influence in purchasing 2,900 acres of cultivated land, with twenty well-built houses on the place.[16]

While it is quite true that individual freedmen initially lacked capital funds to purchase lands and operate them, many apparently heeded the advice to cooperate and thus accumulated impressive amounts of money. An outstanding example was furnished by Wilkes County, Georgia, freedmen organized in a society during the summer and fall of 1865. In November they sent two representatives to the Freedmen's Bureau assistant commissioner on a mission to locate lands they could purchase. The two freedmen leaders said they had $7,000 and could raise it to $10,000. They appear to have pledged their earnings of their first crops as freed people. They decided to leave worn-out lands. They may also have been unwilling to remain in a county where a tense and anxious white grand jury, seeing their public assemblies as potential insurrectionary forces, planned forceful proscription of the freed people. In any event, the two spokesmen presented their society's offer to the Bureau. General Tillson assigned an officer to investigate the possibility of purchase and settlement in Thomas County, in southwestern Georgia. Good lands at $2-$4 per acre were available. But white citizens attached a condition to their acceptance of the plan: A white man must come with the colony to supervise it. The assigned officer, Major G. A. Hastings of the 12th Maine Volunteer Infantry Regiment, rented two plantations for the Wilkes county people not in Thomas but in Dougherty county. One of the two black leaders, Lawrence Speed, emerged in July 1866 as the leader of a militant Equal Rights Society which planters charged with demoralizing labor and "diffusing erroneous ideas" among the workers. The society was a tightly knit orgainzation which, according to complaining planters, required secrecy of its members, monthly dues of one dollar, and military drill. The planters preferred to see conspiratorial and insurrectionary designs behind the freedmen's ostensible goal of securing the right to vote. Their most serious worry about the freedmen concerned the freedmen's independence and supposed insolence to the planters, and their determination "to have lands of their own which they are to get even if they have to fight for them." The Bureau responded to the planters' complaints by twice summoning Lawrence Speed for spreading "erroneous ideas." By September 1866 Speed appears to have been in trouble with his people because of an alleged misappropriation of $400 from the land-buying association. This did not dampen the others, who planned to purchase the same plantation they then lived on. This aspiration prompted probably more than a thousand men to refuse to contract for labor in January 1867. At least that number had come into the city of Albany, where the white county grand jury complained of their idleness as the reason for a rise in crimes.[17]

The Davis Bend experience in 1863 and 1864 proved beyond doubt the wisdom of independent freedmen ownership and operation of land. Unfortunately, this "experiment" by the Freedmen's Bureau on the Joe and Jefferson Davis lands, comprising six plantations twenty-five miles below Vicksburg, was terminated after a year. The land was restored to the original owners under President Johnson's pardon policy. During the experiment, the government parceled out about 5,000 acres to 181 companies and partnerships comprising 1,300 adults and 450 children who lived and worked on these lands and produced crops under their own management. Bureau officers were not permitted to "meddle with the pecuniary or domestic affairs." The Bend people produced $397,700 worth of corn, vegetables, potatoes, melons, and other crops for sale as well as 1,736 bales of cotton worth $347,200. After payments for expenses and supplies the colonists had a balance in hand of $159,200. And although this economic success was most impressive, the exercise of self-government—the freedmen even had their own judicial system—was still more impressive at the Bend. John Eaton, the army's superintendent of freedmen in the Mississippi Valley, found that "The Community distinctly demonstrated the capacity of the Negro to take care of himself and exercise under honest and competent direction the functions of self-government."[18]

Occasionally, individual freedmen asked General Howard in Washington to help save a tract of land or a homeplace fondly remembered from slavery days. John Andrew Jackson, who had received Freedmen's Bureau assistance to reach Boston, asked the general's help in holding money he hoped to collect in order to buy 1,000 acres of land that his old master once owned, probably near Charleston, South Carolina.

There was "a Griss Mill attached," and the whole tract was to be sold
at a sheriff's sale. A friend of Jackson's in Boston had retained a lawyer, and he had ascertained that the owner asked $4,000 for the pro-
perty. But the people, some forty freedmen who had once worked
with Jackson as slaves on it, were poor. Jackson hoped to raise money
among "many of the Clergymen in Europe which knows me." Hopefully, General Howard would consent to hold the money and perhaps
advance $1,000 of the needed sum. In any event, Jackson explained,
"I want to put all those Negroes back on it who once worked there
to earn their living[.] I want to divide it into lots." Reverend B. B.
Spier also wrote to the general, from New Bern, North Carolina, asking
him to prevail upon the government to buy a tract of land on which
he and others had been located, and recently as renters, for the past
four years. They were too poor to pay the price demanded by the sel-
ler, who had just acquired the Peter Evans tract, near the Trent River
settlement of freedmen. If the government would oblige, the freedmen
would pay on time, for they desperately wanted to remain. Reverend
Spier explained:

> We as Freedmen wish to buy it in order that we could keep our
> children massed together as much as possible that they would be
> better attened to by Schools. . . . in this place is grate many poor
> People & if in case they be broken up they could not live as well
> So this thing have raised a in Sieght ment [excitement] among
> our poor People.[19]

That sense of excitement and hunger for land was again aroused briefly after passage of the Southern Homestead Act in June 1866. Public
lands in Alabama, Louisiana, Florida, Mississippi, and Arkansas were to
be opened up for settlement and ownership. The procedure was modeled on that of the 1862 Homestead Act for the western public lands. A
period of six months after passage was reserved exclusively for freedmer
claims. In that brief period hopes were renewed and freedmen made efforts once again to realize their dreams. But Washington did not meet
the need for thoroughgoing action to guarantee lands to freedmen. The
execution of the act was further stymied by the lackadaisical and negli-

gent policies of the U.S. General Land Office. It simply failed to open offices and provide personnel early enough to service freedmen's homestead claims. Within the Freedmen's Bureau itself, on the state level, in Alabama, Florida, and Arkansas, there were insufficient numbers of surveyors and locating agents to help freedmen in finding tracts and entering claims. Their complaints about this deficiency were almost as great as the freedmen's frustration over it.[20]

Unaware of the problems they would have to face in terms of bureaucratic delays and the useless lands opened up to them, freedmen took the Southern Homestead Act at face value and proceeded to organize colonies to settle on the lands. In some parts of Georgia, for example, these efforts began soon after passage of the law. General Tillson reported that transportation was furnished to freed people. In some districts of South Carolina a freedman was chosen by his people to locate lands. So great was the hope and expectation that hundreds of South Carolina black people prepared to go as a colony to Florida, under the leadership of Ralph Ely, a white former army officer. One hundred and twenty-five families were set to sail from Charleston to New Smyrna, Florida, in January 1867. A few days later 250 additional families were to follow. Ely's plan was at best ill conceived because he was totally unprepared to guarantee the social services required in the movement of 1,000 people. Moreover, it appears that Ely never consulted with the freedmen for whom he filed homestead entries in November and December 1866 and for which they paid him $600. But he did show some concern when he demanded the money back upon learning that no action had been taken by the Tallahassee land office. The freedmen's own lack of seed, tools, animals, and materials with which to begin their new venture further doomed their efforts. Worse yet, need compelled them to hire themselves out to planters under contract. Consequently, they had little if any time or energy left for their own homesteads. Whether or not they were aware of such drawbacks before departing Georgia and South Carolina, freedmen did nevertheless pour into Florida in groups to settle there. They met in their churches to formulate plans. Eventually, more than 3,000 freed people entered Florida homesteads, which represented 75 percent of all known homesteads entered by freedmen under the 1866 act.[21]

Louisiana freedmen also organized to take advantage of this opening to the public lands. By July 1, 1867, Dr. J. J. Saville, the state locating agent of the Freedmen's Bureau, reported that "companies of freedmen" were preparing to take up homesteads in the fall. A party of about a hundred persons was expected to begin on September 1, with several hundred more to follow. Saville urged the Bureau to inform Congress that the expired grant of 621,266 acres held by the New Orleans, Opelousas, and Great Western Railroad should be reopened to homestead entry. He was confident that at least 500 families would settle on it in the coming fall and winter.[22]

But Saville's hopes were blocked by the opposition of Northern capitalists to his proposal and by deficiencies in the Southern Homestead Act and the machinery to implement it. Supposed friends of the freedmen, especially the editor of the New Orleans *Republican,* refused to support Saville. They were more interested in railroad speculation than in giving the railroad lands to freed people. Saville took his case directly to Representative George W. Julian, an active foe of railroad special privilege and a proponent of democratic land distribution. Saville maintained that employers and some officers of black regiments were in collusion to divert freedmen away from homestead claims and into contracting for labor. Some officers received $5 apiece for every man they induced to labor for planters, he charged. "The case is freedmen vs. capital," Saville concluded. Finally, Saville deplored that weakness in the Homestead Act that required claimants to travel 100 to 200 miles across the state to a land office, an expense they could not afford. Their ultimate frustration came when they arrived to find no land office at New Orleans, for example. When that office did open on January 17, 1867, it was two weeks past the expiration of the preference period reserved for freedmen and loyal whites. Despite all these obstacles, Saville succeeded in locating eighty-seven homesteads: seventy-three for freedmen and fourteen for white refugees and soldiers. Julian succeeded as well in having Congress take back the railroad lands of the New Orleans and Opelousas in 1870. The federal government opened them to homesteading in 1871 amid interest in settlement. However, by 1873, railroad interests exerted sufficient influence to have the lands restored to the state of Louisiana for railroad purposes. Ten years later the governor conveyed the land to the New Orleans and Pacific Railroad.[23] Clearly, Saville's analysis, of powerful capital versus the freedmen, was precisely on the mark.

Some homestead activity developed in Alabama under the 1866 statute. Although there is little firm data, it appears that if freedmen had

any funds for these purposes, they pooled them to purchase improved
land in the cotton belt and divided it among themselves. In some places,
however, freedmen erected schoolhouses on their homestead entries.
Eventually, about 200 entries were made in the state under the act.[24]

In Arkansas, freedmen quickly moved to take advantage of the act.
Early in September 1866 about 500 freedmen attended a meeting on
the subject at Fort Smith. They decided to seek the aid of the government in obtaining rations and tools over a two-year period. Whether they
succeeded is not made clear by the records, but a colony of squatters
located near the town. By October 1, 1866, 30 families comprising
about 125 persons entered lands in the state and moved onto them.
Advance agents of 150 Georgia families arrived at Little Rock in February 1867 and spent a couple of days with the Bureau surveyor in
examining sites for their colony. They then went on to Fort Smith to
inspect possible sites there before making a final choice, in accordance
with instructions from their people at home. Agents of a second Georgia colony of 18 families also arrived during the month and were expected to locate near Little Rock. As it was, the surveyor settled about
75 families by the end of February. His frustrations over deficiencies
in the Southern Homestead Act moved him to write, "As it *should
have* been I might as well have settled five hundred." Probably the
colony of 150 was unable to attain its objective because the Clarksville land office was not yet open. Belatedly and probably ineffectu-
ally, a Washington, Arkansas, land office was to be opened soon after
August 1867. Freedmen, with meager means to warrant either lengthy
voyages or leisurely exploration of sites, in the end received relatively
small benefit from the Southern Homestead Act. Their own collective
exertions do stand out as notable manifestations of the spirit of community.[25]

The discouragements they met in Washington and in the localities
chosen for settlement did not dissuade freedmen from their efforts.
Their unfulfilled desire for land and community led some groups to
consider schemes for purchase and division of lands as offered by am-
bitious Northern and Southern whites, some of them well meaning.
Such a transaction was attempted in January 1868 by an association
of black war veterans in Natchez (Adams County), Mississippi. They
proposed to purchase at $10 per acre, 10,690 acres cf Natchez planter
A. K. Farrar's large holdings on the Homochitto River in Wilkinson
County. Two hundred and sixty freed men and women, expecting to

receive bounty money from the U.S. government, had formed an association and named a board of directors made up of seven blacks
and one white man (a Presbyterian minister). They had apparently organized during 1867 and had subscribed $30,000 to $40,000 of the
bounty money due them. Moreover, the company created by the freedmen's association to conduct the proposed transaction, Jacobs, Williams,
Wood, and Company, was headed by one of Mississippi's prominent
black Reconstruction leaders, Henry P. Jacobs. Farrar was of course
quite willing to sell and appealed to the government to intervene by
underwriting the scheme. The self-interest is obvious and perhaps in
part accounts for the Freedmen's Bureau's rejection of the plan. A
more decisive reason appears to have been a Bureau officer's report
that cast serious doubt upon the plan's feasibility and upon the capability of the black and white men in the association. But there was
more to the proposal than selfishness by a plantation aristocrat.[26]

Farrar appears to have had genuine concern for the freedmen's welfare and defended his offer in terms that the freedmen probably would
have approved. He had in fact incurred the wrath of other white planters "for even consenting to sell their old Niggers his Plantation." A
meeting of 300 of his peers had met to look into and report on "this
terrible calamity." But one group's calamity may have been another
group's community. Farrar explained that the association's aim was
"to secure to themselves a permanent, social, and industrial establishment." They had "unshaken conviction" that the proposed purchase
had "greater and more varied resources for their settlement . . . to
secure them against want, and social organization." The scheme, he
said, "necessarily embraced a system of industry and social cultivation
that should overcome the prevailing distrust of the capacity of the
freedman to sustain himself, and improve permanently his condition,
without the presence and co-operation of the white race." If the colony
was to be realized, Farrar concluded, "Other communities will be associated together at eligible localities, throughout the country . . . and
if, as it is yet believed, this people is susceptible of a high degree of
Civilization, and of a wise administration of the affairs of a Common-
wealth," no better starting place, in the planter's opinion, could be
found than in this transfer of land from himself to the association of
black men.[27]

In spite of these abortive attempts, freedmen's longing for settlement and stability was made evident not so much by Farrar's brand

of eloquence as by the freed people's actions and status. A sampling
of forty of the association's male subscribers and a comparison of those
names with regimental rosters, Freedmen's Bureau marriage records,
and military pension records reveal that a slight majority of those in
the sample for whom birthplaces are known (thirteen out of twenty-
four) were born in Mississippi counties and nearby Louisiana parishes.
It should be noted that thirty-two wives of men whose names appear
in the land association roster gave their places of residence at the time
of their marriages (1864-1865) as Natchez (twenty-six) or nearby Vidalia,
Louisiana (five), and one woman gave Good Hope, Louisiana. The men
had served in several black regiments during the war. The muster rolls
of the 6th U.S. Colored Heavy Artillery Regiment helped to identify
thirty-five persons in the total sample of forty. Of the twenty-five
whose occupations were named in the records, eighteen were laborers,
farm hands, field hands, or farmers. A carpenter, two teamsters, a mu-
sician, and a cook were the skilled men; and two were servants. The
majority of the applicants appear to have been in their twenties (twenty-
two of thirty-six with known ages were between twenty and twenty-
nine years old). The immediate families of twenty-eight men in the
sample are important to our appreciation of their aims. Three of them
with children in their households appear to have had no wives at the
time the marriage registers were compiled in 1864 and 1865. But all
of the twenty-five couples and the three unwed men had seventy-eight
children. The ratios of men, women, and children are much like those
of the Louisiana family groups applying for leaseholds in 1865. The
Mississippi freedmen households consisted of husband and wife and
from one to six children. Most had fewer than four children per household. These records do not indicate whether aged persons or other relatives were in the households. These Mississippi veterans appear to have
wished to settle on homesteads close to their places of birth or their
wives' residences and where they entered military service (Natchez)
and where they were mustered out (Natchez). They were young married men who appear to have opted for independence on their own
land and in their own community.[28] Finally, the failure of the 1867
crop and the falling price of cotton were felt with great force among
Adams County laborers and plantation owners. Planters were not expected to clear expenses at the end of the year. Freedmen, who had
contracted for a share of the *net* crop, were expected in November to
receive nothing in cash for their labor at year's end. Applications for re-

lief in the Freedmen's Bureau headquarters rose. The 28,000 freed people in the subdistrict embracing Adams County faced "indescribable destitution and suffering."[29] The chance to bid their military bounty money for a vast plantation was irresistible for 260 freed people with almost another 1,000 persons dependent upon their labor and their luck. Some of them, unable to wait for the outcome of negotiations with Farrar and with the government, took possession of portions of Farrar's vast farmland. They had begun working, in January 1868, to prepare the land for a crop. They said they were determined to keep their families from starving. By mid-February other freedmen were making inquiries about how soon they could move onto the farm.

Notwithstanding the intervention on behalf of the association by Charles Sumner, the Bureau officers found the scheme impracticable. General Howard refused a request from Jacobs to furnish transportation for interested freedmen and disapproved the company's plans. As Farrar lamented, if the plan was to be rejected, the "munificent bounty of the Government now about to come to the hands" of the freedmen, "will soon be recollected only, as the bauble of a brief holiday."[30]

Despite broken government promises, freed people persevered. Relying on their own resources, they continued to make collective purchases. In 1868 about 200 freedmen in Charleston formed a cooperative land association. They bought a 600-acre farm at Remley's Point, opposite the city, for $10 per acre. A year earlier about 100 "poor colored men" in the same city organized the Charleston Land Company. In 1868 the company purchased 600 acres. They financed it by their dollar-a-month payments toward a $10 share per member. Another cooperative, the Atlantic Land Company, was organized in Charleston County in 1868. However, it failed to complete its purchase of Bull's Island for $15,000. The group could not raise the final $6,000 and faced foreclosure in 1870. In that year ten Savannah freedmen combined the proceeds from their crop and paid cash for a 700-acre plantation on the Sea Islands. Each man and his family held a 70-acre farm. Additional clubs were forming on the islands off the Georgia city. The traveler who reported these efforts in 1870 found them also in the interior of Georgia and South Carolina. A community of families in South Carolina extended cooperation to marketing their cotton in Augusta, Georgia. They chartered a railroad car for $140 round trip to take their cotton and corn and other crops to the city. There they exchanged them for "clothing, furniture, implements of husbandry, and supplies for putting in their next crop." They tried to get a teacher for their settlement, offering to pay all the expenses. Back on the coast, in 1872, another coopera- tive purchased a 750-acre tract on Edisto Island. By 1873 some of the largest plantations in Colleton County, South Carolina, the former do- main of the noblesse oblige planters, were owned by freedmen's cooper- ative societies. Some had been in operation three or four years, with self-government including tribunals to adjudicate disputes and violations of the societies' bylaws. The land was equally distributed. All sick per- sons were cared for by the society if they were unable to care for them- selves. Officers were elected and charged with the responsibility of re- porting on their conditions to the society's weekly meeting or special emergency meetings.[31]

A rare glimpse of the familial-collective mode of migration and set- tlement comes from Hortense Powdermaker's anthropological studies in Mississippi during the 1930s. A group of twenty to thirty Alabama black families, most of them former slaves, migrated in 1873 to the Mississippi-Yazoo delta. Through their six-week trek they brought all their worldly goods in covered wagons and their livestock to begin life anew in a frontier setting. They cleared a desolate land and planted and cultivated it, women and children working the land while men per- formed day labor splitting rails and cutting logs for white employers. A Texas Quaker who owned the land made the transition easier by choosing to sell only to blacks. The settlers built log cabins, a school, a church, and roads. The leader of the community had been a slave shoemaker. His wife had been a house slave, a seamstress. The minister of the church was another community leader. Eight years after their arrival some of the people returned to Alabama to lead about 200 peo- ple to the Mississippi community. Similar recruitments followed in later years. The "Cottonville" community, as it was known, endured until 1934.[32]

In 1874 a group of laborers in Montgomery, Alabama, formed an association to buy land at $4 to $5 per acre. A fund for the purpose was to be amassed from member payments of $1 to $10. Late that year, the Alabama Convention of Colored People, composed of dele- gates from every county in the state, met to consider their economic depression and their political and social repression. Among other actions, the convention organized an emigration association to seek lands in the west. It was authorized to settle a colony of families as a pilot venture. If successful, it would become the nucleus for thousands of Alabama laboring-class families. The effort may have enjoyed some success. In any event, the creation of the Emigration Association implemented an intention of the labor convention of Alabama that had been held in Montgomery on January 2, 1872. At that earlier meeting an agent of the convention had reported optimistically on an August 1871 inspection tour of land in Kansas. The 1874 convention's committee on homesteads reported that its inquiry showed that at least 100 homestead claims in Kansas had been entered by "colored Alabamians," in addition to the 200 that were entered in Alabama under the Homestead Act. The committee urged that Alabama blacks hasten to make claims before available public land east of the Rocky Mountains was removed from their reach. The report predicted that within twenty years no worthwhile land in that area would be left for black men on which to settle. In conclusion the committee discouraged en masse emigration but recommended experimental colonization of a small number of families. [33]

The convention's urging reflected the deep longing of freed people. Granville Bennett, a Livingston, Alabama, freedman illustrated this when he testified to the Klan investigation committee two months before the labor convention. Bennett stated that the people of Sumter County generally agreed that they would prefer to go to Kansas to escape harassment by night riders. As for himself, the old man wished to spend his last days in peace, "in a place called Kansas, way up here somewhere." "I've got it mighty strong in my head," he declared. "I have only got so long to live, and I want to live in the comfort of my life while I do live, and it is no comfort now. I am afraid to lie down, and if there is ary other place to go to and inherit the happiness of my life, I want to go, if it is only for ten days." [34]

Finally, black men in Texas actively organized during the 1870s and early 1880s to obtain lands and homesteads. In one case they enjoyed the collaboration of a white man who purchased or took options on land in Fort Bend County and sold tracts to blacks at $1 to $7 per acre. In 1874 1,000 black people were reported moving from Washington County to join the colony. But freedmen had by this time organized the Colored Farmers' Association. At its 1876 convention in Huntsville, 150 delegates from eleven counties made plans to open cooperative stores in the larger Texas towns. A Colored State Grange was organized at Dallas in 1880 for the express purpose of helping its members to acquire homesteads. Two years later Navarro County freedmen with the same aim organized the Colored Men's Land and Commercial Joint Stock Company, with a capital stock of $25,000. In 1883 a Texas Homestead and Colonization Association grew out of a black men's convention in Waco. Unfortunately, little is known of the affairs of these organizations, and further research is needed in this area.[35]

Reconstruction failed the freed people in large measure because they were unable to revolutionize landownership. Given the power arrayed against the black sharecroppers and laborers in the South, that class fared little better than other peasant classes in industrializing societies.[36] Nevertheless, freedmen did not allow themselves to fall into serfdom and tried to rise out of their rural proletarian status. Cooperation and collective action on the scale of a village movement became one of several strategies. It linked the desire for land and schools with the desire for family stability and community.

The American village movement, as the remarks at the opening of this chapter indicated, appear to have been but a variant of the more pronounced and successful Jamaican and Guyanese village movements. The parallels are intriguing. First of all, the similarities in Jamaican, Guyanese, and American black peoples' aspirations are distinct. In each, freedmen displayed a boundless land hunger. Although separated in time by a generation, the desire to be independent landowners was made palpable. The motivations to seek peasant proprietor status in freedmen communities were virtually identical: escape from the controls of slavery or of postemancipation labor systems resembling slavery. Even though in all three there was strong attachment to homeplaces, to slave quarters in the South, to yards and houses and provision grounds in the Caribbean, freedmen clearly sought to escape them when they could not be free of planters' controls over their lives. In other words, freedmen in the South Atlantic system from Virginia to British Guiana, at least, asserted their own identities and programs.

Another motivation probably was supplied by the prototypes of proprietorship enjoyed in limited and small-scale fashion during slavery in Jamaican provision grounds, British Guiana "nigger yards," and North American garden plots. Indeed, this reflected an economic concern, for family subsistence depended in considerable measure upon the vegetables

raised in such holdings and upon the fowl and occasional cow attached
to them. But there was more to the yard and the house of the slave
and of the freedmen. In Caribbean societies, Sidney Mintz demonstrates
quite discriminately, considerable variation marks the phenomenon of
house and yard. Yet the similarities are persistent. Among them is their
historically common origin in the slave provision grounds, although differing at least according to ecological systems and economies (sugar,
coffee, tobacco, and so on). But, as Mintz shows, the house and the
yard in the Caribbean were and are a powerful cultural force. They are
the sites of daily life, of familial interaction.[37]

In Caribbean peasant society the house accommodates one sexually
cohabiting couple; conjugal unions usually depend upon access to independent houses. But this does not necessarily mean removal at a
great distance from the parent's house. A separate home may be in
the same yard. There, kin are linked not only in the present but across
the generations. The dead are buried in Haitian and Jamaican yards,
and the reverence they receive is one such link. Another is the custom
in Jamaica, West Africa, and among Gullah blacks in the South Carolina Sea Islands of burying the placenta of a newborn child beneath
a door stoop or of burying the child's umbilical cord at the foot of
a fruit-bearing tree in the yard. In these and in other profound ways
the house and the yard take on great symbolic importance as expressions of the ties binding kin groups and of the reverence for dead ancestors and for newborns. "But the yard is an extension of the house,
and land remains immensely important for Caribbean peasants," Mintz
has written.[38] It is the site of myriad activities and interchanges. One
may adopt Mintz's analysis to suggest that yards were the nuclei of
slave communities and that in them values, beliefs, and behavior patterns were passed on to the freedmen who came out of them, throughout the Americas. The anthropological study aids our appreciation of
the village movements.

During the 1840s in Jamaica and British Guiana and during the 1860
and 1870s in the Southern states, such collective efforts were responses
to the rigorous work routines of plantation and estate. The exodus from
sugar estates was equaled in quality and tone by the exodus from cotton plantations. Jamaican freedmen succeeded in making individual land
purchases and in establishing model village communities under the aegis
of the Nonconformist Church missionaries, who had been active aboli-

tionists. Some acquired lands by becoming squatters on abandoned estates. Generally, Jamaican and British Guiana landowners, like North American planters, resisted and refused to sell lands to freedmen. Owners feared loss of social control over black laborers and devised similar racial justifications for their continued domination.

The freedmen wished to be respected and independent, to realize freedom. In Jamaica, Phillip Curtin informs us, freedmen retained some African views on landownership, suggesting the assertion of an identity retained but altered from its origins across the generations.[39] All three groups of freedmen used a form of organization common to the modern world, the joint-stock company, to acquire and redistribute lands. Cultural retention and acculturation are both evident in the freedmen's strategies. It is evident in their aspirations as well: to live in communities governed by themselves and free to live as other people in culturally plural societies.

The tragic irony was that the liberal forces that participated with them in abolishing slavery sooner or later abandoned the freed people, and some became their employers and exploiters. Revived sugar markets and planter control of political machinery in Jamaica and British Guiana combined to force villages back to a reliance on plantation labor. The prospects of extracting the Southern states' natural resources for great profits weakened the wartime liberals' will to struggle for equality. They tired of the "Negro question" and participated in the fruits of the new "labor question." Freedmen were denied the opportunity to obtain lands and to develop prosperous communities.

A Fiat to Go Forth 8

There is an exodus of agricultural labor. . . . The committee find that the primary cause of this lies in the absence of a republican form of government to the people of Louisiana. . . .All rights of freedmen [are] denied. . . . The constantly recurring, nay, ever present, fear which haunts the mind of these our people . . . is that slavery in the horrible form of peonage is approaching. —The Colored State Convention, New Orleans, Louisiana, April 21, 1879.

Landless Southern black and white agricultural laborers and sharecroppers felt the same economic stranglehold on their lives. Where the first sprouts of interracial political collaboration appeared among them, superior force suppressed them. This left black farmers almost totally isolated. In black majority counties and electoral districts, freedmen were able to maintain some presence in local governments into the mid-1870s. But this was short-lived, once the bourbon planters initiated violence against blacks, particularly in northern Louisiana and Mississippi. Tensas Parish, Louisiana, illustrates the problem that planters attacked with a shotgun policy. In the 1870 census Tensas counted 11,000 blacks and 1,400 whites. In the 1872 election, Republicans received 2,300 votes, Democrats 182; in 1876, Republicans received 3,200 votes, Democrats, 500. Bourbons prepared to reverse the results in the 1878 elections. During October, false alarms of armed black attacks on Waterproof, Louisiana, in Tensas Parish, provided the pretext for the governor to dispatch troops against the blacks and for private gangs to "bulldoze" black people. Six to ten blacks were killed. The policy of terror was applied to much of the cotton plantation and sharecropper population in the lower Mississippi Valley.[1]

By 1880 the vast former slave population in the area was terrorized into virtual political silence and forced to settle for the planters' terms

and conditions of labor. Thousands of freed people, however, refused
to remain and began to head for Kansas. Their migration was a village
movement away from repressive living conditions and toward a free
life in a peaceable community. The northwestward movement, first by
a few hundred brave souls from the Mississippi River communities,
then by thousands, was the reenactment of British Guiana and Jamaica
freedmen movements. It was a much more desperate effort than the
one attempted more passively ten years earlier by Adams County freedmen to create a community on their own land.

Driven by terror at home and enticed by higher wages and above all
by the vision of a promised land on the other side of the Mississippi
River, freedmen communities had organized and prepared for emigration and colonization throughout the Reconstruction period. Much of
this busy activity came to light in 1880 during the spectacular exodus
of some 60,000 people from Louisiana, Mississippi, Alabama, Texas,
Georgia, South Carolina, Tennessee, and other Old South states to
Kansas. But, quite significantly, black rural laborers, and a few articulate, educated, politically minded and other middle-class black people,
initiated a serious emigration.

Parties of freedmen or single ambassadors traveled to Kansas and
other states to investigate the possibilities. In June 1879 Kansas governor John St. John met with "100 leading colored men" from Alabama
and Mississippi, and spent an hour talking with them in the senate cham-
ber. The governor told them what they could expect to find if they
should come with their people. Delegates replied that they had reached
the limits of endurance under oppression; they would risk their lives
to be free rather than live in the South any longer. But such probes
were a well-known practice, even a decade earlier. Romulus Moore of
Georgia's Taliaferro County, for example, was dispatched to Louisiana
in 1869 to search for land on which his people could live more peaceably. The 10,000-acre estate on which they lived as tenants or owners
was the target of systematic Klan attacks. Moreover, their unsettled
state was aggravated by the dismissal of black members of the Georgia
legislature, of which Moore was a member. He declared that, "We calculated to collect a large body of colored people and go on some land
there."[2]

At about the same time, white terror seriously disturbed the Tennessee black community, which then pressed for protection. Frustrated by

the unrelieved harassments, some of its members organized for emigration. The 1866 black men's convention at Nashville had heard speeches extolling western lands and urging black men to move to Kansas.[3] Three years later, another such assembly in Nashville was strongly reminded of the western state as a desirable place to settle.[4] A Nashville undertaker and cabinetmaker, Benjamin Singleton, appears to have assumed the leadership in organizing a Tennessee Real Estate and Homestead Association in 1869; and in creating a local group, the Edgefield Real Estate Association, in 1874. He claimed to be the "father" of the 1879-1880 exodus that had aroused the interest of the press and Congress. His claim is enhanced by his having established colonies on Kansas soil. Singleton's first hegira was completed in 1875 when he led a colony to Baxter Springs, Kansas. During the next five years, he made several moves back and forth between Tennessee and Kansas. A Topeka black people's newspaper credited him with bringing 7,432 colonists, according to figures the editors gleaned from railroad and steamboat companies. Singleton had spent his own money, he said, in printing circulars and distributing them throughout the South. They bore the promise of a peaceful life in Kansas and the possibility of owning land. Black men working on the steamboats or on railroad trains touching at Nashville circulated these papers in their travels.[5]

We do not know if one of them reached Granville Bennett, who had the idea of Kansas "strong in his head" or "Jones," a Demopolis, Alabama, freedman. Jones was the subject of a white lawyer's testimony in which the black freedman emerged as an agitator for emigration to Kansas and for higher pay to local farm laborers. Aberdeen, Mississippi, freedmen were understandably receptive to the idea of emigration after about eight months of terror in 1870-1871. Unable to endure more of the violent attacks on them, they gathered in their church to discuss emigration. They were merely representative of the condition of affairs in the so-called late insurrectionary states. "Pap" Singleton, a man of seventy when he spoke to a Senate committee in 1880, may have enlarged his role in the great exodus movement. He did not exaggerate when he gave its causes: "Well, my people, for the want of land—we needed land for our children—and their disadvantages—that caused my heart to grieve and sorrow; pity for my race, sir, that was coming down, instead of going up—that caused me to go to work for them."[6]

As a convention of black men in New Orleans in 1879 declared, "The fiat to go forth is irresistible."[7] Ever since the Reconstruction

Acts in 1867 had enfranchised freed blacks, the people had endured relentless harassment. There appeared to be no end to the killing and "bulldozing" of Louisiana and Mississippi freedmen to disfranchise and bring them under virtual slavelike control. The 1876 presidential election arrangement ostensibly was to bring peace to the nation, to quiet the turmoil of Reconstruction. However, President Rutherford B. Hayes's hands-off policy merely left the way open to retaliatory violence by whites against freedmen laborers and voters. The freedmen's distress brought them to the edge of despair.

As distressed peoples in other societies and other times awaited justice, so did the sugar and cotton laborers look to a savior for relief and deliverance. Insistent men like Singleton stimulated hope and confidence. When they also possessed charismatic qualities, such men contributed to a revitalization of the people. Thus it should not be surprising to learn that in the economically depressed Mississippi River counties in 1878 a black man by the name of Dr. Collins appeared to be a Moses assembling the Israelites for the trek to New Canaan. His frenzied oratory carried the message of mass migration to Liberia, a land of plenty, with food growing on trees, where no one would be required to work. In a style common to leaders and exhorters of crisis cults among distressed peoples, Collins promised salvation from outside of Mississippi's freedmen community. He told the people to get ready and that a boat would come for them.[8] Similarly, Singleton, although not quite so emotionally high pitched as Collins, claimed divine sanction for his leadership.

> Right emphatically, I tell you today, I woke up the millions
> right through me! The great God of glory has worked in me.
> I have had open air interviews with the living spirit of God for
> my people; and we are going to leave the South. We are going
> to leave if there ain't an alteration and signs of change.[9]

There were no alterations and no signs of change. Singleton's move to Kansas appeared to be the fulfillment of the leadership role he claimed.

In Tennessee as in Mississippi and Louisiana, freedmen required higher wages and more equitable distribution of the earnings from their crops. In all three states they required protection of their rights as citizens, lower rents to be paid for land, and an opportunity to purchase lands.

Anyone who could promise or imply the promise of land and peaceable opportunity—as did Singleton, Collins, the railroad companies, and labor agents in their propaganda—met with almost unquestioning support and acceptance. And when, in one year, the governor of Kansas received 3,000 letters of inquiry from Southern blacks, we have a measure of their yearning to escape economic misery and to realize their dreams.[10]

Henry Adams further illuminates this link between land and community. Both Adams and Singleton reveal to us aspects of the culture and potential power of a laboring class attempting independently to solve its problems. And although Adams, a Shreveport, Louisiana, former slave, exhibited far less personal magnetism than Singleton and Collins, he also possessed leadership qualities. He demonstrated a gift for organizing that appears to have been fed by his political and class consciousness. Adams was born into slavery in Georgia in 1843. At the age of eight he was taken to Louisiana with his slave family. He was emancipated in 1865, and joined the U.S. Army in 1866 for a three-year hitch. When he came out of the army, he had learned the rudiments of reading and writing and continued to teach himself. He succeeded well enough to draw up lengthy records of white planters' abuses of black laborers, and he submitted these records to a Senate committee in 1880. He also took a leading part in Radical Republican politics in Caddo Parish. He had been a faith doctor ever since he was nine years old and claimed to have treated and cured numbers of blacks and whites who sought him out. In much of his organizing work he revealed a distrust for many preachers, although his father was one, but he did collaborate with them in a black men's convention in New Orleans in 1879.[11]

Adams also expressed a distrust of politicians when, in 1880, he described a committee of 500 freedmen that he and other concerned black army veterans had organized and led since 1870. Politicians, black and white, were barred from the committee and from the councils that it in turn organized over a decade. By 1880 these astonishingly unpublicized efforts, Adams claimed, resulted in an enrollment of 98,000 black rural laborers prepared for migration. The committee of 500 initially set out to investigate the conditions of the black people. When they learned of widespread misery, debt, illness, economic exploitation, political skullduggery, and murder, and with no sign of countermeasures to provide protection or give relief, they concluded that no viable community could be maintained in the Deep South states.

Their enlarged organization aimed at migration to a western territory that they said should be set aside for them. Failing that, the government should appropriate funds for transportation to Liberia.

Singleton also had indicated that "political" blacks were not permitted in his movement. Adams explained that they might endanger the movement by revealing it to the "republican politicianers" who would in turn divulge its efforts. This would lead to violent retaliation.

Then who was eligible for this great work of protection and liberation? Singleton had said that "it was the muscle of the arm, the men that worked that we wanted." Adams affirmed this class consciousness in discussing his political opinions with senators who quizzed him. When a senator asked Adams if he knew what the sentiments of his people were, Adams replied, "Well, what I wants and what I know the laboring classes wants —for I speak for them as much as for myself, for I am amongst them there, and I am considered a leading man among them there—" The senator interrupted to ask if Adams considered himself a leading man among the people. Adams carefully made a distinction when he answered, "No, I am considered a leading man with the people there."[12] He then explained that "the laboring class of people down there" preferred Grant, as Adams did, but that some black politicians were working toward a nomination of General Sherman for president. Adams regarded his role in organizing the field workers to defend their economic and civil rights as the most important of his assumed duties. He explained that a kind of flying squadron of 150 men in the committee of 500 had the responsibility to live and work among the people, "in the fields, everywhere to see what sort of living our people lived." These worker-organizers "went to the masses" in a style to be repeated during the next century by Russian, Chinese, French, and other radical and revolutionary movements. They traveled to nearby states, found jobs, and paid all their own expenses. The man assigned to Louisiana and Mississippi was supported by the funds these workmen paid out of their own pockets.

This black "rail splitter and wood chopper" stunned the senators and aroused their curiosity and disbelief. They doubted a laborer's capacity to perform such feats as Adams claimed. With what must have been a mixture of admiration and incredulity, these political sophisticates probed the puzzle of Adams's striking talents. How did you get to be so prominent if politicians were not allowed in your group? Did your people not regard you as a politician? Adams explained that his leadership did not necessarily derive from his being a politician:

The committee always say that they could not control a great many
people of the laboring class without I spoke to them how they ought
to vote, or something of that sort in behalf of their own interests
to better their own condition, and so I would speak to them and
tell them how I thought it would be best for them to vote. And I
would have to tell a great many of them whether they ought to
take part in politics.[13]

One senator wanted to know if it was helpful that Adams was a faith doctor. He replied, "They have more confidence in me in every way on that
account." He denied practicing voodoo, when asked by a senator.

Much of his prominence was due to his intimate involvement in the
affairs of the plantation laborers. He examined their contracts and compared them with accounts of cotton sales; and he demonstrated how the
laborers were being swindled. He led groups of former soldiers in defending
threatened black men and women. Above all, despite his disclaimers to
the senators, the document that he placed in the record did show that
he was a local political leader. He was president of the "Mother Club"
(apparently the main Republican club) in Shreveport. Adams reported
that during the 1874 elections Democrats and others unleashed a wave
of violence in five Red River counties that destroyed their Republican
organizations. Adams claimed his club in the city was the only one to
withstand that campaign because black and white men in the city resisted
armed attacks. He played a leading role, risking a tour into the countryside to speak in hostile, remote, and unprotected surroundings.

The exodus that appeared spontaneous in 1879 was the ultimate black
village movement. It was long in the making, and the people who participated constituted whole communities. When they departed, they gave
the impression of a massive uncontrolled force. But we know that laborers in Tennessee, Louisiana, Mississippi, and other states organized for
an event like this. By the time it took place, the exodus had acquired the
collaboration of black middle classes and religious and philanthropic organizations in St. Louis, Topeka, New Orleans, and other places in the
United States. The "exodusters" traveled in groups on the roadways,
steamboats, railways, and on foot and in wagons. Adams was a member
of a committee on arrangements and transportation in New Orleans,
seeking out steamboat captains courageous enough to stop at river land-
ings for black folk and their families and bundles and to charge reasonable fares.

Not all of the exodusters were so poor as to lack cash for transportation. Late in 1879, Texas blacks left for Kansas at the rate of about 1,000 to 1,200 a week, some having sold or left behind prospering farms. A reporter counted 90 men, women and children in one railroad car who had paid over $1,000 in fares. Hundreds gathered at remote country rail stations, while other hundreds traveled together with their teams of mules and wagons. A Shreveport correspondent told a local newspaper about the "Kansas fever" in his district. One morning in December 1879 the railroad depot was a scene of great excitement as 65 persons prepared to depart on the 11:30 A.M. train, "and each was well provided with money, well dressed, bought their tickets like American citizens going to a free country where they could breathe the air of freedom." The cars were crowded every day, and at the end of the week in which he wrote, 150 families were due to leave on the morning train for Kansas. A few days earlier 25 families had started for "that great and free land, Kansas" in seven wagons with two mules to each. When the river rose and boats began again to ply the waters between Shreveport and the mouth, he expected a brisk and massive departure. North Louisiana would be free of black faces "as she is of rice growing." "I hope to see a day," he wrote, "when these powerless people will have a home, vote as they please, pay only one rent, and at the end of the year when they go to the land owner to pay, he will not say 'nought is a nought, figure a figure, figure belongs to me and nought to the poor nigger.' " The exodusters heeded Singleton's advice, and that of Kansas residents, in going with money and other means. The Shreveport and Texas scenes were reenacted in 1881 when emigration societies in South Carolina's Edgefield district led out 5,000 people in the last week of December bound for better conditions in Arkansas.[14]

A relatively small number of freed people were exodusters. They nevertheless symbolized the lengths, literal and symbolic, to which they would go to maintain their communities. It is clear that not all of the migrants found the land they sought. Singleton's 7,000 colonists and the 5,000 persons who settled in Arkansas appear to be our firmest statistics. Another estimate, by Henry King, Topeka's postmaster, asserted that 15,000 to 20,000 black people settled in Kansas during the year ending April 1, 1880. Thirty percent of them came from Mississippi, 20 percent from Texas, 15 percent from Tennessee, 10 percent from Louisiana, 5 percent each from Georgia and Alabama, and 15 percent from other Southern states. About 20,000 acres were taken by the freedmen during the first year, and 3,000 acres of it was cultivated in grains.[15]

Although our knowledge of the numbers of emigrants remains impre-
cise, the emigrants' actions are significant. Their exodus raised the black
rural laborer's communal movement above the local level. Falling short
of a declaration of nationality and of national independence, it merely
sought protection for a community and was shaped by a community consciousness. For a moment in 1873, it wrung from Mississippi white leaders
a conciliatory pledge to reduce violence and harassment. It could be argued that had the exodus been even more voluminous—a general strike
on a grand scale—even greater equity could probably have been won by
the Afro-American community. But the numbers were small, and the
demand for a territory was insufficiently propagated.

It was a tactic among tactics in a grander strategy that most post-Civil
War Afro-Americans shared. Within that consensus, there was room for
debate over tactics, as Frederick Douglass and Richard T. Greener demonstrated in their controversy over the wisdom of emigration. As it turned
out, there was more "huddling together" in the South than flight. Despite
the oppressions and low wages, freed people found a measure of security
and personal freedom in this era, when they could join larger communities of their own. W. E. B. Du Bois executed a sharply cut word-engraving
of such a community in describing late nineteenth-century Dougherty
County, Georgia. It was part of what he designated the "Black Belt,"
the "huddling together for self-protection." In retrospect it was a passive
and conservative tactic but ironically one with revolutionary implications.

The exodus arose ironically from the freedman's quest for stability
and community. He had been emancipated for fourteen to fifteen years
and had failed to gain ownership of the land. The cotton field laborers
who worked the rich and almost boundless acres of the lower Mississippi
Valley particularly felt this defeat. It was especially intolerable to them,
for they had begun in early Reconstruction years to enter sharecropping
agreements as a viable alternative to wage labor under the old gang-labor
system. They perceived a measure of self-control and self-determination
in their ability to operate farms and make decisions with respect to farm
management as well as to family affairs. But planters swindled croppers
out of earnings and maintained their political and social domination by
forceful means. Throughout northern Louisiana's cotton parishes in the
mid-1870s freedmen were cheated of their just share of the crops. Some
who had settled homesteads on government lands were driven off, and
some were killed. Freedmen refused to send their wives to work in the

fields and tried to send their children to schools, despite a white terror
that drove them back to picking cotton. White planters were determined
to keep a tight-fisted control over the lives of their laborers and tenants.
The croppers and their families simply wanted to live peacefully and pro-
ductively in their communities.

Explanations of the exodus in 1879 and 1880 were contemporaneous
with the Irish agitation and movement to free the land and the peasant.
The common-class character of the Afro-American and the Celt was ex-
pounded by George Ruby, an educated black man and leader among Louisiana and Texas blacks. He found a basic cause common to the Kansas
exodus and the Irish migration to America, and to other peoples' migra-
tions to the New World, "the class oppression to which the Englishman,
Irishman, Frenchman, German were subjected, and the want of an independent home for themselves and their families." The most striking of
the cases, Ruby said, was that of the Irish laborers who were forced to
become "toilers by day upon the lands of others."[17]

Spokesmen of the Irish in America and Ireland made the same analysis.
The danger of widespread starvation in Ireland in 1879 and the crisis in
landlord-tenant relations stimulated the organization of the Irish National
Land League. Its principal objectives were neatly expressed in its slogans:
"Down with landlordism" and "The land for the people." Branches of
the Irish-American-organized Irish National Land and Industrial League
proliferated in the United States by the summer of 1880. Two years later,
the land struggle was introduced into the American industrial workers'
movements. A newly organized Central Labor Union in New York in
1882 adopted a stirring statement of Dr. Thomas Nulty, the bishop of
Meath: The land of every nation belongs to the people of that country.
The real owner was the Creator, who made a gift of the land to the people. They must share their common inheritance. Among the banners on
the platform at a mass labor demonstration in New York on July 5, 1882,
was one stating "The No Rent Battle of Ireland Is the Workingmen's Battle the World Over." Land monopoly in America and in Ireland lay at
the root of the troubles. George Ruby voiced the same sentiments in
1880 when he declared Afro-American laborers could not obtain homes
because planters were generally disposed to hold lands in large tracts.
"They would rather have the whole country lie waste than see it in the
hands of the colored people." For their part, Anglo-Irish landlords refused to relinquish their grip on Irish soil, and Irish peasants were reduced

to an abject tenantry.[18] Neither the Afro-American farmer and rural laborer nor the Irish peasant succeeded in loosening the landlord's hold on the land.

Migration to American and English cities transformed Irish peasants into industrial wage earners and deepened their yearning for their own lands. Migration to Kansas relieved a small number of Afro-Americans of their depressed conditions. The bulk of the laboring blacks and whites remaining as tenants and sharecroppers on the Southern plantations and farms was visible proof that the progressive reconstruction of Southern society had passed them by. The Kansas exodus was the last organized act of black reconstruction. It was too late and too feeble to alter the power relationships developing in the South. But it remains a symbol of Afro-American lower-class communalism.[19]

A Spirit of Combination   9

It is a weariness to labor for the same masters and be ruled by them.—Heraclitus.

There must have been moments when I felt the sorrows of a motherless child, but what I most remember from my youngest days was an abiding sense of comfort and security. I got plenty of mothering, not only from Pop and my brothers and sister when they were home, but from the whole of our close-knit community. Across the street and down each block were all my aunts and uncles and cousins—including some who were not actual relatives at all. . . .

Hard-working people, and poor, most of them, in worldly goods—but how rich in compassion! How filled with the goodness of humanity and the spiritual steel forged by centuries of oppression.—Paul Robeson, *Here I Stand* (1958).

Sometime between 1910 and 1920 black landownership reached a peak of about 15 million acres. Almost 220,000 nonwhite farm owners were noted in the census of 1910. Obviously, some freedmen and their descendants had managed to acquire homesteads or small pieces of residential property. By 1972 the estimated total of black landownership had sunk to 5 million acres. Nonwhite farm owners as a percentage of all farm owners in the United States reached its high point of 7.1 percent in 1910 and declined steadily after that. It was down to 5.8 percent in 1969.[1]

The longing for land was not lost after Reconstruction. Nor did the striving for it cease. Freed people were forced to contend with the frustrating crop lien system, depressed wages and debt peonage, sharecropping on onerous terms, and a political dictatorship. Against such an array of power and coercion the freedman would appear to have been totally stripped of his protection and power. Most were the victims of postemancipation capitalistic agriculture, which was itself in the grip of Northern

financial powers. Some escaped its excesses by both their organization
and their effort to construct a community. Some managed through their
family efforts to acquire land and realize their aspirations. As yet, we do
not know much about the process or the extent of individual purchase
or inheritance. However, a pattern of farm ownership may be derived
from the 1910 census. It showed that among all nonwhite farm operators
(owners, renters, and combinations of the two) in the Southern states,
owners were in the majority in Maryland (61.9 percent), Virginia (66.9
percent), Kentucky (50.5 percent), and Oklahoma (53.9 percent). Black
owners came close to a majority in Florida, with 49.5 percent. In the
Deep South states and through the cotton belt, much of which during
the generation from 1880 to 1910 was undergoing intensive industriali-
zation and urbanization, black farm owners constituted small percentages:
15.1 and 15.4 respectively in Mississippi and Alabama; 19.5 in Louisiana
and 23 in Arkansas. The lowest proportion was reached in Georgia, with
12.7 percent.[2]

That state had collected the most reliable data over the final twenty-
five years of the nineteenth century. Ironically, this was because it was
the only one in which tax collectors separated taxpayers according to
color. This record supplied Du Bois with the raw material for his investigation of black landholders. He demonstrated that about 8,450 Georgia
blacks owned 338,769 acres by 1874. Twenty-five years later such ownership had risen to 1,075,073 acres. A high point had been reached in 1898
when 1,097,087 acres were recorded. More than a million acres had been
owned since 1892, and the figures fluctuated closely around the peak for
eight years. The relative stability lasted through the decade. It would be
fair to assume that it continued for the succeeding decade. Thus, in 1910,
probably a million acres were owned by 12.7 percent of the farm operator.
It was a small part of the land, and a disproportionately small part of the
black population was represented in that figure. The fact remained that
between emancipation and 1874, Georgia freedmen had acquired at least
338,769 acres.[3]

A sampling of estimates for black landownership in other states reveals
similarly small proportions. By 1880, South Carolina freed people owned
about 100,000 acres, and Virginians 80,000 to 100,000 acres. Ten thousand of the South Carolina acreage was owned by freedmen on four of
the Sea Islands: Edisto, Wadmalaw, John, and James. The people on them
had been among the most militant and persistent in resisting eviction in

the 1860s, and their communities appear to have been among the most durable. Small numbers managed to purchase land and homes in other parts of the state. Nordhoff in 1875 found about 2,000 freedmen in Arkansas who owned a farm or a house or a town lot. A bare hint at North Carolina black ownership comes from a witness in the exodus investigation. He asserted that blacks in Halifax County owned 16,000 acres and those in Edgecombe County 6,000 acres. Wharton found 10,000 owner-occupants among Mississippi blacks. Fifteen hundred held equity in their places at that time. Among the available statistics on black landownership none is more devastatingly representative than Wharton's for Mississippi: Not one in a hundred blacks in seventeen counties owned the land on which he worked; in twelve counties less than one in twenty and in others less than one in fifty owned the land. There, as in most of the other southern states, wage labor and a lopsided system of farm tenantry triumphed over freed blacks and increasing numbers of whites.[4]

Small farmers who were blocked from obtaining land of their own became sharecroppers. By 1880, the nine large Southern cotton states— Alabama, Arkansas, Georgia, Louisiana, Mississippi, North Carolina, South Carolina, Tennessee, and Texas—contained 1,110,294 farms. Sharecroppers operated 301,738 of them with family labor. In the case of black farmers the family replaced the slave gang that was the mark of prewar plantation production methods. Ironically, freedmen had attempted through sharecropping to free themselves from gang labor and from the direct subjugation by masters, overseers, and drivers. Instead, they were thrust into a new morass of debt, subordination, and poverty and were denied the least semblance of equality.[5]

The freedmen's choice of sharing the crop in 1863 and later appeared at first to be satisfactory to them. Army commanders on the Virginia peninsula early in the war put their contrabands to work in and around the camps, paid wages, and furnished subsistence rations. Freedmen earning their own livelihoods were soon removed from the ration rolls, for they provided their own food. Some officers responsible for contraband affairs employed former slaves in cultivating crops on nearby abandoned plantations on a share basis. In Virginia, this arrangement seemed to be making freedmen partners with the government. Similarly, in the lower Mississippi Valley, freedmen who shared crops with Northern farmers and capitalists on abandoned plantations appeared to be quite successful and provided an example for free enterprise ideologists to tout the system. Partly on this basis, some of the best and most dedicated of the officers and chaplains in charge of black or contraband affairs had urged that the government distribute abandoned and confiscated lands to the freed people. But even men such as Conway, Saxton, Eaton, and others yielded to the pressures of the "New Order." This was best represented by the Pittsburgh capitalist and Republican Congressman William "Pig Iron" Kelley, who denounced land confiscation, and by William Trescot, spokesman for defeated wealthy South Carolina planters, who succeeded in winning their pardons and the restoration of their lands. Their victory over the freed people in the summer and fall of 1865 was evident in the contract system that foreclosed the opportunity for landownership. Freedmen's Bureau officers and agents, taking a lead from General Howard, urged this as the best course for freedmen to take. In working for wages, they were told, they would be demonstrating their self-reliance. In contracting the labor of their families and others in their kin groups, for a share of the crops, the freedmen were told, they would be gaining a measure of economic independence.

The bitter fruit of these urgings was widespread planter violation of contracts, nonpayment of wages, swindling of sharecroppers, and eviction of their families. Aged and infirm freed people were especially the victims of such mistreatment, and freedmen reacted against the contract system on that ground. Moreover, freedmen protested that they were denied the full prerogatives of partners. They claimed that they were used as laborers but were not permitted to make management decisions with respect to the cultivation, harvesting, processing, packing, and marketing of their cotton and corn crops. Finally, planters continued to use physical violence against the freed people. For example, a group of able-bodied Greensboro, Georgia, laborers discovered in March 1866 that slavery had not been abolished. They had been thrown into jail for refusing wages of $7 and $8 per month. But "their master," according to local black leader Abram Colby, had them released and "dragged them back to their plantation with as much power and assurance as could have been exhibited three or five years ago."[6]

The freedmen's first response in 1865 and 1866 was to refuse to contract. But this position was overcome by a combination of trust in the Freedmen's Bureau's friendly persuasiveness, the coercive actions of many of its agents, and the real threat of starvation, since rations were withheld and the promise of land was broken. Forced to make contracts, freedmen then attempted to get the best possible conditions. For some, wage labor appeared to give them independence. For others, sharecropping or renting land and working it for themselves appeared the next best alternative to ownership. Some continued to resist contracting for as long as they could hold out.

These strategies were used in making contracts for 1868 in Mississippi. After the disastrous 1867 cotton crop, planters and laborers were placed in difficult positions. Sharecroppers suffered as did planters from the effects of the poor crop. But wage workers avoided the pitfall of debt into which croppers sank. Their contract choice was wages. This experience was recorded in the Natchez Freedmen's Bureau headquarters. Other contracts provided a lease of land for a share of crops, with some freedmen agreeing to provide their own food. William McFeely's study of Mississippi Bureau records indicated that freedmen preferred sharecropping because it gave them a chance to manage their own production, and a condition of contract was their own provision of food and maintenance of their aged folk and children. That labor was hired in family units is revealed in the voluminous Bureau contract files for 1865 and 1866. Frequently, the first "X" or signature on the agreement was the headman's. Similar names indicate family members in contracts and in complaints written up by Bureau agents. For example, South Georgia mainland laborers who were sent away without pay in August 1865 and who sought refuge on St. Simon Island appear to have been groups of families: 7 Palmers, 2 Wades, 9 Grants, and 6 Staffords. A contract on a large South Carolina plantation in 1865 covered 35 families embracing 121 persons, 32 of those families headed by husband and wife. Most agreed to share crops with the landowner.[7]

A variety of labor contracts and tenure agreements was revealed by the 1880 census figures for nine cotton states. Wage agreements stipulated monthly pay from $5 to $10 in Georgia to $8 to $15 in Texas and Arkansas. At least one planter rented, contracted for wages, for shares, and for swapping work. For example, a Yallabousha County, Mississippi, contract in 1868 contained monthly and annual wage stipulations as well as crop-sharing provisions.[8]

Mississippi Bureau agents reporting the progress of contracts in January 1868 confirmed this varied pattern. In the Philadelphia subdistrict a majority of the contracts were for shares of crops or for the rental of lands to farmers working for themselves. "Quite a number of the freedmen,"

the Bureau agent wrote, "have rented land with the intention of making
a crop without the assistance of white citizens." Very few contracts for
wages were made in this vicinity. Most of the contracts at Grenada and
Greenville were for wages. At DeKalb the contracts varied. At Corinth
freedmen contracted for a stipulated portion of the crops. In the Columbus subdistrict, freed people complaining about the nonpayment of wages
left to seek work elsewhere.[9]

The Grenada Bureau office also reported freedmen refusing to work,
in this case because planters would take families only for their board and
clothing. Many freedmen refused such contracts and said they would prefer charity. But many moved to the cities seeking work. Planters who thus
refused to provide for or who excluded families forced a few hapless women to regard their children as encumbrances. One atypical case of infanti-
cide was attributed to a woman's belief that she could get higher wages
if not burdened by children. But most Mississippi freedmen accepted sharecropping and/or wages because they hoped to make the best of a bad situation.[10]

Large numbers of them refused to give up hope of purchasing their own
lands or of receiving a government grant. At Natchez, veterans depended
"upon the daily expectation of receiving their bounty money." The Yazoo
City agent reported "a large class lying idle, not induced to go to work."
They were still under the impression that the government would help them
At Port Gibson most contracts were for stated wages but "a class of freedpeople" refused to contract on any terms. They said they were waiting
for the new law that would give them lands, mules, and provisions. The
Bureau agent knew of no such law. By 1880 many of these Mississippi
laborers and farmers were among the sharecroppers who made up half
of all Southern black farmers.[11]

The revived postwar plantation system supplanted small owners with
sharecroppers and renters. Georgia farm tenure patterns make this clear.
In 1880, owners operated 55 percent of the farms but dropped to 46 percent in 1890, although the absolute number of owners increased from
76,451 to 79,477. Cash renters jumped from 13 percent in 1880 to 17
percent a decade later. Farms worked on shares increased from 31 percent in 1880 to 36 percent in 1890. Numbers of renters and croppers had
grown rapidly in ten years, from 62,000 to 91,000. Du Bois's study of
black landholders in Georgia in 56 counties in 1899 revealed 8,450 owners
of farms assessed at $1,795,416. According to the 1890 census, there

was a total of 171,000 farms assessed at $189,249,198. Black ownership
in monetary terms was a tiny affair, a mere nine-tenths of 1 percent of
the state's total farmland values.[12]

The disproportionately small black land tenure in the South is further
illustrated in two recent quantitative studies of 1880 census materials.
One is by Herbert G. Gutman, who chose to examine land tenure in two
localities: St. Helena Island, South Carolina, and rural Adams County,
Mississippi. Of the 1,425 black adult males in St. Helena Island and township, landowners comprised 49 percent. Fifteen percent were cash tenants,
and 31 percent were farm laborers. The remaining 5 percent were in other
occupations, most of them artisans. The size of units owned by 702 farmers suggests that they might have succeeded in holding on to grants
made by General Sherman's Special Field Order No. 15. Thirty-two percent owned fewer than ten acres; 47 percent owned ten to fourteen acres;
9 percent owned fifteen to nineteen acres; and 12 percent owned twenty
and more acres. However, rural Adams County, Mississippi, freedmen had
failed to achieve such tenures. Among them sharecroppers and farm laborers predominated. Of 2,976 adult males listed in the manuscript census,
only 6 percent were landowners and some of these were whites. Sharecroppers, the largest group, comprised 40 percent. Sixteen percent of the men
were farm laborers and 22 percent were classed as "other laborers." Only
1 percent were artisans, and another 1 percent were "other."[13]

A more comprehensive sampling of the 1880 census by Richard Sutch
and Roger Ransom involved 4,695 farms throughout the South. These
investigators found that half the black farmers rented for a share of the
crop. Black farmers, whether owners or renters and sharecroppers, had
to support themselves on smaller farms per family member than did white
families. Blacks owned 7.3 percent of all farms, a proportion almost identical to the national distribution of land ownership thirty years later.
Concordia Parish, Louisiana, makes this pattern of tenure dramatic. One
of the most important cotton regions, and with a black majority population, the parish listed 200 farming units in 1860 and 1,499 in 1880. Tenants operated 1,382 of them. In 1860 25 units with more than 1,000 improved acres being cultivated as a unit grew to 43 in 1880. The total of
land in tenantry and of land owned in units of more than 100 improved
acres discloses a concentration of ownership unchanged from 1860.[14]
Moreover, the rigid terms by which owners controlled farmlands in the
South appear to have been unbroken since the Reconstruction period.

When considered against the background of freedmen's aspirations and plans in the 1860s, the losses to the Afro-American community were great.

The losses were dramatic in the light of Thaddeus Stevens's estimates of land available for redistribution in 1865. The 1872 land proposals by the Negro National Labor Union (NLU) further emphasize the loss. Protesting the low wages paid to laborers by politically powerful planters, the NLU sought redress by protection of the freedman's political equality and by distribution of 46 million acres of public lands in the South. One-fourth of the able-bodied black males of the South would thus have a chance to homestead in five southern states. Two hundred thousand men taking 40 acres each under this proposal would have occupied only 8 million acres. In addition, if a federal land commission, probably modeled on the South Carolina commission, were to purchase lands in the remaining Southern states at a cost of $2 million, additional thousands of 40-acre tracts could be taken up by freedmen. The NLU finally recommended that lapsed grants of public lands held by railroad companies should revert to the United States and be immediately made available to settlers under the 1862 Homestead Act.[15] Congress may have heard this petition from the Afro-American community leadership. Obviously, by its inaction it displayed no inclination to listen.

In Kansas, freedmen found some relief from their situation, as we have seen. But this too was for a small number among the millions requiring a beneficial change. Even for Kansas black people the exodus proved inadequate. By the spring of 1882, they renewed the call for a portion of the Oklahoma Territory. A convention of black men met in Parsons on April 27 and 28. Delegates assembled from many points in southern Kansas and petitioned Congress for every third section of land in the neighboring territory to be set aside for Southern black emigrants. As usual, the memorial to Congress that spelled out the plan was referred to the committee on public lands, and it died there.[16]

Variants of the same basic proposal with its nationalist overtones were heard in the Afro-American community through the end of the century. The all-black-state concept was advanced by Edward McCabe (the black auditor of the state of Kansas). In practice it resulted in the establishment of about twenty-five all-black self-governed towns in Oklahoma, some existing down to the 1960s. One of the earliest was Boley, in Okfuskee County. After the Oklahoma Territory was opened for settlement, the

Fort Smith and Western Railroad began to build its way from the Oklahoma and Arkansas border to the territorial capital at Guthrie. The railroad hired southern blacks who had emigrated with their families in search of new land. Some role in the establishment of the town was played by Thomas M. Haynes, a Texas black man who was made Boley town-site manager by the railroad. Most significantly the town appears to have been established as a settlement of railroad section hands.[17]

A similar working-class origin of all-black and probably freedmen communities or enclaves in larger communities appeared in Iowa coal-mining towns. Not far from Oskaloosa, the town of Muchachinock embraced 20,000 people, of whom 1,500 were blacks mostly from Virginia. By 1884 the latter had established a community containing a mutual-benefit association, two frame schoolhouses for 200 children, a brass band, and Methodist and Baptist churches. They maintained an Odd Fellows Hall, and there was a considerable number of Masons. Small eating saloons and a dry-goods store were owned and patronized in the community. Black men operated boarding houses, presumably for the miners. Above all, the community boasted that none of its members was buried by the county. The mutual benefit association took care of that problem. And it was the recipient of funds from fines imposed on offenders of the community's regulations. It was a self-governed entity, with no justice of the peace, constable, or police force. A committee elected by mutual agreement tried all offenses.[18] Black coal miners in settlements around Mystic also appear to have woven a fabric of community self-determination in the newly created United Mine Workers (UMW) union of the 1890s. Here the focus was not necessarily on obtaining land but on strengthening working-class effectiveness and the community of coal miners. One of the miners, O. H. Underwood, praised the UMW for doing more than the Fourteenth Amendment to wipe out the word "white" and discrimination from the Constitution. He also informed us of numbers of black men who held responsible positions in the mine union locals as presidents, vice presidents, and secretaries.[19] Too little is known at this writing of the fabric of community life, and of the black working class, but in this instance we catch glimpses. They deserve a major study.

Further encouragement and establishment of black communities came from Booker T. Washington's Tuskegee Conference self-help programs. Notwithstanding his reputation as an accommodationist to white rule, Washington's philosophy stimulated a number of self-created black agrarian

communities. Weak and disarming as Washington's surrender to the giants
of industrial capitalism proved to be in the realm of the New South, he
offered a path toward that upright and Puritanical agrarian community
that he admired in the white world. Oakland, Texas, blacks created such
a village community. Seeking relief from the crushing crop mortgage system that pressed them into endless debt, they rallied in 1889 to agree on
cooperative buying and selling of supplies and crops. In addition, they
organized a mutual-aid society to support the sick and offer a death benefit to families. The title of "Improvement Society" covered its communal
concerns and self-help activity. Thirty-two heads of Oakland families, of
whom thirty were property owners, with 1,225 acres among them, formed
the first branch. Two years later a second one was established by another
thirty heads of families, with eleven property owners among them holding
490 acres. By 1900, R. L. Smith, a black representative in the Texas state
legislature, had led the movement to embrace 86 branches with 2,340
members. They had purchased by that time 46,000 acres, with a 30 percent indebtedness. Smith claimed the most salutary effects upon the communities: crime eliminated, a death rate averaging only 2 per 1,000 population, an all-embracing membership of persons sixteen to eighty years
of age. This suggests that many in this cooperative community endeavor
were former slaves. Further benefits accruing to the movement were in
Smith's words: "self-reliant manhood and womanhood free from the
bondage of debt," a "spirit of combination." Finally, the enduring gains
were the fulfillments of the freedmen's dreams: ". . . the roving tenant
changed into a fixed freeholder," and "the family relation idealized and
made the unit of civilization."[20] It remains a tempting question whether
this movement complemented or contradicted contemporary black agrarian
protest movements.

The Texas "success story" was not shared by the overwhelming mass
of black freedmen and their children. "The shadow of the plantation"
hung heavily over most of them, for they did not obtain ownership of the
land they worked. Dougherty County, Georgia, in the 1890s was a micro-
cosm of the post-Reconstruction world. Du Bois wrote about that community in his *Souls of Black Folk*. Coming within a few years of Smith's
account of the Texas village movements, Du Bois's description stands in
stark contrast. It is a story of depression and impoverishment and denied
opportunity. At the end of 1898, when low prices for cotton prevailed,
175 out of 300 tenant families owed $14,000; 50 could show nothing

for their labors; 75 cleared a total of $1,600. Instead of becoming "fixed freeholders," they had been forced into peonage. They became a black variant of the world's "ground down peasantries," and symbolized the defeat in the struggle for land.[21]

The rapid process of peonization is graphically conveyed in two views of postbellum labor relations. *DeBow's Review,* the Southern planters' journal, carried an article in 1866 that called upon the Louisiana state government to compel blacks to work in "coarse, manual labor" and to punish them "for dereliction of duty or non-fulfillment of contract." This was at a time when freedmen were still seeking and hoping for lands of their own. Thirteen years later an emigrant black laborer stopping over in St. Louis en route to Kansas told an interviewer why he and others like him fled. He observed that during slavery masters cared for slaves because they were property. In 1879, the emigrant stated, no one cared for them and "massa and his friends wants we uns to be slaves of 'ciety."[22]

Not all was lost when the land was lost, however. The history of Afro-Americans is one of continuous subjugation, and the loss of land only underscores the iniquities. But that history is at the same time a record of a community making and remaking itself in order to confront, first, the world that the slaveholders dominated and, second, the one fabricated by railroad, mine, cotton plantation, and banking corporations. During slavery, Afro-Americans suffered the division of the family and the sale of its members, the blows of disciplinary fists and whips, deprivation and insecurity in a system proclaimed by its apologists to be the apogee of paternalistic providence and security. On the other hand many slaves did subsist on a modicum of planter social welfare practices. The slaves created their own mechanism for survival through 200 years of that system: their families, their pride in skills and labor, a music and literature of the spoken word, a durable and distinctive adaptation of the dominant religion, their struggles to be free, and a fundamental conception of right. Without space of their own, without full free status, slaves created a community not so much of place but of feeling, thought, and action.

Their habits of mutuality persisted and proved influential in creating the freedmen's community. When the slave was transformed legally into a freedman, he was thrust at the same time into the marketplace as an economic thing. But he resisted that transformation into a commodity. The planters' and industrialists' values clashed with the freedmen's sense

of right and community. The power of the two propertied classes obstruc-
ted the emergence of a freeholder class. The freedman was made unequal
in the contest with railroad and iron manufacturing tycoons and planters.
Shortly after passage of the Fourteenth Amendment, declaring freed people equal citizens, it was rapidly undermined by corrosive court decisions
fashioned with sophistries necessary to disarm the freed people. Nonethe-
less, and because of those juridical attacks, freedmen recognized their
situation and strove to improve it against severe odds.

Agricultural wage workers no less than industrial wage workers fashioned instruments to improve their condition. They organized cooperatives,
communities, political parties, and farmers' alliances. They "huddled"
in their churches and benevolent and fraternal societies. The independence
and enlargement of the Afro-American church deservedly enjoy reputations as "enduring accomplishments" of the Reconstruction period.[23]
Yet the black church and religious leader did not stand apart from or
alone in the community's struggle for survival and improvement. At least
as powerful was the freedmen's struggle to find the lost members of families and to settle them on land and in communities of their own.

One aged black woman remembered much in the 1930s—the slave days
and the free, the hard work to earn enough for the farm acquired at $10
per acre, the happy times when her husband played the fiddle up and
down the countryside at dances, his establishment of the first black church
in their Texas community, her own "cooking, washing and ironing," and
the rearing of her ten children, her husband's election to the state legislature, and his hauling lumber from Waco to build their home. They were
models of classical frontier settlers, individuals who appear to have arrived
at "fixed freeholder" status, the American dream fulfilled. But Mariah
Robinson left us with yet another sign of her community's active effort
to define itself and its future. She told an interviewer, "Us held by the
committee call 'Free Committee Men.' "[24] Could she have meant Henry
Adams's committee of 500? And were she and her husband among those
98,000 who signed up for a territory in the West? Or did she refer to the
Colored Farmers Alliance, with more than a million members in 1891?
Or to some other unknown group imbedded in the fabric of the freedmen's self-created community? Whatever the answer may be, it is clear
that Mariah Robinson, crossing from slavery to freedom and into the historical record during a profound American crisis, reaffirmed the role of
the freed people in thousands of local and temporary situations. Taken
together, they comprised a significant movement with enduring effects.

The freed people had attempted to change the South by their acqui-
sitions of land, individually and through their "village movements." The
Afro-Americans had taken the initiative in demanding and winning emancipation, citizenship, voting rights, schools, and a bit of land. Limited as
each of them proved to be, their attainment demonstrated the Afro-American's active role in making his community and in making America. The
Afro-American destroyed the myth of his inferiority and incapacity, of
his domination by the masters to the point of infantilization. Briefly he
was a political force through the collaboration of middle-class blacks
and freed field laborers. The alliance with abolitionists, Radical Republicans, some sympathetic Freedmen's Bureau agents and Southern planters, and some Southern white artisans and farmers also contributed to
the making of the freedmen's community. But the freed people, like their
Radical Republican allies, were abandoned and isolated by conservatives
who had a greater stake in a prospering national industrial capitalism
than in an agrarian economic and political democracy. As a result, the
mass of Southern whites and blacks paid a heavy price in poverty and
exploitation. The cynical manipulation of the race question by ruling
political and economic interests denied the mass effective roles in Southern society. In this connection, Genovese's use of the concept of hegemony is probably more appropriate in explaining white internalization
of ruling class ideology —racism and paternalism—than it was in explaining
the slave's surrender to paternalism. While paternalism suffered rejection by
the slaves, antebellum nonslaveholding whites, and postwar Populists,
racism proved almost invincible for more than a century and corrosive
of attempts at democratic alliance. Nevertheless Reconstruction era Afro-
Americans advanced their own community by participating in such an
alliance, and by acting in their own behalf, they impelled their allies to
adopt radical democratic principles and measures. The Afro-Americans
marshaled their meager means to attempt the creation of a more felici-
tous world for themselves. Thus, they kept the democratic faith and put
America in their debt.

Notes

INTRODUCTION

1. Stanley M. Elkins, *Slavery: A Problem in American Institutional and Intellectual Life* (Chicago: The University of Chicago Press, 1959); Robert W. Fogel and Stanley M. Engerman, *Time on the Cross: The Economics of American Negro Slavery* (Boston: Little, Brown, 1974); Eugene D. Genovese, *Roll, Jordan, Roll: The World the Slaves Made* (New York: Pantheon, 1974).

2. Louis S. Gerteis, *From Contraband to Freedman, Federal Policy Toward Southern Blacks, 1861-1865* (Westport, Conn.: Greenwood Press, 1973).

3. Ira Berlin, *Slaves Without Masters: The Free Negro in the Antebellum South* (New York: Pantheon, 1974).

4. Herbert G. Gutman, "The World Two Cliometricians Made: A Review Essay of $F + E = T/C$," *Journal of Negro History* (January 1975); Paul David and Peter Temin, "Slavery: The Progressive Institution," *Journal of Economic History,* (September 1974); Richard Sutch, "The Treatment Received by American Slaves: A Critical Review of the Evidence Presented in *Time on the Cross,*" *Explorations in Economic History* 12, no. 4 (October 1975); Oscar Handlin, "The Capacity of Quantitative History," *Perspectives in American History,* 9 (1975).

5. Genovese, *Roll, Jordan, Roll,* p. 273.

6. Thornton Testimony, *Report* of the Joint Committee on Reconstruction, 39th Cong., 1st sess. vol. II, pt. 1: 52-53.

7. Raymond Williams, "Base and Superstructure in Marxist Cultural Theory," *New Left Review,* 82 (December 1973), pp. 8-10; James D. Anderson, "Aunt Jemima in Dialectics: Genovese on Slave Culture" (Review Essay), *Journal of Negro History,* 61 (January 1976), 107-111.

8. Ralph Ellison, *Shadow and Act* (New York: Signet, 1966). Although discussing music when he wrote, "Technique was then, as today, the key to creative freedom . . ." the statement may be applied to social process in general (pp. 247-248).

9. Sidney W. Mintz, *Caribbean Transformations* (Chicago: Aldine, 1974).

10. A. Irving Hallowell, *Culture & Experience* (New York: Schocken, 1967; originally Philadelphia, University of Pennsylvania Press, 1955), p. 75.

11. John S. Mbiti, *African Religion and Philosophy* (New York: Anchor, 1970), p. 279.

12. Willie Lee Rose, *Rehearsal for Reconstruction: The Port Royal Experiment* (New York: Vintage, 1967), p. 367.

13. Anthony F. C. Wallace, "Revitalization Movements," *American Anthropologist,* 58 (April 1956), p. 265.

14. Leonard B. Glick, commentary on an essay by Weston La Barre ("Materials for a History of Crisis Cults: A Bibliographic Essay"), *Current Anthropology,* 12 (February 1971), p. 29.

CHAPTER 1

1. *The War of The Rebellion: A Compilation of the Official Records of the Union and Confederate Armies.* (Washington, D.C.: U.S. Government Printing Office, 1880-1901), Series 2, Vol. I, pp. 649-652, 750-812. Hereafter cited as *O.R.*

2. Edward Magdol, "Martin R. Delany Counsels Freedmen, July 23, 1865," *The Journal of Negro History,* 61 (October 1971), 306.

3. George P. Rawick, *From Sundown to Sunup: The Making of the Black Community* (Westport, Conn.: Greenwood Publishing Co., 1972).

4. John W. Blassingame, *The Slave Community: Plantation Life in the Antebellum South* (New York: Oxford University Press, 1972).

5. Eric R. Wolf, *Peasants* (Englewood Cliffs, N.J.: Prentice-Hall, 1966) p. 92; Manuel Gottlieb, "The Land Question in Georgia During Reconstruction," *Science and Society,* 3 (Summer 1939), 356-357.

6. Melville J. Herskovits, *The Myth of the Negro Past* (Boston: Beacon Press, 1958; originally New York, Harper & Brothers, 1941), pp. 62-63, 182 ff.; Melville J. Herskovits and Mitchell Harwitz, eds., *Economic Transition in Africa* (Chicago: Northwestern University Press, 1964), especially Daniel Diebuyck, "Land Holding and Social Organization," p. 104, and E. P. Skinner, "West African Economic Systems," pp. 80-81; Basil Davidson, *The African Genius* (Boston: Little, Brown and Company, 1969), p. 81.

7. Philip Curtin, *The Atlantic Slave Trade: A Census* (Madison: University of Wisconsin Press, 1969).

8. Peter H. Wood, *Black Majority: Negroes in Colonial South Carolina, from 1670 Through the Stono Rebellion* (New York: Alfred A. Knopf, 1974), pp. 35-62; Gerald W. Mullin, *Flight and Rebellion: Slave*

Resistance in Eighteenth-Century Virginia (New York: Oxford University Press, 1972); Ira Berlin, *Slaves Without Masters: The Free Negro in the Antebellum South* (New York: Pantheon Books, 1964), pp. 219-220; Herbert G. Gutman, "The World Two Cliometricians Made," *Journal of Negro History* (January 1975), pp. 121-127.

9. Harvey Wish, ed., *A Journey in the Back Country* (New York: Capricorn Books, 1959), p. 202 (originally published in New York in 1860).

10. Ibid., pp. 202-204.

11. Charles S. Sydnor, *Slavery in Mississippi* (New York: Appleton-Century, 1933), pp. 9-15; Ulrich B. Phillips, *American Negro Slavery* (Baton Rouge: Louisiana State University Press, 1966; originally published in New York, 1918), pp. 247-249; J. Carlyle Sitterson, *Sugar Country: The Cane Sugar Industry in the South, 1753-1950* (Lexington: University of Kentucky Press, 1953); Willie Lee Rose, *Rehearsal for Reconstruction* (New York: Bobbs-Merrill, 1964), pp. 81-82; Joel Williamson, *After Slavery: The Negro in South Carolina During Reconstruction, 1861-1877* (Chapel Hill: The University of North Carolina Press, 1965), p. 127.

12. *From Sundown to Sunup,* pp. 32, 38; Blassingame, *The Slave Community,* p. 66.

13. Berlin, *Slaves Without Masters,* pp. 11-12; Rawick, *From Sundown to Sunup,* pp. 35, 45-49.

14. E. Franklin Frazier, "The Negro Slave Family," *The Journal of Negro History,* 15 (1930) 198-259; cited in Rawick, *From Sundown to Sunup,* pp. 91-93.

15. Rawick, *From Sundown to Sunup,* pp. 80-89; Orville W. Taylor, *Negro Slavery in Arkansas* (Durham, N.C.: Duke University Press, 1958), chap. 11, "Jumping the Broomstick," pp. 189-202.

16. Herbert G. Gutman, *The Black Family in Slavery and Freedom, 1750-1925* (New York: Pantheon, 1976), p. 20; Gutman, "The World Two Cliometricians Made," pp. 180-181; *New York Independent,* March 16, 1865; for a sample of durable slave "cohabitations" in Robeson County, North Carolina, see also Edward Magdol, "Against the Gentry: An Inquiry into a Southern Lower-Class Community and Culture, 1865-1870," *Journal of Social History* 6 (Spring 1973), 265-266.

17. Blassingame, *The Slave Community,* pp. 92-93, 102; Rawick, *From Sundown to Sunup,* p. 93.

18. Allan Kulikoff, "Black Society and the Economics of Slavery," *Maryland Historical Magazine* 70 (Summer 1975), 203-210.

19. Frederick Douglass, *Life and Times of Frederick Douglass* (New York: Collier Books, 1962; reprinted from 1892 rev. ed.), p. 42.

20. Mullin, *Flight and Rebellion*. Fictive kinship appeared among European and Latin American peasant societies over five centuries. The godparenthood, or ritual coparenthood, is its specific mechanism. It frequently operates in a class grouping to create a "security network of ritual kinfolk." Clearly, this was an influential device in the making of peasant or folk communities, of which the slave community may be considered a type. See Sidney W. Mintz and Eric R. Wolf, "An Analysis of Ritual Co-Parenthood (Compadrazgo)," *Southwestern Journal of Anthropology* 6 (Winter 1950), 341-368.

21. James W. C. Pennington, *The Fugitive Blacksmith* (London, 1849), cited in E. Franklin Frazier, *The Negro Family in the United States* (Chicago, 1939), p. 31.

22. The discussion of slave songs and slave ideology depends upon LeRoy Moore, Jr., "The Spiritual: Soul of Black Religion," *American Quarterly*, 23 (December 1971), 670-676; Lawrence W. Levine, "Slave Songs and Slave Consciousness: An Exploration in Neglected Sources," in Tamara K. Hareven, ed., *Anonymous Americans: Explorations in Nineteenth-Century Social History* (Englewood Cliffs, N.J.: Prentice-Hall, 1971) pp. 99-130; Sterling Stuckey, "Through the Prism of Folklore: The Black Ethos in Slavery," *The Massachusetts Review* (Summer 1968), 417-437; Blassingame, *The Slave Community*, pp. 67-76.

23. J. L. Dillard, "On the Beginnings of Black English in the New World," *Orbis*, 21 (1972), 523-536; Eugene D. Genovese, *Roll, Jordan, Roll: The World the Slaves Made* (New York: Pantheon, 1974), p. 440.

24. William W. Freehling, *Prelude to Civil War: The Nullification Controversy in South Carolina, 1816-1836* (New York: Harper & Row, 1968, Torchbook ed.)

25. Richard Maxwell Brown, *The South Carolina Regulators* (Cambridge, Mass.: Harvard University Press, 1963); Richard Price, ed., *Maroon Societies: Rebel Slave Communities in the Americas* (New York: Anchor Press/Doubleday, 1973); Roger Bastide, *African Civilizations in the New World* (London: C. Hurst & Co., 1967); Wood, *Black Majority*, pp. 312-326.

26. Eric J. Hobsbawm, *Primitive Rebels, Studies in Archaic Forms of Social Movement in the 19th and 20th Centuries* (New York: W. W. Norton & Co., 1965).

27. Brown, *South Carolina Regulators;* Herbert Aptheker, *Negro Slave Revolts* (New York: International Publishers, 1963), pp. 280-281; Magdol, "Against the Gentry."

28. Kenneth W. Porter, "Negroes and the Seminole War, 1835-1842," *Journal of Southern History*, 30 (November 1964), 427-440.

29. Donnie B. Bellamy, "Free Blacks in Antebellum Missouri," *Missouri Historical Review,* 67 (January 1973), 198-227. Mullin, *Flight and Rebellion,* pp. 188 ff.; William G. Paul, "The Shadow of Equality: The Negro in Baltimore, 1864-1911," (unpublished Ph.D. dissertation, University of Wisconsin, 1972), pp. 21-22, 29-31; William Allen Letters, Columbia, S.C., July 6, 1865, and Allen diary, pp. 132-133.

30. Stanley Elkins, *Slavery: A Problem in American Institutional and Intellectual Life* (Chicago: University of Chicago Press, 1959); Sidney W. Mintz, *Caribbean Transformations* (Chicago: Aldine, 1974), p. 76.

31. Marc Bloch, *The Historian's Craft* (New York: Alfred A. Knopf, 1953).

CHAPTER 2

1. Bloch, *The Historian's Craft,* p. 89

2. Cornelius King, "Cooperation—Nothing New," *Opportunity: A Journal of Negro Life,* 18 (1940), 328

3. Miguel Gual Camarena, "Una Cofradia de Negros Libertos en el Siglo XV," *Estudios de edad media de la Corona de Aragon,* 5 (1952), 457-466. I am indebted to Gerald Kamber and Frank Longoria, formerly of the Foreign Languages Department at State University College at Postdam, N.Y., for a translation of this article. A. J. R. Russell-Wood, "Black and Mulatto Brotherhoods in Colonial Brazil: A Study in Collective Behavior," *The Hispanic American Historical Review,* 54 (November 1974), pp. 567-602.

4. Herskovits, *Myth of the Negro Past,* p. 161; Shirley Ardener, "The Comparative Study of Rotating Credit Associations," *Royal Anthropological Institute Journal,* 94, 1st Series (July 1964), pp. 201-209; William R. Bascom, "The Esusu: A Credit Institution of the Yoruba," *Royal Anthropological Institute Journal,* 82 (1952), 63-69.

5. W. E. B. Du Bois, *The Philadelphia Negro: A Social Study* (New York: Schocken Books, 1967; reprint of 1899 first ed.), pp. 18-22; *A Statistical Inquiry into the Condition of the People of Colour in Philadelphia* (Philadelphia: The Society of Friends, 1849), pp. 22-23, cited in Benjamin Quarles and Leslie H. Fishel, Jr., *The Negro American: A Documentary History* (Glenview, Ill.: Scott, Foresman, 1967), pp. 160-161; In New York City, black workers, both skilled and unskilled, established the New York African Society for Mutual Relief in 1808. By 1870 the society boasted $40,000 in real estate. See Herbert Aptheker, ed., *A Documentary History of the Negro People in the United States* (New York: Citadel Press, 1951), p. 623. Benjamin Quarles, *Black Abo-*

litionists (New York: Oxford University Press, 1969), pp. 101-102; Paul, "The Shadow of Equality," p. 134; Edgar G. Thomas, *The First African Baptist Church of North America* (Savannah, 1925). See Berlin, *Slaves Without Masters,* chap. 9, "The Free Negro Community," pp. 284-315, for a discussion of the free black communities in the antebellum South, where similar institutions of mutuality served mulattoes and blacks.

6. Howard Bell, "National Negro Conventions of the Middle 1840's: Moral Suasion vs. Political Action," *Journal of Negro History,* 42 (October 1957), 253-255.

7. William H. Pease and Jane Pease, *Black Utopia, Negro Communal Experiments in America* (Madison: State Historical Society of Wisconsin, 1963)

8. Aptheker, *Documentary History,* pp. 526-528.

9. Memoranda, May 1863 (Inspection of Fortress Monroe), American Freedmen's Inquiry Commission Papers, Houghton Library, Harvard University. Hereafter cited as the AFIC Papers.

10. Herbert Aptheker, "Organizational Activities of Southern Negroes, 1865," in *To Be Free, Studies in American Negro History* (New York: International Publishers, 1948), pp. 136-162

11. Wilmington *Herald,* September 8, 1865, cited in W. McKee Evans, *Ballots and Fence Rails: Reconstruction of the Lower Cape Fear* (Chapel Hill: University of North Carolina Press, 1967), p. 87.

12. Aptheker, "Organizational Activities," pp. 143-144.

13. Ibid., 154-155; *New York Times,* August 1, 1867; Hamilton James Eckenrode, *The Political History of Virginia During Reconstruction* (Baltimore: The Johns Hopkins Press, 1904), pp. 82; J. P. McConnell, *Negroes and Their Treatment in Virginia from 1865 to 1867* (Pulaski, Va., 1910), pp. 116-118. Alrutheus A. Taylor, *The Negro in the Reconstruction of Virginia* (Washington: The Association for the Study of Negro Life and History, 1926), p. 214.

14. Austin Marcus Drumm, "The Union League in the Carolinas," Ph.D. dissertation, University of North Carolina, 1955, pp. 128-132.

15. Peter Robert Kolchin, "First Freedom: The Responses of Alabama's Blacks to Emancipation and Reconstruction," Ph.D. dissertation, Johns Hopkins University, 1970, p. 80; Frances Butler Leigh, *Ten Years on a Georgia Plantation Since the War* (London, 1883), p. 11; Charles Stearns, *The Black Man of the South, and the Rebels* (New York: Negro Universities Press, 1969; reprint of original edition, New York: American News Company, 1872); p. 208; Albert T. Morgan, *Yazoo, or on the Picket Line of Freedom* (Washington: Published by the author,

1874), pp. 232-238; Clifton L. Ganus, "The Freedmen's Bureau in Mississippi," Ph.D. dissertation, Tulane University, 1953, p. 278.

16. *Annual Report of the Secretary of War for 1867,* 40th Cong., 3rd sess., I (Washington, D.C., U.S. Congress Serial No. 1367, 1868), p. 404; see also the discussion of local black leadership in Chapter 5.

17. *New York Times,* April 7, 1867; testimony of George Houston in *(Ku Klux Klan Conspiracy) Conditions of Affairs in the Late Insurrectionary States,* 42 Cong., 2nd sess., Senate Report No. 41 (Washington, D.C.: U.S. Government Printing Office, 1872), Alabama, p. 1003.

18 Ibid., Alabama, pp. 1086, 1790-1797, 1838-1839, Georgia, pp. 9, 739; Mississippi, p. 725. For similar Democratic pressures in Louisiana see William E. Highsmith, "Some Aspects of Reconstruction in the Heart of Louisiana," *Journal of Southern History* 13 (November 1947), 460-491.

19. Ganus, "Freedmen's Bureau in Mississippi," p. 208; Stearns, *Black Man of the South,* pp. 116, 170-171; *Antislavery Reporter,* 13 (April 1865), 78; J. Carlyle Sitterson, *Sugar Country: The Sugar Industry in the South, 1753-1950* (Lexington: University of Kentucky Press, 1953), p. 221; A Mississippian complained in 1871 that black laborers "worked when they pleased and let it alone when they pleased." *KKK Conspiracy,* Mississippi, p. 233.

20. *National Freedman,* 2 (March 1866), 92.

21. Henry Edwin Tremain, *Two Days of War: A Gettysburg Narrative and Other Excursions* (New York: Bonnell, Silver and Bowers, 1905), p. 272.

22. Nordhoff, *Freedmen of South Carolina,* pp. 12-13.

23. William F. Allen Diary, June 3, 1864, p. 205.

24. E. Merton Coulter, *The Civil War and Readjustment in Kentucky* (Chapel Hill: University of North Carolina Press, 1926), p. 346; James McKaye, *The Mastership and Its Fruits* (New York: 1864), pp. 16-17.

25. *Savannah Daily Republican,* September 5 and 6, 1865.

26. Gerteis, *From Contraband to Freedman,* pp. 89-90; 112-114; William F. Messner, "Black Violence and White Response: Louisiana 1862," *Journal of Southern History* 41 (February 1975), 19-38.

27. Kolchin, "First Freedom," pp. 285-286; freedmen strikes in Louisiana sugar fields are noted by Sitterson, *Sugar Country,* pp. 245-248; for strikes among Richmond and City Point, Virginia, stevedores and among tobacco warkers see A. A. Taylor, *The Negro in the Reconstruction of Virginia* (Washington, 1926), pp. 120 ff.; see also James S. Allen, *Reconstruction: The Battle for Democracy* (New York: Interna-

tional Publishers, 1937), pp. 166-167, and W. E. B. Du Bois, *Black Reconstruction in America* (New York, 1935).

28. Joel Williamson, *After Slavery: The Negro in South Carolina During Reconstruction, 1861-1877* (Chapel Hill: The University of North Carolina Press, 1965), p. 104.

29. Ibid., p. 102.

30. Kolchin, "First Freedom," p. 71.

31. Stopping in Port Royal, South Carolina, in November 1865 during his travels through the postwar South, John Richard Dennett reported to his readers in *The Nation* that freedmen working for wages planted one acre in cotton for their employers but insisted on two for themselves. One disgruntled employer complained that it was impossible to induce laborers to plant more cotton than would "supply them with spending money. Their living they expected to make off their own land." Dennett, *The South as It Is, 1865-1866* (New York: The Viking Press, 1965) p. 214.

32. U. S. Grant to President Andrew Johnson, December 18, 1865.

33. New York *Herald,* September 1, 1865.

34. *Statistics of the Operation of the Executive Board of the Friends Association of Philadelphia for the Relief of Colored Freedmen* (Philadelphia, 1864), pp. 21-22.

35. Reverend Joseph Warren, D.D., *Extracts from Reports of Superintendents of Freedmen* (Vicksburg, Miss.: Freedmen Press Print, 1864), p. 22.

36. Whitelaw Reid, *After the War: A Southern Tour, May 1, 1865 to May 1, 1866,* C. Vann Woodward, ed. (New York: Harper & Row, 1965), p. 115.

37. American Freedmen's Inquiry Commission Testimony (hereafter AFIC Testimony), December 1-14, 1863. War Department, Adjutant General's Office, Record Group 94, National Archives.

38. *Statistics of the . . . Friends Association of Philadelphia,* pp. 32-33; Freedmen were responsible for a change in shoe style in 1865 when they demanded something better than the mass-produced and drab brogans that their masters bought for them when they were slaves. They developed an aversion to what were called "russets." The Boston *Shoe and Leather Reporter* wrote that "Finer leather, better trimmings, and more expensive workmanship" were now in demand, and the Massachusetts factories found the trade lucrative (reported in *Savannah National Republican,* December 6, 1865).

39. Colonel J. M. Alexander to AFIC, September 1, 1863, AFIC Papers.

40. D. B. Nichols, Superintendent of Contrabands, South Potomac, Camp Springdale, Va., to AFIC, September 8, 1863, AFIC Papers.

41. *House Executive Documents,* No. 70, 39th Cong., 1st sess., p. 370.

42. Albion W. Tourgee, *The Invisible Empire* (New York: Fords, Howard, & Hulbert, 1880), p. 451.

43. *5th Annual Report,* New York Branch, Freedmen's Union Commission (New York, 1867), pp. 16-17.

44. McConnell, *Negroes and Their Treatment in Virginia,* p. 24.

45. New York *Herald,* July 16, 1865.

46. Ibid., August 11, 1865.

47. AFIC Testimony, 1863, RG 94, National Archives.

48. Reid, *After the War,* p. 564.

49. B. K. Lee, Jr., in AFIC Testimony; AFIC Papers, Col. J. M. Alexander to AFIC, September 1, 1863.

50. Admiral D. D. Porter, General Letters, Press Book, July 27, 1863, Record Group 45, National Archives.

51. Nordhoff, *Freedmen of South Carolina,* pp. 12, 20, 26.

52. AFIC Testimony.

53. *KKK Conspiracy,* Georgia, p. 817.

54. William A. Phillips, Talequa, Cherokee Nation, to Samuel G. Howe, Freedmen's Commission, October 10, 1863, AFIC Papers.

55. *The Examiner,* March 9, 1865 (at the Baptist Historical Society, Colgate-Rochester Divinity School, Rochester, New York)

56. John Eaton, *Report of the General Superintendent of Freedmen, Department of the Tennessee and State of Arkansas for 1864* (Memphis, 1865).

57. Ibid.

58. Magdol, "Against the Gentry," p. 266; Kolchin, "First Freedom," p. 106; Elaine C. Everly, "Marriage Registers of Freedmen," *Prologue* (Fall 1973), pp. 150-154.

59. Robert H. Abzug, "The Black Family During Reconstruction," p. 31, in Nathan I. Huggins, Martin Kilson, and Daniel M. Fox, eds., *Key Issues in the Afro-American Experience, vol. 2* (New York: Harcourt Brace Jovanovich, Inc., 1971).

60. Wilder, AFIC Testimony.

61. Kolchin, "First Freedom," p. 120.

62. Assistant Commissioner, Georgia, Letters Received, Bureau of Refugees, Freedmen and Abandoned Lands. Toney Golden, Gabriel Andrews, Tony Axon to Col. H. F. Sickles, November 28, 1865. Record Group 105, National Archives. Hereafter cited as BRFAL . . . , RG 105, N.A.

63. Crandall A. Shifflett, "The Household Composition of Rural Black Families: Louisa County, Virginia, 1880," *Journal of Interdisciplinary History,* 6 (Autumn 1975), 256-257.

64. Wade W. Nobles, "Africanity: Its Role in Black Families," *Black Scholar,* June 1974, p. 12; Allison Davis, B. B. Gardiner, and M. R. Gardiner, *Deep South* (Chicago: The University of Chicago Press, 1941); Charles S. Johnson, *Shadow of the Plantation* (Chicago: The University of Chicago Press, 1934); W. E. B. Du Bois, *The Negro* (New York: Henry Holt & Co., 1915; reprinted New York: Oxford University Press, 1970), p. 72.

65. Elizabeth Kilham, "Sketches in Color," *Putnam's Magazine,* new series, 13 (December 1869), 744-745; Abzug, "The Black Family During Reconstruction," p. 33; Elizabeth Hyde Botume, *First Days Among the Contrabands* (Boston, 1893), pp. 143 ff. Sandy Conor, a private in Co. C, 34th Regiment, U.S. Colored Troops, asked the chaplain to write a letter, from Jacksonville, Florida, to the Freedmen's Bureau in Savannah, inquiring if his wife was still alive, "and if so how is she faring." They had become separated after he went into the army. She had four children, he wrote, and she could be found trading near the dock in Savannah. H. H. Moore, Chaplain, to Freedmen's Bureau, Savannah, October 8, 1865. Savannah Letters Received, RG 105, N.A.

CHAPTER 3

1. *O.R.,* ser. 3, vol. III, pp. 73-74.
2. Nordhoff, *Freedmen of South Carolina,* p. 2.
3. Carney to Commission, September 9, 1863, AFIC Papers.
4. Lt. Col. G. W. Hoyt to Commission, September 15, 1863, ibid.
5. AFIC Testimony, December 14, 1863.
6. Eaton Report, 1863, AFIC Papers.
7. John Eaton, *Report of Superintendent of Freedmen, Department of Tennessee,* pp. 23-27.
8. Ibid, p. 50; W. F. Allen Diary, September-October 2, 1864; Reid, *After the War,* p. 286.
9. John A. Saxton to Professor F. J. Child, Deerfield, Mass., June 19, 1865, reprinted in *The Freedmen's Record,* August 1865, p. 127, courtesy of Herbert G. Gutman.
10. John Eaton, *Grant, Lincoln and the Freedmen* (New York: Longmans, Green, 1907), p. 166.
11. James Redpath, December 24, 1863, AFIC Testimony.
12. AFIC Testimony.

13. Ibid.

14. Testimony of Holcombe and Harree Stokes (white), December 26, 1865. "Reports of Racial Violence in the South . . . April 1865 to January 1866," Letters Received, Office of the Adjutant General, Main Series, 1861-1870, Record Group 94, N.A. (Microcopy 619, Roll 505); Thomas to Major General Carl Schurz, Vicksburg, Miss., September 28, 1865, *Senate Executive Documents*, No. 2, 39th Cong., 1st sess. (Washington, D.C.: U.S. Government Printing Office, 1866), p. 97.

15. Records of the Assistant Commissioner, BRFAL, Georgia, 1865-1867. Unbound Miscellaneous Papers, n.d., RG 105, N.A. (Microcopy 798, Roll 36); William F. Allen Diary, Savannah, July 1865.

16. Col. H. Scofield to S.G. Howe, Milliken's Bend, La., October 4, 1863, AFIC Papers; Hoyt to Commission, September 15, 1863 AFIC Papers; Captain R. J. Hinton, AFIC Testimony, New York, December 14, 1863.

17. Reuben Tomlinson, to J. M. McKim, St. Helena, S.C., April 10, 1864, *Philadelphia Press*, April 24, 1864, reprinted in *Second Annual Report*, New England Freedmen's Aid Society, pp. 66-67

18. A. Pettijohn, M.D., U.S.A., to Reverend Mr. Hawkins, Alexandria, Va., August 16, 1864, in *Freedmen's Advocate*, September 1864. For a modern scholar's sensitivity to the freedmen's self-confidence and capability, see Edwin D. Hoffman, "From Slavery to Self-Reliance," *Journal of Negro History*, 41 (January 1956), 8-42.

19. Worthington C. Ford, ed., *A Cycle of Adams Letters*, 2 vols, (Boston: Houghton, Mifflin, 1920), II, pp. 212-219; Thomas Wentworth Higginson, *Army Life in a Black Regiment* (Boston, 1870; reprinted in Collier Classics paperback edition, 1962).

20. *New York Commercial Advertiser*, n.d., in *American Missionary* 9 (November 1865), 258.

21. New Orleans *Tribune*, January 20, 1865.

22. W. E. B. Du Bois, *The Negro Church* (Atlanta: Atlanta University Press, Atlanta Study No. 8, 1903), p. 57; Inabel Burns Lindsay, "The participation of Negroes in the Establishment of Welfare Services, 1865-1900," (doctoral thesis in social work, University of Pittsburgh, 1952), p. 56.

23. Francis Butler Simkins and Robert Hilliard Woody, *South Carolina During Reconstruction* (Chapel Hill: The University of North Carolina Press, 1932), p. 395.

24. George Alfred Townsend, *The Swamp Outlaws: Or the North Carolina Bandits, Being a Complete History of the Modern Rob Roys and Robin Hoods* (New York, 1872), p. 33.

25. Aptheker, "Organizational Activities of Southern Negroes"

26. See Chapter 5.

27. Ibid.

28. Virginia Writers' Project, *The Negro in Virginia* (New York: Hastings House, 1940), pp. 248-249.

29. John L. Bell, Jr., "Baptists and the Negro in North Carolina During Reconstruction," *North Carolina Historical Review,* 42 (May 1965), pp. 391, 400.

30. Du Bois, *The Negro Church,* p. 40.

31. Roberta Sue Alexander, "North Carolina Churches Face Emancipation and the Freedmen: An Analysis of the Role of Religion During Presidential Reconstruction, 1865-1867," *University of Dayton Review,* 9 (Winter 1972), 47-65.

32. Lindsay, "The Participation of Negroes in the Establishment of Welfare Services," pp. 112-114.

33. Thomas Conway to Major General Otis Oliver Howard, New Orleans, La., August 30, 1865, BRFAL, Louisiana, Letters Sent, RG 105, N.A.

34. New York *Tribune,* February 13, 1865; James M. Simms, *The First Colored Baptist Church in North America* (Philadelphia, 1888), pp. 138, 141.

35. Morgan, *Yazoo,* p. 358; New York *Tribune,* February 13, 1865.

36. Alexander, "North Carolina Churches Face Emancipation," p. 51; Vernon Lane Wharton, *The Negro in Mississippi, 1865-1890* (Chapel Hill: The University of North Carolina Press, 1947; reprinted 1965 in Harper Torchbooks paperback edition), pp. 256-258; Edwin Archer Randolph, *The Life of Rev. John Jasper* (Richmond, Va.: R. T. Hill & Co., 1884), p. 30; Virginia Writers, *The Negro in Virginia,* p. 248; Margaret R. Neary, "Some Aspects of Negro Social Life in Richmond, Virginia, 1865-1880," *Maryland Historian,* 1 (Fall 1970), 106.

37. W. C. Whitaker, *History of the Protestant Episcopal Church in Alabama, 1763-1891* (Birmingham, 1898), pp. 197-198, cited in Kolchin, "First Freedom," p. 199.

38. Morgan, *Yazoo,* p. 358.

39. Benjamin Franklin Riley, *A History of the Baptists in the Southern States East of the Mississippi* (Philadelphia: American Baptist Publication Society, 1898), pp. 320-321.

40. Brigadier General Charles Howard, Report, in *House Executive Documents,* No. 70, 39th Cong., 1st sess., pp. 354-355; Du Bois, *The Negro Church,* 57.

41. Kolchin, "First Freedom," pp. 208-210.

42. Wesley J. Gaines, *African Methodism in the South; or Twenty-five Years of Freedom* (Atlanta, 1890), pp. 18-19.

43. "A Black Belt County, Ga.," in Du Bois, *The Negro Church*, p. 57.

44. Smalls, AFIC Testimony.

45. Charles Octavius Boothe, *The Cyclopedia of the Colored Baptists of Alabama; Their Leaders and Their Work* (Birmingham, 1895) p. 107.

46. Ibid., p. 69.

47. *O.R.*, ser. III, vol. IV, p. 371 (final report of the American Freedmen's Inquiry Commission).

48. Report of Brevet Major General Clinton B. Fisk, Assistant Commissioner, BRFAL, Nashville, Tenn., February 14, 1866, *House Executive Documents*, No. 70, 39, I, p. 240.

49. Lindsay, "The Participation of Negroes in the Establishment of Welfare Services," p. 109.

50. Kolchin, "First Freedom," p. 227; Joe M. Richardson, *The Negro in the Reconstruction of Florida, 1865-1877* (Tallahassee: Florida State University Press, 1965), p. 35; Wharton, *The Negro in Mississippi*, 129; *KKK Conspiracy*, Mississippi, p. 723.

51. *House Executive Documents*, 39th Cong., 2nd sess., (Serial No. 1293) (Washington, D.C.: Government Printing Office, 1867), p. 69.

52. Indexes to Deposit Ledgers, The Freedmen's Savings Bank and Trust Company, Norfolk, Va., New Bern, N.C., Jacksonville and Tallahassee, Fla., New Orleans, La., and Washington, D.C., branches, Record Group 101, National Archives; Neary, "Negro Social Life in Richmond," pp. 114-117.

53. Samuel Harris, Inspector, Freedmen's Savings and Trust Company, to J. W. Alvord, Secretary, Charleston, S.C., April 20, 1867, RG 105, N.A.; New York *Tribune,* June 7, 1871; D. L. Eaton, Actuary, FS&T Co., to Hon. D. L. Morrell, Washington, D.C., February 3, 1868, Legislative Records, House Committee on Freedmen's Affairs, Record Group 233, N.A.

54. Wharton, *Negro in Mississippi,* chap. 20, pp. 268-272, indicates a considerable range of leisure-time activities organized in clubs and on a community scale. Especially notable were the picnics to which freed people came "in families or as organized clubs. Some came with drums and music, carrying banners."Baseball games between neighboring towns, volunteer fire companies, parades, barbecues, and other social activities among freedmen communities occurred in Florida, South Carolina, and North Carolina. See Richardson, *The Negro in the Reconstruction of Florida,* p. 36; Williamson, *After Slavery,* p. 312; Evans, *Ballots and Fence Rails,* p. 118.

55. J. W. Alvord, Report on Schools, *House Executive Documents,* No. 70, 39th Cong., 1st sess., p. 334; Nordhoff, *Freedmen of South Carolina,* p. 1.

56. A. P. Peabody, 2nd Annual Report, New England Freedmen's Aid Society, p. 78.

57. James McKaye, *The Mastership and Its Fruits; The Emancipated Slave Face to Face with His Old Master* (New York, 1864), p. 18.

58. Richardson, *The Negro in the Reconstruction of Florida,* p. 98.

59. Alvord, Report on Schools, p. 344.

60. Augustus A. Low, "The Freedmen's Bureau in the Border States," in Richard O. Curry, ed., *Radicalism, Racism and Party Realignment; The Border-States During Reconstruction* (Baltimore: Johns Hopkins Press, 1969), pp. 260-261.

61. Alvord, Report on Schools, p. 334.

62. Ibid., p. 344; *American Missionary,* April 1867, pp. 86-87.

63. Ibid, pp. 338-339; Petition of Colored Children of City Schools of Louisiana, December 18, 1865, BRFAL, Louisiana, Assistant Commissioner, Letters Received, RG 105, N.A.; ibid., petition for capitation tax to support schools, November 27, 1865.

64. W. E. B. Du Bois, *Efforts for Social Betterment Among Negro Americans* (Atlanta, Ga.: Atlanta University Press, Atlanta Study No. 14, 1909), p. 34. See also Henry Allen Bullock, *A History of Negro Education in the South* (Cambridge, Mass.: Harvard University Press, 1967), pp. 26-28. Bullock found blacks in Louisiana, Tennessee, and Virginia who "through their own resources," entirely sustained forty-six schools and contributed to the support of forty-two others. They also purchased through their own resources thirty-three school buildings in the three states. Of a total $9 million expended on schools for blacks in the South from 1862 to 1874, freedmen paid $1,172,989: $672,989 in taxes and tuition and $500,000 in church organizations' contributions; $3.9 million came from benevolent societies nationally, but the figure is based on receipts from sixteen out of sixty-five societies. The Freedmen's Bureau and Congress (through other appropriations) were responsible for $5.1 million.

65. H. M. Johnson, Secretary, African Civilization Society, to Reverend J. W. Alvord, General Superintendent of Schools, BRFAL, Brooklyn, N.Y., April 15, 1869, RG 105, N.A.; Quarles, *Black Abolitionists,* p. 217.

66. Linda Warfel Slaughter, *The Freedmen of the South* (Cincinnati, Ohio: Elm Street Printing Co., 1869; Kraus reprint, 1969), pp. 158-160.

67. William Slade, President, Social, Civil and Statistical Association of Washington, D.C., in AFIC Testimony, 1863.

68. Alvord, Report on Schools, p. 341; Paul, "The Shadow of Equality," p. 27. Alvord reports the donor's name as Nelson Willis; Paul names Nelson Wells as the free black who bequeathed $10,000 in 1835.

69. Alvord, Report on Schools, pp. 336, 340.

70. William F. Allen Letters, Columbia, S.C., July 6, 1865; *American Freedman,* June 1867, p. 239.

71. New York *Herald,* September 2, 1865.

72. *House Executive Documents,* 70, 39th Cong., 1st sess., p. 354.

73. Joseph Warren, Superintendent for Education, Miss., BRFAL, Reports for October and November 1865. At Pontotoc, freedmen had purchased a lot for a school but early in 1868 they looked to the Freedmen's Bureau for aid in raising $375 for a building (Ganus, "The Freedmen's Bureau in Mississippi," p. 350. See also, for early schools in 1863 and 1864 in the Natchez district, American Missionary Association Archives, Mississippi records.

74. Dr. Shakespeare Allen to Major General O. O. Howard, Centreville, St. Mary's Parish, December 28, 1866. Letters Received BRFAL, RG 105, N.A.

75. *American Missionary,* July 1868, p. 154.

76. *Freedmen's Record,* March 1866, p. 11.

77. Louis T. Harlan, *Booker T. Washington: The Making of a Black Leader, 1856-1901* (New York: Oxford University Press, 1972), pp. 34-37.

78. H. R. Pease to O. O. Howard, February 1, 1868, RG 105, N.A. cited in Ganus, "The Freedmen's Bureau in Mississippi," p. 347.

79. Joe M. Richardson, "Christian Abolitionism: The American Missionary Association and the Florida Negro," *Journal of Negro Education,* (Winter 1970), 39-40. In St. Augustine, early in 1867, black people complained of the inadequacy of the Catholic schools. One mother withdrew her little girl and sent her instead to a school supported and taught by Quakers (*American Freedman,* June 1867, p. 239).

80. They also appear to have recognized an ally in shaping the new South. On Wadmelaw Island off the Georgia coast, Mary A. Sharp, a Northern schoolteacher, conducted the "Thaddeus Stevens School" *(Pennsylvania Freedmen's Bulletin,* September 1866, p. 4). In 1868 when the trustees of the black schools in the District of Columbia decided to build a four-story brick building on 21st Street between K and L Streets in Washington, they named it "The Stevens School-House," "in honor of

the late Hon. Thaddeus Stevens, of Pennsylvania, the champion of free schools for all" *(The American Journal of Education,* vol. 3, 1870, p. 256).

CHAPTER 4

1. The best brief histories of the contraband policy and of slaves becoming free persons under army protection are W. E. B. Du Bois, *Black Reconstruction in America* (New York, 1935), chap. 4, "The General Strike," pp. 55-83, and Allan Nevins, *The War for the Union* (New York, 1971), vol. 3, *The Organized War, 1863-1864,* chap. 11, "Under the Trampling Armies: The Tragic Lot of the Freedmen," pp. 413-444; and Louis S. Gerteis, *From Contraband to Freedman* (Westport, Conn.: Greenwood Press, 1973).

2. *The National Freedman,* September 1865, p. 267.

3. Horace James, *Annual Report of the Superintendent of Negro Affairs in North Carolina for 1864* (Boston, 1864); see also James's correspondence with the American Freedmen's Inquiry Commission, April 1863 and November 13, 1863, New Bern, N.C., AFIC Papers (Harvard University, Houghton Library); "Letter from Captain James," Newbern, N.C., April 24, 1864, *Second Annual Report, New England Freedmen's Aid Society* (Boston, 1864), Appendix, Hereafter cited as *NEFAS, 2 Report.*

4. *The Freedmen's Advocate,* September 1864; *NEFAS, 2 Report,* p. 86.

5. *House Executive Documents,* No. 70, 39th Cong., 1st sess. (Washington, D.C.: U.S. Government Printing Office, 1866), p. 380; New York *Herald,* July 3, 1865; Byron Sunderland et al., *Addresses and Ceremonies at the New Year's Festival to the Freedmen, on Arlington Heights; and Statistics and Statements of the Educational Condition of the Colored People in the Southern States and Other Facts* (Washington, D.C.: McGill and Witherow, 1867); Lindsay, "The Participation of Negroes in the Establishment of Welfare Services, 1865-1900," pp. 90-94; Brevet Brigadier General Charles H. Howard, Assistant Commissioner, BRFAL, for the District of Columbia and West Virginia, *Annual Report* for the year ending October 22, 1867 (Washington, D.C., 1867), p. 12.

6. Ibid., p. 11; Lindsay, "The Participation of Negroes," pp. 96-100.

7. Isaac Jones Wistar, *Autobiography of Isaac Wistar Jones 1827-1905; Half a Century in War and Peace* (New York, 1938), pp. 417, 438.

8. Elizabeth Kilham, "Sketches in Color," *Putnam's Magazine* (February 1870), 205-209. Chapels like the rough-hewn one Kilham found

were also described by two other workers: one on Roanoke Island, N.C., the other on President's Island in the Mississippi Valley. Vincent Colyer, *Brief Report of the Services Rendered by the Freed People to the United States Army in North Carolina in the Spring of 1862 After the Battle of Newbern* (New York 1864), p. 36; Levi Coffin, *Reminiscences* (Cincinnati, 1880), p. 629.

 9. John Eaton, April 29, 1864, AFIC Testimony; Coffin, *Reminiscences,* p. 629.

 10. Howard H. Harlan, *Zion Town—A Study in Human Ecology* (Charlottesville: University of Virginia Press, 1935), pp. 14-16, 46.

 11. John Eaton, Report of Superintendent of Freedmen, p. 12;

 12. E. Merton Coulter, *The South During Reconstruction* (Baton Rouge: Louisiana State University Press, 1947), p. 261.

 13. J. T. Trowbridge, *The South, a Tour of Its Battle Fields and Ruined Cities, a Journey Through the Desolated States, and Talks with the People, Etc.* (Hartford, Conn.: L. Stebbins, 1866), pp. 251-252.

 14. AFIC Testimony, May 11, 1863.

 15. John G. Fee, *Autobiography* (Chicago, 1891), pp. 182-183.

 16. J. A. Hawley to Col. Samuel Thomas, Vicksburg, Miss., December 8, 1865, in *House Executive Documents,* No. 70, 39th Cong., 1st sess., pp. 266-267.

 17. William F. Allen Papers, September 26 and November 30, and December 23, 1864; John Eaton, AFIC Testimony, Memphis, April 29, 1863.

 18. This account of the camp at Corinth, Mississippi, is based on Cam Walker, "Corinth: The Story of a Contraband Camp," *Civil War History* (March 1974), 5-22. See also Coffin, *Reminiscences,* pp. 635-638; Eaton, AFIC Testimony, April 29, 1863.

 19. *Senate Executive Documents,* No. 28, 38th Cong., 2nd sess., pp. 11, 21; *House Executive Documents,* No. 85, 37th Cong., 2nd sess., p. 5.

 20. James, *Annual Report,* p. 30; In his response to the American Freedmen's Inquiry Commission, April 1863, James had reported 932 of the 2,384 freedmen in the camps and villages under his superintendence who could read "a little." Of these readers, 182 "can write," he stated. It appears reasonable he could have managed better than he did, had he tried to work with these literate freedmen (Horace James, Census of Blacks, April 1863, AFIC Papers).

 21. Walter L. Fleming, "Jefferson Davis, the Negroes and the Negro Problem," *Sewanee Review* (October 1908), pp. 410-411; *House Executive Documents,* No. 70, 39th Cong., 1st sess., pp. 264-267; Wharton, *The Negro in Mississippi,* pp. 38-42. Clifton L. Ganus, "The Freedmen's

Bureau in Mississippi," pp. 130-246. Fanny Johnson, who had been a child in Nashville when Davis Bend was operated by the freedmen, recalled in 1938 at the age of 76 that she had been taken there. "It was the most beautiful place I ever see," she remembered. "All the cabins was whitewashed good. The trees was big and the whole place was just lovely. It was old man Jeff Davis' place" (Federal Writers Project, Slave Narratives, Arkansas, part iv, p. 88).

22. American Freedmen's Union Commission, *The Results of Emancipation in the United States of America* (New York, 1867); Eaton, AFIC Testimony, April 29, 1863.

23. AFIC Testimony.

24. *House Executive Documents,* No. 70, 39th Cong., 1st sess., p. 368.

25. Trowbridge, *The South,* p. 533.

26. Alexander Wayman, *My Recollections of 40 Years' Experience,* p. 107.

27. W. H. Tiffany to L. H. Birge, Ogeechee, Georgia, September 29, 1865, BRFAL Georgia, Letters Received, Savannah, RG 105, N.A.; *Savannah Daily Republican,* September 29, 1865; New Orleans *Tribune,* August 4, 1865.

Sea Islands freedmen continued an antebellum precedent of limited self-regulation. On Sapelo Island during the eighteenth century, Thomas Spalding ordered a village of huts to be built for his slaves on his vast estate. One of them was Bu Allah, a Mohammedan who wore a fez and with his family remained aloof from the other 400 slaves. Yet he was "implicitly obeyed." See Caroline C. Lovell, *The Golden Isles of Georgia* (Boston: Little, Brown, 1932), pp. 99-100. Ogeechee freedmen followed that precedent to some extent in 1865 when they elected a committee of three on each plantation to represent their neighborhoods and constitute a Cabinet of Advisers to the local Freedmen's Bureau general superintendent. Three years later, on nearby Ossabaw Island, freedmen agreed to legitimize the practice in making a contract for labor. Five headmen were named by the freed people on the island with the approval of the Bureau agent and the firm of Magill, Fly, and Middleton, which employed them. When the company installed its own man as plantation superintendent, the five headmen responsible for "civil administration and preservation of law and order" objected. They petitioned the Bureau for his removal on the ground that he knew nothing about planting of Sea Island cotton and they feared that they would suffer losses under his administration (Louis Bond, John Mungin, Peter Bowen, Sheet Baker, and Prince Brown to Freedmen's Bureau Agent, Savannah, April 28, 1868, Savannah, Contracts, RG 105, N.A.).

28. H. E. Tremain, *A Gettysburg Narrative and Other Excursions* (New York, 1905), p. 270.

29. Trowbridge, *The South,* p. 252.

30. Tunis G. Campbell to Colonel A. P. Ketchum, St. Catherine's Island, May 20, May 30, June 15, 1865. BRFAL Georgia, Savannah, Letters Received by A. P. Ketchum, RG 105, N.A.: *KKK Conspiracy,* Georgia, pp. 846, 854, 936-937, 941; E. Merton Coulter, *Negro Legislators in Georgia During the Reconstruction Period* (Athens: University of Georgia Press, 1968), pp. 124-125.

31. BRFAL Georgia, Register of Land Titles, Savannah, 1865, RG 105, N.A.; *Savannah Daily Republican,* June 19, 1865; *National Freedman,* April 1865, pp. 82-83; New York *Tribune,* February 13, 1865; Willie Lee Rose, *Rehearsal for Reconstruction: The Port Royal Experiment* (New York: Bobbs-Merrill, 1964; Vintage Books, 1967), p. 331.

32. Records of the Bureau of Refugees, Freedmen, and Abandoned Lands, Georgia, Sub-District of Savannah, "Papers re: Belleville" RG 105, N.A.

33. New York *Tribune,* December 5 and 23, 1867.

34. James S. Allen, *Reconstruction, The Battle for Democracy* (New York: International Publishers, 1937), p. 123.

35. Nashville *Daily Press and Times,* August 11, 1866.

36. Elizabeth Hyde Botume, *Firts Days Among the Contrabands* (Boston: Lee and Shepard, 1893), p. 48; see also the discussion of "primordial sentiments" in Clifford Geertz, ed., *Old Societies and New States* (New York: The Free Press of Glencoe, 1963), pp. 105-157.

37. Botume, *First Days,* pp. 57, 60, 137 ff; see also Williamson, *After Slavery,* pp. 312 ff.

38. Carol K. Rothrock Bleser, *The Promised Land: The History of the South Carolina Land Commission, 1869-1890.* (Columbia: University of South Carolina Press, 1969), p. 152.

CHAPTER 5

1. Herbert Aptheker, *Documentary History of the Negro People in the United States* (New York: Citadel Press, 1951), pp. 7-16.

2. Higginson, *Army Life in a Black Regiment;* Rose, *Rehearsal for Reconstruction,* pp. 384, 390-392; Okun Edet Uya, *From Slavery to Public Service, Robert Smalls, 1839-1915* (New York: Oxford University Press, 1971).

3. W. E. B. Du Bois, *Black Reconstruction in America,* p. 721. Class division among South Carolina Afro-Americans affected political actions.

A recent study concludes that black former slaves in the state legislature were more radical than the freeborn, mulatto representatives on the land confiscation issue (Thomas Holt, "Radical Blacks and Conservative Browns: The Voting Behavior of Negro Legislators in the South Carolina House of Representatives, 1868-1871," unpublished paper, presented at the annual meeting of the Organization of American Historians, Chicago, 1973). This revises an older view that white racism tended to erase class lines in the black and mulatto Afro-American community. The test of voting behavior in Holt's study is limited to one state and one brief period. Even though similar divisions on the confiscation issue appeared in New Orleans, the general thrust of the communities on many other issues unified Afro-Americans.

4. *Condition of Affairs in the Late Insurrectionary States,* 42nd Cong., 2nd sess., Senate Report No. 41 (13 vols., Washington, D.C., 1872). The committee investigated Klan violence in six states, most of it perpetrated after the passage of the 1867 Reconstruction Acts. The testimony reveals a wealth of information on violent deeds committed in many southern counties but omits mention of those committed on the gulf coast of Alabama and Mississippi, tidewater South Carolina, coastal Georgia, and those committed around the towns of Natchez and Vicksburg, and in almost all Southern cities. References in this chapter to parts of the *Ku Klux Klan Conspiracy,* the short title of the thirteen volumes, will be cited by state and page in the volume covering that particular state under consideration (for example, "Alabama, 422").

Artisan leaders were generally ignored in the Dunning school monographs in Reconstruction history and treated lightly in revisionist interpretations of the times. See Vernon Lane Wharton, *The Negro in Mississippi, 1865-1890* (Chapel Hill: The University of North Carolina Press, 1947); Joel Williamson, *After Slavery: The Negro in South Carolina During Reconstruction* (Chapel Hill: The Univeristy of North Carolina Press, 1965); Alrutheus Ambush Taylor, *The Negro in South Carolina During Reconstruction* (Chapel Hill: The University of North Carolina *construction of Virginia* (Washington, D.C.: Association for the Study of Negro Life and History, 1926); Horace Mann Bond, "Social and Economic Forces in Alabama Reconstruction," *The Journal of Negro History,* 23 (July 1938), 290-348, and *Negro Education in Alabama: A Study in Cotton and Steel* (Washington, D.C.: Association for the Study of Negro Life and History, 1939). Wharton, for example, found some local black leaders among former urban slaves, "blacksmiths, carpenters, clerks or waiters in hotels and boarding houses," and a few former servants of wealthy whites (p. 164). Williamson found native South Caro-

lina black men "fresh from the cotton fields" at the 1868 Charleston
constitutional convention. Thirty-eight former slaves were among the
seventy-four delegates. Williamson identified twenty-six of them as
"trades-, profession or business men," the eleven tradesmen making up
the largest group. Most had used their skills while slaves. Eight of the
twenty-six were clergymen, and some of them were tradesmen as well.
No further information was disclosed to identify the convention delegates (p. 376); Allen Trelease, *White Terror: The Ku Klux Klan Conspiracy and Southern Reconstruction* (New York, Harper & Row, 1971),
is a meaningful narrative constructed from the congressional testimony
of 1871 and local newspaper and other sources. However, the work does
not deal with the black community and its culture from the freedmen's
viewpoint. Until recently slaves, freedmen, and other lower-class persons
were believed to be "inarticulate" from the point of view of historians
searching for their direct testimony. They left few written records in the
forms familiar to historians and other educated and middle-class persons.
This may possibly explain in part the Dunning school treatment of them.
Nevertheless, their actions expressed their ideas and aspirations. A helpful effort to clarify the concept of inarticulateness in history is in Jesse
Lemisch and John K. Alexander, "The White Oaks, Jack Tar, and the
Concept of the 'Inarticulate,' " *The William and Mary Quarterly,* 3rd ser.,
29 (January 1972), 129-134.

    5. Chandler Davidson, *Biracial Politics, Conflict and Coalition in the
Metropolitan South* (Baton Rouge: Louisiana State University Press, 1972),
pp. 280-282; Daniel C. Thompson, *The Negro Leadership Class* (Englewood Cliffs, N.J.: Prentice-Hall, 1963), p. 24; Everett Carll Ladd, Jr.,
Negro Political Leadership in the South (Ithaca, N.Y.: Cornell University Press, 1966), pp. 113-114.

    6. Of course, many persons are not included. Of dozens of witnes-
ses who said they were persecuted for voting the Radical Republican
ticket, some seemed to be leaders, but the evidence is inconclusive. In
addition, many witnesses told of others who had been beaten or killed
and who seemed at least in such testimony to have been leading figures.
Again, the evidence was lacking or very slight. The Union League of America was established on a national basis in May 1863. It was organized to
rally support for the U.S. government and the Lincoln administration
during the Civil War. When peace came, the Union League became a par-
tisan political group, an arm of the Republican party. The black masses
in the South filled the chapters organized there. Under the circumstances the leagues were secret at first, with oaths and passwords and rituals.
Members were sworn to loyalty to the United States and the Republican

party, and to support only Republican candidates. The name Loyal
League soon displaced that of Union League in the South. For black
members the leagues were not only political but also fraternal and mu-
tual-aid societies. The leagues disbanded after the 1870 election. See
Guy James Gibson, "Lincoln's League: The Union League Movement
During the Civil War" (unpublished Ph.D. dissertation, University of
Illinois, 1958); Wharton, *The Negro in Mississippi,* pp. 164-166; Trelease,
White Terror, pp. xxix-xxxi.

7. Alabama, 1001, 1623, 1691; South Carolina, 1015-1016.

8. Georgia, 735, 923-928; South Carolina, 1158-1163.

9. From tables compiled by the author. See also Mississippi, 9-10,
773; Georgia, 1, 706, 930; South Carolina, 328, 1165; Florida, 109. A
former governor of Georgia, Joseph E. Brown, the president of Western and Atlantic Railroad, testified, "Well, I should say that the
majority of them, (the blacks) where they are of proper age, have families and the husband and wife live together and I think the majority of
them during the time of slavery did so" (Georgia, 817).

10. Georgia, 1060; Alabama, 334.

11. Similarly, the occupations of artisan leaders of the Parisian masses
are to be found in George Rudé, *The Crowd in the French Revolution*
(New York: Oxford University Press, 1959)

12. *Captain Swing: A Social History of the Great English Agricultural
Uprisings of 1830* (New York: Pantheon, 1969), especially pp. 242-246.
Slave-artisan mobility and leadership is best appreciated by Gerald W.
Mullin, "Gabriel's Insurrection," in Peter I. Rose (ed.), *Americans from
Africa: Old Memories, New Moods* (New York: Atherton Press, 1970),
pp. 53-74.

13. Alabama, 1003.

14. South Carolina, 587; Georgia, 401-402

15. Alabama, 88-89.

16. Georgia, 9, 739; South Carolina, 1175, 1216; Mississippi, 253, 363,
497; Alabama 1790-1797, 1838-1839.

17. Alabama, 1086; Mississippi, 725. Robert Gleed, a black state senator in Mississippi, considered them to be traitors and in a class with Bene-
dict Arnold. When challenged by white congressmen, Gleed conceded the
right of blacks to be Democrats but, comparing it with Arnold's betrayal
of the army, said "that does not make it justice and equity because he
did." W. H. Harrison declared that his election in Georgia rested on black
voters "en masse." He said, "Only three or four colored people were simple enough to vote the democratic ticket." At the age of twenty-eight,
Harrison had already become one of the most astute of these local black
leaders, his testimony displaying sophistication, wit, and eloquence.

18. William C. Ford, a Meridian lawyer, said that blacks collected and "shouted, halooed, and sang very obnoxious songs." He could not recall what songs they were. The committee chairman suggested, "Old John Brown," but Ford's memory slipped on this point; he had only heard about the incident. In York, South Carolina, a witness affirmed that black people at an open meeting of Democrats and Republicans did indeed heckle a speaker by singing "Old John Brown" (South Carolina, 1440-1441).

A vivid demonstration of freedmen political consciousness and Afro-American identity was the three-mile-long parade of 4,000 persons in Charleston on March 21, 1865. Black soldiers led the way, followed by bands, contingents of black schoolchildren. Butchers, tailors, and coopers marched with tools of their trade in their hands. Units of painters, blacksmiths, carpenters, wheelwrights, barbers, and other tradesmen followed *(New York Times,* April 4, 1865).

19. Georgia, 254.

20. South Carolina, 683.

21. Alabama, 1016-1022.

22. Alabama, 334-335, 1607, 1773-1774, 1781, 1808; see also Eugene D. Genovese, "Rebelliousness and Docility in the Negro Slave: A Critique of the Elkins Thesis," *Civil War History,* 13 (December 1967), 293-314; Stanley M. Elkins, *Slavery: A Problem in American Institutional and Intellectual Life* (Chicago: University of Chicago Press, 1959).

23. Alabama, 996-1004, 1622-1623, 1640-1641, 1662-1665, 1688, 1690-1691.

24. Ibid., 856, 886; Wilson Carey, in the North Carolina constitutional convention of 1868, voiced similar views: "The Negro planted the wilderness, built up the state to what it was. Therefore, if anything was to be given, the Negro was entitled to it." Cited by Leonard Bernstein, "The Participation of Negro Delegates in the Constitutional Convention of 1868 in North Carolina," *The Journal of Negro History,* 24 (October 1949), 408. James S. Allen, in his *Reconstruction: The Battle for Democracy* (New York: International Publishers, 1937), pp. 105-106, tells us that Lewis Lindsay, "a Negro worker of Virginia," threatened to use arms to resist the imposition of hunger through an employers' boycott of freedmen laborers. "Before any of his children would suffer for food, the streets of Richmond would run knee-deep in blood; and he thanked God that the Negroes had learned to use guns, pistols, and ramrods." General John Schofield, the U.S. Army commander in Virginia, found a (Joseph) Lindsay (or Lindsay) Lewis to be "an ignorant illiterate man who makes fiery speeches to his class." Lewis was a former slave and a leader of a brass band in the city of Richmond, according to Richard

G. Lowe, "Virginia's Reconstruction Convention, General Schofield Rates the Deputies," *Virginia Magazine of History and Biography,* 80 (July 1972), 341-360.

25. Mississippi, 9-11, 49-50, 66, 70, 171; Reverend Elias Hill, a licensed Baptist preacher of York County, South Carolina, believed that republicanism was God's will. "I believe the republican party advocates what is nearer the laws of God than any other party, and therefore, I feel that it is right." But he denied that he preached "political" sermons on "republicanism" (South Carolina, 1412-1413). See also Edward Magdol, "A note on Authenticity: Eliab Hill and Nimbus Ware in *Bricks Without Straw,*" *American Quarterly,* 22 (Winter 1970), 907-911.

26. Mississippi, 49-50, 116, 157.

27. Ibid., 31, 32, 109, 157, 171-172.

28. Alabama, 1581, 1962-1963

29. Georgia, 701, 1040; the black man's desire for land is established in William S. McFeely, *Yankee Stepfather: General O. O. Howard and the Freedmen* (New Haven, Conn.: Yale University Press, 1968); *Reconstruction: The Battle for Democracy;* Manuel Gottlieb, "The Land Question in Georgia During Reconstruction," *Science and Society,* 3 (Summer 1939), 356-388; Martin Abbott, *The Freedmen's Bureau in South Carolina, 1865-1872* (Chapel Hill: University of North Carolina Press, 1967).

30. Du Bois, *Black Reconstruction;* Wharton, *The Negro in Mississippi,* pp. 59-61; Williamson, *After Slavery,* pp. 54-63; Herbert Aptheker, *A Documentary History of the Negro People in the United States* (New York: Citadel, 1951). pp. 543, 546; South Carolina, 445; Alabama, 1131, 1133.

31. South Carolina, 605.

32. Georgia, 702; one such place was in Warren County, Georgia. Another was near Sparta, Georgia, where W. H. Harrison told of a fairly substantial black landownership. He lived in a settlement where blacks owned some 800 acres. One of the benefits, he asserted, was that he suffered no personal injury from the Klan because he lived in so large a settlement. Colby reported that many black people had purchased up to 100 or 150 acres but had to live "poorly as they can" or be driven away. Many had 15 or 20 acres each but could not go near them.

33. Georgia, 213, 701, 926, 1041.

34. Mississippi, 54, 357, 436, 993-996; similarly, freedmen in Tennessee had established what they called "protective Union Stores" on capital furnished by $10 shares, in order to overcome price exploitation by merchants. McFeely, *Yankee Stepfather,* p. 300.

35. Mississippi, 48, 54, 357, 436, 723, 993-996; Georgia, 662; Alabama, 1662.

36. *House Executive Documents,* 39th Cong., 2nd sess., (Serial No. 1293) (Washington, D.C.: U.S. Government Printing Office, 1867), pp. 67-71; Pike County Court Records, August term, 1866. BRFAL Georgia, Miscellaneous Papers. RG 105, N.A.
37. Nashville *Daily Press and Times,* August 11, 1866.
38. Thompson, *Making of the English Working Class,* pp. 456-469. See also P. H. J. H. Gosden, *The Friendly Societies in England,* 1815-1875 (Manchester: Manchester University Press, 1961).
39. Mississippi, 325-340; 1188; South Carolina, 1407-1408.
40. Georgia, 702, 931.
41. Ibid., 616.
42. Ibid.
43. Albion Tourgée, *A Fool's Errand and the Invisible Empire* (New York, 1880). The second of these two works, which are bound together in one volume, is the nonfictional basis of the first, a well-known novel. Tourgée cited copiously from the Klan hearings; he emphasized the violence and brutality and reproduced the testimony of some men whose names appear in this article. He was, of course, endeavoring to demonstrate to his readers that his novel was based on real situations. However, he made no effort to use the hearings, as is attempted here, as an indication of the black lower-class world and its leaders.
44. South Carolina: (Wilkes), 1043, 1058-1059, 1427-1433, 1582-1583; (Williams), 1712, 1750-1768, 1775, 1791-1792; A former slave in Hinds County, Caldwell had been commissioned a captain in the short-lived Mississippi Infantry during a period of intense terror against blacks. He had been a member of the county board of police and then had been one of five black men elected in 1870 to the state senate. He served for five years. He had been a blacksmith. Behind the assault on leading black men in Hinds County lay the resentment of white planters over Loyal Leagues that protested there and elsewhere in the South against sharecropping in 1869 and 1870. Those organized black freedmen called instead for the chance to rent land at a maximum rent of $1.50 per acre. Herbert Aptheker, "Mississippi Reconstruction and the Negro Leader, Charles Caldwell," in *To Be Free* (New York: International Publishers, 1948), pp. 163-187.
45. Mississippi, 1158.
46. Alabama, 998, 1382, 1663, 1689, 1955-1956, 1962; Mississippi, 8. Similar interracial artisan collaboration may have occurred in the 1868 Beaufort, South Carolina, Republican convention to name district delegates for election to the state general assembly. Two of the six nominees were white: C. J. Stolbrand, tailor, and George A. Bennett, whom an opposition paper attacked as "a bankrupt tavern keeper." The four blacks

were W. J. Whipper (Northern-born middle-class black leader), R. Smalls, the pilot who abducted *The Planter,* Philip Ezekiel, tailor, and W. C. Morrison, tinner. See *The Free Press* (Charleston and Beaufort), April 4, 1868.

47. National Archives, Record Group 105. Bureau of Refugees, Freedmen and Abandoned Lands, Virginia Assistant Commissioner: Reports of Leading Whites and Freedmen, March 8, 1867, to May 1, 1867; see also Luther P. Jackson, *Negro Office Holders in Virginia 1865-1895* (Norfolk, Va.: Guide Quality Press, 1945) for a compilation drawn from local sources; Charles Nordhoff, *The Cotton States in the Spring and Summer of 1875* (New York: D. Appleton & Co., 1876), pp. 83-84.

Confidential reports from seventy-nine of the state's hundred counties, as well as from cities such as Alexandria, Charlottesville, Norfolk, Portsmouth, and Williamsburg, furnished 462 names of freedmen who appeared to be leaders in their communities. Remote mountain counties as well as those of the Tidewater were heard from. The identification of ninety-nine men by occupation showed (1) artisans and laborers and (2) teachers and clergymen as the two largest categories. Some clergymen may have had other occupations, however. Unfortunately, the letters of the officers of the Bureau did not make this distinction clear in all cases. Twelve businessmen and eighteen farmers made up the other categories. The Columbus blacklist of sixty-eight "unworthy" Negroes, accompanied by a list of those considered worthy, was privately circulated among the city's white businessmen prior to the mayoralty election in December 1874. Among the "unworthy," forty-eight were identified by occupation. Artisans predominated: carpenters (fifteen), blacksmiths (two), cabinet makers (two), a shoemaker, a brick-mason, a ginhouse builder. Those in the laborer category on the "unworthy" list included a gardener, a laborer, and two woodchoppers. Only three of the sixty-five on the "worthy" list were identified by trade or occupation: a carpenter, a cemetery sexton, and the keeper of a livery stable. One was labeled "dead." How he was expected to vote was not explained. Among the "unworthy," one was "bad" and another "awful." Like their fellow "unworthies," they were considered sure to vote against the Democratic candidate and possibly influence other black voters to follow their lead.

Schofield's private assessment of black delegates to the Virginia constitutional convention in 1867 reveals that of the twenty-one men with known occupations, 43 percent, or nine, were artisans. A biographical survey of the thirty-four black legislators of North Carolina from July 1868 to February 1872 disclosed occupational information for eleven, five of whom were artisans. Most prominent among them was James H. Harris, a mattress maker prior to his involvement in politics. Thus, from

all the sources examined in this essay, 40 percent of the black leaders
with known occupations were artisans (see Table 5). Lowe, "Virginia's
Reconstruction Convention, General Schofield Rates the Deputies,"
pp. 341-360; Elizabeth Balabanoff, "North Carolina Negro legislators,
July 1868-February 1872," *North Carolina Historical Review,* 49 (Winter 1972), 22-56; eighteen skilled occupations were recorded for politically active black men among the sixty listed as registrars in the six
counties surrounding Greensboro, N.C., in 1867. See Otto H. Olsen,
Carpetbagger's Crusade: The Life of Albion Winegar Tourgee (Baltimore:
Johns Hopkins University Press, 1965), p. 80.
    48. David C. Rankin, "The Origins of Black Leadership in New Orleans
During Reconstruction," *The Journal of Southern History,* 40 (August
1974), 429-431.
    49. John W. Blassingame, "Before the Ghetto: The Making of the
Black Community in Savannah, Georgia, 1865-1880," *Journal of Social
History,* 6 (Summer 1973), 476-477.
    50. Robert E. Perdue, "The Negro in Savannah 1865-1900," Ph.D.
dissertation, University of Georgia, 1971, pp. 67-68; *National Freedman,*
April 1865, p. 82; New York *Tribune,* February 13, 1865; Howard,
Autobiography, vol. 2, p. 189; McFeely, *Yankee Stepfather,* p. 47;
Savannah Republican, January 16, 1865.
    51. Virginia Writers' Project, *The Negro in Virginia,* pp. 220-222.

CHAPTER 6

    1. *O.R.,* ser. 1, 47, part 2, pp. 60-62; La Wanda Cox, "The Promise
of Land for the Freedmen," *Mississippi Valley Historical Review,* 45
(December 1958), 413-440; Christie Farnham Pope, "Southern Homesteads for Negroes," *Agricultural History,* 44 (April 1970), 201-215.
    2. Federal Writers' Project, *Slave Narratives, a Folk History of Sla-
very in the United States from Interviews with Former Slaves* (Washington, D.C.: Library of Congress, 1941), Alabama narratives, pp. 314-315;
Walter L. Fleming, *Civil War and Reconstruction in Alabama* (New York:
Columbia University Press, 1905), p. 446; Kolchin, "First Freedom,"
p. 67.
    3. *House Executive Documents,* No. 70, 39th Cong., 1st sess., pp.
310-311.
    4. *Report of the Joint Committee on Reconstruction, House Report,*
No. 30, 39th Cong., 1st sess., part II, p. 192.
    5. James Sinclair to Charles J. Wickersham, Lumberton, N.C., Octo-
ber 23, 1865, BRFAL, North Carolina, Letters Received, RG 105, N.A.;
W. McKee Evans, *To Die Game: The Story of the Lowry Band, Indian*

Guerrillas of Reconstruction (Baton Rouge: Louisiana State University Press, 1971), p. 63; Lt. O. B. Todd, Semimonthly report, Lumberton, N.C., subdistrict, December 11, 1865, RG 105, N.A. In September the white grand jury of Wilkes County, Georgia, became alarmed over the mass meetings and parades of 2,000-3,000 freed people in Washington, Georgia. The white citizens were especially upset by what they called "exaggerated views and expectations." These were said to be that "some great enhancement of their condition is to take place at Christmas. Many believe that there will then be a general division among them of the lands of the country" (Grand Jury, Wilkes County, Ga., to Major General James B. Steedman, Commanding, Department of Georgia, September 27, 1865, BRFAL Georgia, Miscellaneous Letters, RG 105, N.A.).

6. New York *Tribune,* September 8, 1865.

7. S. D. Barnes to Lieutenant E. Bamberger, December 30, 1865, cited in Ganus, "The Freedmen's Bureau in Mississippi," p. 187; *House Executive Documents,* No. 70, 39th Cong., 1st sess., p. 174; *The Freedmen's Record,* January 1866, pp. 6-7, 10-11.

8. New York *Tribune,* October 4, 1865.

9. Whitelaw Reid, *After the War; A Southern Tour, May 1, 1865 to May 1, 1866,* C. Vann Woodward, ed. (New York: Harper & Row, 1965), pp. 335-336 ff.

10. John Richard Dennett, *The South as It Is, 1865-1866,* Henry Christman, ed. (New York: The Viking Press, 1965), pp. 187 ff, 248, 342.

11. William S. McFeely, *Yankee Stepfather, General O. O. Howard and the Freedmen* (New York: W. W. Norton, 1970), p. 134.

12. B. H. True to O. O. Howard, Commissioner BRFAL, Madison, Georgia, February 22, 1868, Letters Received, RG 105, N.A.

13. Myrta Lockett Avary, *Dixie After the War* (New York: Doubleday, Page & Co., 1906), p. 346; *Senate Executive Documents,* No. 6, 39, 2, p. 114.

14. Friends Association of Philadelphia, *6th Annual Report* (Philadelphia, 1870), p. 9.

15. Fleming, *Civil War and Reconstruction in Alabama,* pp. 447-448.

16. November 23, 1861, cited in James M. McPherson, *The Negro's Civil War* (New York: Vintage Books, 1965), pp. 293-294.

17. Allen, *Reconstruction,* p. 43.

18. Joseph Carrol Vance, "The Negro in the Reconstruction of Albemarle County, Virginia," unpublished M.A. thesis, Univerisity of Virginia 1953, p. 63.

19. Jesse Thomas Wallace, *A History of the Negroes of Mississippi from 1865 to 1890* (Clinton, Miss., privately published, 1927), pp. 23, 152.

20. Fleming, *Civil War and Reconstruction in Alabama,* p. 412.

21. William W. Davis, *The Civil War and Reconstruction in Florida* (New York: Columbia University Press, 1913), p. 359.

22. Joe M. Richardson, *The Negro in the Reconstruction of Florida, 1865-1877* (Tallahassee: Florida State University Press, 1965), p. 55.

23. Herbert Aptheker, "Organizational Activities of Southern Negroes," p. 148. Soldiers in Tennessee played active roles in freedmen's affairs. In addition to the black civilian delegates to the Colored People's State Convention on August 7, 1865, soldier delegates came from six regiments: the 13th, 14th, 15th and 17th U.S. Colored Troops; the 1st U.S. Colored Heavy Artillery; and Battery A, 2nd Light Artillery, U.S. Colored Troops. See *The Colored Tennessean* (Nashville), August 12, 1865.

24. *Report of the Joint Committee on Reconstruction,* p. 66.

25. Ibid., part III, Report by Charles Howard, p. 42.

26. James E. Sefton, *The United States Army and Reconstruction, 1865-1877,* (Baton Rouge: Louisiana State University Press, 1967), pp. 50-52.

27. Ibid., p. 42.

28. December 28, 1865.

29. Thomas W. Conway, *Final Report of the Bureau of Free Labor, Department of the Gulf* (New Orleans, 1865), pp. 34-35; Howard, *Autobiography,* II, pp. 188-189.

30. *The Liberator,* November 15, 1865; BRFAL Land Division, Letters Received. Jonathan Cory, Jr., to Major General O. S. [sic] Howard, Jacksonville, Fla., April 16, 1866. RG 105, N.A.

31. Commissioner, BRFAL, Letters Received, 1867, RG 105, N.A.; Civil War pension records; muster rolls, 6th U.S. Colored Heavy Artillery Regiment, Old Military Records, N.A.

32. New York *Herald,* October 21, 1865.

33. *The Freedmen's Record,* September 1866, pp. 111-112; Thomas W. Conway to Benjamin Flanders, New Orleans, La., October 24, 1864. Treasury Department, 3rd Special Agency, Record Group 366, National Archives.

34. *Report of the Joint Committee on Reconstruction,* part III, p. 36; *House Executive Documents,* No. 70, 39th Cong., 1st sess., p. 347.

35. AFIC Testimony, 1863.

36. Ibid.

37. Howard, *Autobiography,* II, p. 242; Writers Project, *Slave Narratives,* Arkansas, p. 183.

38. *Ku Klux Conspiracy,* Alabama, p. 1810.

39. Ibid., Georgia, p. 861.

40. *Joint Committee on Reconstruction,* part III, p. 77.

41. William F. Allen Diary, Charleston, S.C. July 10, 1865.

42. *House Executive Documents,* 70, 39, I, p. 356.

43. John Preston McConnell, *Negroes and Their Treatment in Virginia from 1865 to 1867* (Pulaski, Va., 1910), pp. 35-37.

44. *Ku Klux Conspiracy,* Mississippi, p. 590.

45. Ibid., South Carolina, p. 605.

46. August 1, 1865.

47. *House Executive Documents,* No. 70, 39, I, p. 240. Such treatment of freedmen was widespread in Georgia, North and South Carolina, as restoration went on apace. The Freedmen's Bureau subcommissioner at Orangeburg, South Carolina, wrote that "large numbers of freedmen with their families and baggage are coming into my district, from the North and Western districts. They are entirely destitute; and their statements are, an outrage upon humanity. They were working on the plantations, and are now driven away without having received any share in the crop they helped to raise and gather" (Colonel E. A. Kozlay to Major O. D. Kinsman, Adjutant General, October 13, 1865. BRFAL South Carolina, Assistant Commissioner, Letters Received, RG 105, N.A.

Of 600 people on St. Simon's Island 200 were driven from the mainland after crops were made (BRFAL Georgia, Letters Received by A. P. Ketchum, W. F. Eaton to A. P. Ketchum, August 25, 1865, RG 105).

Sixteen Roanoke Island, North Carolina, freedmen petitioned on their own behalf and for others against their eviction from the island where they were born, had worked, and of which they had fond memories. Their offer to pay rent or purchase lots had been spurned by property-owning whites. The freedmen said they made a living "fishing, fowling, and 'progging' " and feared separation from their familiar settlements and occupations (BRFAL North Carolina, Letters Received, December 14, 1866, RG 105, N.A.).

48. Vance, "Negro in Reconstruction of Albemarle County," pp. 49, 98-100.

49. Semimonthly Reports, June 30-September 7, 1866, BRFAL, North Carolina RG 105, N.A.

50. *House Miscellaneous Documents,* No. 52, 40th Cong., 3rd sess. (Washington, D.C.: U.S. Government Printing Office, 1869), p. 119.

51. The following discussion of the land question relies upon Du Bois, *Black Reconstruction in America,* pp. 66-67; Howard, *Autobiography,* II, pp. 229-244; Williamson, *After Slavery,* pp. 54-63; Wharton, *Negro in Mississippi,* pp. 58-62; Allen, *Reconstruction,* pp. 43-53; Rose, *Rehearsal for Reconstruction,* pp. 272-296; John A. Carpenter, *Sword and Olive Branch: Oliver Otis Howard* (Pittsburgh: University of Pittsburgh Press, 1964); McFeely, *Yankee Stepfather, passim.*

52. McFeely, *Yankee Stepfather,* pp. 98-99.

53. La Wanda Cox and John H. Cox, eds., *Reconstruction, the Negro, and the New South* (New York: Harper & Row, 1973), p. 320.

54. McFeely, *Yankee Stepfather,* p. 102.

55. Ibid., chap. 6, pp. 107-129. BRFAL Land Division, Letters Received, Saxton to Howard, Charleston, S.C., January 14, 1866, RG 105, N.A.

56. *Speech of the Hon. Thaddeus Stevens, Delivered in the city of Lancaster,* September 7th, 1865 (Lancaster, Pa.: Examiner & Herald Print, 1865); New York *Tribune,* September 12, 1865.

57. *Congressional Globe,* 39th Cong., 1st sess., part 1, pp. 655-658; Cox and Cox, *Reconstruction,* pp. 43-53.

58. Patrick W. Riddleberger, "George W. Julian: Abolitionist Land Reformer," *Agricultural History,* 5 (July 1955), p. 110.

59. Howard A. White, *The Freedmen's Bureau in Louisiana* (Baton Rouge: Louisiana State University Press, 1970), pp. 59-60; Pope, "Southern Homesteads for Negroes," pp. 203-206; Commissioner BRFAL, Letters Received (Louisiana), J. J. Saville to William H. Sterling, January 28, 1867, and July 1, 1867, RG 105, N.A.

60. Du Bois, *Black Reconstruction,* pp. 55-83.

61. New York *Herald,* September 26, 1865.

62. Washington *National Intelligencer,* January 16, 1866.

63. White, *Freedmen's Bureau in Louisiana,* p. 57.

64. Howard, *Autobiography,* II, pp. 238-239.

65. Tremain, *Other Excursions,* pp. 278-280.

66. Ibid., pp. 271-283; *Joint Committee on Reconstruction,* pp. 238-239; *South Carolina Leader,* December 9, 1865.

67. Mary Ames, *From a New England Woman's Diary in Dixie in 1865* (Springfield, Mass., 1906), pp. 99-103.

68. Allen, *Reconstruction,* pp. 62-63.

69. Tremain, *Other Excursions,* p. 250.

70. McFeely, *Yankee Stepfather,* p. 157, citing New Orleans *Tribune,* November 20, 1865.

71. *Joint Committee on Reconstruction,* part III, p. 41; Williamson, *After Slavery,* p. 82.

72. Simkins and Woody, *South Carolina During Reconstruction,* p. 229.

73. Gottlieb, "The Land Question in Georgia," p. 368.

74. George C. Rogers, Jr., *History of Georgetown County, South Carolina* (Columbia: University of South Carolina Press, 1970), p. 433; Avary, *Dixie After the War,* p. 345.

75. Joseph Manigault to General D. E. Sickles, December 16, 1865, Savannah, Georgia, BRFAL, Letters Received, RG 105, N.A.

76. New York *Herald,* October 22, 1865.

77. Manigault to Sickles, December 16, 1865.

78. New York *Herald,* August 14, 1865.

79. *House Executive Documents,* No. 70, 39th Cong., 1st sess., p. 138.

80. John T. Trowbridge, *The South,* chap. 75, pp. 537-545, is the source for the discussion of the James Island visit; New York *Herald,* December 25, 1865.

81. New York *Herald,* September 17, October 15, 1865; Martin Abbott, *The Freedmen's Bureau in South Carolina* (Chapel Hill: University of North Carolina Press, 1967), pp. 72-73.

82. W. McKee Evans, *Ballots and Fence Rails,* p. 69; Allen, *Reconstruction,* p. 65; Washington *National Intelligencer,* January 13, 1866; Thomas C. Arnold to General Sickles, December 27, 1865, BRFAL Savannah, Georgia, Letters Received, RG 105, N.A. In Bryan County, Georgia, white farmers complained in December 1865 that freedmen would not work nor contract for 1866 (BRFAL Waynesboro, Ga., Agent, Letters Received, December 1865, RG 105, N.A.).

83. Sylvester Soper, Captain, 26th U.S. Colored Infantry to Captain A. P. Ketchum, Robertsville, S.C., July 1, 1865. Letters Received by A. P. Ketchum; Ketchum to Soper, Savannah, July 5, 1865, ibid., RG 105, N.A.; W. H. Gibbons, Affidavit, in Subassistant Commissioner Records, Savannah, RG 105; *Savannah Daily Republican,* November 7, 1865; Davis Tillson to O. O. Howard, Commissioner BRFAL, Savannah, February 23, 1866; Margaret U. Downes, Brunswick, Ga., to Lieutenant Douglas G. Risley, Subassistant Commissioner, May 24, 1867. BRFAL, St. Mary's, Ga., RG 105, N.A.

84. *Savannah National Republican,* December 12-16, 1865; Davis Tillson to Colonel H. F. Sickles, Augusta, Ga., December 6, 1865. BRFAL Georgia, Assistant Commissioner, Register of Letters Sent, p. 280. RG 105, N.A.

85. The occurrences were numerous enough to indicate a general freedmen's response. J. Carlyle Sitterson, *Sugar Country: The Sugar Industry in the South, 1753-1950* (Lexington: University of Kentucky Press, 1953), pp. 209-210; Augustine J. H. Duganne, *Camps and Prisons: Twenty Months in the Department of the Gulf* (New York, 1865), pp. 63-64; Rogers, *History of Georgetown County,* p. 421; Willis Young to O. O. Howard, November 7, 1865, BRFAL Georgia, Letters Received, Savannah, RG 105, N.A.; ibid., Flye, Middleton and Magill to Lieutenant Nelson Bronson; Avary, *Dixie After the War,* p. 342; Coulter, *The South During Reconstruction,* p. 110; Kolchin, "First Freedom," pp. 85, 89; *see also* Tiffany to Sickles, December 12, 1865, BRFAL Savannah, Letters Received, RG 105, N.A.; Senate Executive Documents, No. 6, 39th

Cong., 2nd sess., p. 53; White, *Freedmen's Bureau in Louisiana*, p. 54; Davis, *Civil War and Reconstruction in Florida*, p. 427; New York *Herald*, May 23, 1866.

86. *Joint Committee on Reconstruction*, III, p. 185; *National Freedman*, May 1865; Vance, "Negro in Reconstruction of Albemarle County," p. 7; *Freedmen's Advocate*, January 1865, p. 3; *Free South* cited in *Freedmen's Advocate*, April 1864.

87. *The Pennsylvania Freedmen's Bulletin*, March 1867, pp. 15-16. Wyatt was not alone, claiming a right to the land and offering a labor theory of value. Georgia freedmen in the summer of 1865 divided up a farm among themselves and explained to the irate owner, "they had been working for massa all their lives, they had a right to the land in payment for their labor." *(The Weekly Reporter*, Henderson, Ky., August 24, 1865, from Richmond *Whig* and New York *Journal of Commerce*.) Samuel Childress, writing from Nashville, Tennessee, November 29, 1865, underscored the gloomy outlook for freedmen unable to purchase land. "Our race," he wrote, "has tilled this land for ages; whatever wealth has been accumulated South has been acquired mainly by our labor.—The profits of it, have gone to increase the pride and wickedness of our old masters. . . . The small oppressor was the State; the great oppressor was the United States." Childress wanted only the opportunity to purchase land at prices freed people could afford, "and on such terms as would enable our people in a reasonable time to have a home of their own, on which they might hope to earn a living, and educate their children" (New York *Anglo-African*, December 16, 1865). I am much in the debt of Leslie Rowland for these items.

88. Aptheker, *To Be Free*, p. 144; Richardson, *Negro in Reconstruction of Florida*, p. 132; "Colored Convention in Augusta," *Southern Recorder*, January 30, 1866, cited in Ethel Maude Christler, "Participation of Negroes in the Government of Georgia, 1867-1870," unpublished M.A. thesis, Atlanta University, 1933, p. 5.

89. *New York Times*, April 19, May 30, 1867; Hamilton James Eckenrode, *The Political History of Virginia During Reconstruction* (Baltimore: The Johns Hopkins Press, 1904), pp. 68, 81; McConnell, *Negroes and Their Treatment in Virginia*, pp. 43-44, 112.

90. Carol K. Rothrock Bleser, *The Promised Land: The History of the South Carolina Land Commission, 1869-1890* (Columbia: University of South Carolina Press, 1969), p. 159.

CHAPTER 7

1. William H. Pease and Jane Pease, *Black Utopia, Negro Communal Experiments in America* (Madison: University of Wisconsin Press, 1963).

2. Michael Moohr, "The Economic Impact of Slave Emancipation on British Guiana, 1832-1852," *The Economic History Review,* 2nd ser., 25 (November 1972), 588-608; Raymond T. Smith, *British Guiana* (New York: Oxford University Press, 1962), pp. 188-189; William Grant Sewell, *The Ordeal of Free Labor in the West Indies* (1859) in Lydia Maria Child, *The Right Way, the Safe Way, Proved by Emancipation in the West Indies, and Elsewhere* (New York, 1862); Leo Despres, "Differential Adaptations and Micro-cultural Evolution in Guyana," in Norman E. Whitten, Jr., and John F. Szwed, eds., *Afro-American Anthropology, Contemporary Perspectives* (New York: Free Press, 1970), pp. 279-280; Rawle Farley, "The Rise of the Peasantry in British Guiana," *Social and Economic Studies,* 2 (March 1954), 93-95.

3. *Freedmen's Advocate,* April 1864; Willie Lee Rose, *Rehearsal for Reconstruction: The Port Royal Experiment* (New York and Indianapolis, 1964), p. 315. In the March 1863 sales, several plantations went to blacks who pooled their small savings. About 2,000 acres were obtained in this manner. See Rose, *Rehearsal,* p. 215.

4. A. P. Ketchum to Brigadier General R. Saxton, Beaufort, S.C., April 30, 1864, in *Freedman's Advocate,* July and August, 1864; Rose, *Rehearsal,* pp. 284-285.

5. Ketchum to Saxton, April 30, 1864; Preemption Papers, January 1864, Bureau of Internal Revenue, U.S. Direct Tax Commissioners, RG58, National Archives; *The American Baptist,* April 26, 1864.

6. Rose, *Rehearsal,* pp. 287-290, 282; Ketchum to Saxton, April 30, 1864. The direct tax commissioners issued 617 certificates for ten- to twenty-acre homesteads sold to black heads of families between December 10, 1863, and the termination of the program on May 17, 1865. *National Intelligencer,* December 30, 1865.

7. Ketchum to Saxton, April 30, 1864.

8. James M. McPherson, *The Negro's Civil War* (New York: Vintage Books, 1965), from Philadelphia *Press,* May 31, 1864.

9. U.S. Congress, *Senate Executive Documents,* No. 26, 37th Cong., 3rd sess. (Serial 1149), pp. 5-6; American Freedmen's Inquiry Commission interviews in Letters Received by the Office of the Adjutant General, Main Series, 1861-1870, National Archives, RG94; Whitelaw Reid, *After the War* (repr., New York: Harper & Row, 1965), pp. 146-147, 564.

10. *National Freedman,* April 1865; Rose, *Rehearsal for Reconstruction,* p. 331.

11. Records of the Bureau of Refugees, Freedmen and Abandoned Lands, Louisiana, National Archives, RG105, N.A.; Howard A. White, *The Freedmen's Bureau in Louisiana* (Baton Rouge, 1970), p. 56; New

Orleans *Tribune,* September 5, 1865, August 30, 31, 1865.

12. BRFAL, Louisiana, Applications for Land, 1865, RG105, N.A.

13. New Orleans *Tribune,* January 15, 1865; Oliver Otis Howard, *An Autobiography* (New York, 1908), vol. II, p. 224; McFeely, *Yankee Stepfather, General O. O. Howard and the Freedmen* (New Haven, Conn.: Yale University Press, 1968), p. 168; W. E. B. Du Bois, *Black Reconstruction in America,* (New York, 1935; reprint ed., S. A. Russell, 1956), pp. 456-458.

14. New Orleans *Tribune,* February 2, 23, 24, 28, 1865; April 11, 1865; August 3, 1865.

15. U.S. Congress, *House Executive Documents,* No. 70, 39th Cong., 1st sess., pp. 390-391; Reid, *After the War,* pp. 221-222; *New York Times,* April 29, 1866.

16. Virginia Writers' Project, *The Negro in Virginia,* pp. 222-223; Du Bois, *Black Reconstruction,* p. 666; Du Bois, *The Negro Landholder in Georgia,* pp. 735-736; Bleser, *Promised Land,* pp. 38-39.

17. Davis Tillson to Major Hastings, ASAC, Albany, Ga., November 15, 1865; Tillson to Hastings, November 30, 1865; Tillson to General O. O. Howard, December 20, 1865. BRFAL Georgia, Letters Sent, RG 105, N.A.; Hastings to Tillson, Albany, Ga., January 7, 1866, in *House Executive Documents* No. 70, 39th Cong., 1st Sess., pp. 316-317; Citizens of Dougherty County to Freedmen's Bureau, Albany, Ga., July 17, 1866, and Samuel Brown to Tillson, September 14, 1866, Georgia Assistant Commissioner, Unregistered Letters (Box 11), RG 105, N.A. (Both letters courtesy of Leslie Rowland.)

18. *House Executive Documents* No. 70, 39th Cong., 1st sess., pp. 264-267; Vernon Lane Wharton, *The Negro in Mississippi,* pp. 39-42; John Eaton, *Grant, Lincoln and the Freedmen* (New York, 1907), p. 166.

19. John Andrew Jackson to O. O. Howard, Boston, March 10, 1868. Letters Received, Office of the Commissioner BRFAL, RG 105, N.A.; Reverend B. B. Spier to O. O. Howard, Newbern, N.C., January 13, 1869. Papers of the House Committee on Freedmen's Affairs, RG 233, N.A.

20. Christie Farnham Pope, "Southern Homesteads for Negroes," *Agricultural History,* 44 (April 1970), 202-205, 210-211; W. W. Granger to Brevet Major John Tyler, Little Rock, February 1, 1867, BRFAL Arkansas, RG 105, N.A.

21. *Senate Executive Documents,* No. 6, 39th Cong., 2nd sess., p. 57; O. Morgan to Joseph S. Wilson, Commissioner, General Land Office, Tallahassee, May 30, 1867, BRFAL, RG 105; Joe M. Richardson, *The Negro in the Reconstruction of Florida* (Tallahassee: Florida State University Press, 1965), pp. 75-76; Pope, "Southern Homesteads for Negroes," p. 205.

So eager were freedmen to begin work that some of them did not wait for the paper work to be completed. They began to improve the lands on which they were located. But most freedmen endured the bureaucratic halters. One of four Florida locating agents reported that he had located 573 homesteads on U.S. lands between April 1867 and October 1868. Some of the freedmen thus settled also rented improved lands, where they raised provision crops. Besides these public-land occupants, an unknown number of freedmen purchased or leased small farms from private sources and planted ten acres or more "under their own control." See Locating Agents Reports, BRFAL Florida, especially those of S. F. Halliday, May 14, 1867, to September 15, 1868, RG 105.

22. J. J. Saville to William H. Sterling, New Orleans, July 1, 1867, Commissioner, Letters Received, BRFAL, RG 105.

23. J. J. Saville to G. W. Julian, *Congressional Globe,* 40th Cong., 2nd sess., p. 807 (read by Julian in the House of Representatives, January 28, 1868, during his fight to return the Opelousas grant to the federal government); Claude F. Oubre, " 'Forty Acres and a Mule': Louisiana and the Southern Homestead Act," *Louisiana History,* 17 (Spring 1976), pp. 143-157; Saville to Sterling, January 17, 1867, Commissioner, Letters Received BRFAL, RG 105.

24. John B. Meyers, "Education of Alabama Freedmen During Presidential Reconstruction, 1865-1867," *Journal of Negro Education,* 40 (Spring 1971), 168; *Senate Reports,* No. 693, part 3, 46th Cong., 2nd sess. (Washington, D.C.: U.S. Government Printing Office, 1880), p. 142. Hereafter *Exodus Testimony.*

25. Warren Hofnagle, "The Southern Homestead Act: Its Origins and Operation," *The Historian,* 32 (August 1970), 612-629; W. W. Granger to Dr. Kirkwood, Little Rock, February 24, 1867; General E. O. C. Ord to O. O. Howard, March 18, 1867; Joseph S. Wilson to O. O. Howard, August 23, 1867, Commissioner, BRFAL, Letters Received, RG 105, N.A. Mississippi's locating agent and the freedmen he tried to aid were even more frustrated by the general resistance or indifference to their efforts. J. L. Roberts finally resigned in September 1868 after failing to obtain authorization to hire a surveyor. He charged that General A. C. Gillem, assistant commissioner of the Bureau in Mississippi, did not favorably consider his requests and suggestions. Moreover, white citizens refused to give him information about government lands, and he could not find maps. Roberts to John Tyler, Acting Assistant Adjutant General, BRFAL, Jackson, Miss., September 8 and 14, 1868, Locating Agent, Jackson, Miss., Letters Sent, RG 105, N.A.

26. A. K. Farrar to Colonel James Biddle, Kingston, Miss., February 19 1868; Commissioner, BRFAL, Letters Received, RG 105, N.A.

27. Ibid.

28. BRFAL, Mississippi, Letters Received; Mississippi Marriage Records, 1864-1866; both in RG 105, N.A.; Muster Rolls, 6th U.S. Colored Heavy Artillery Regiment, 1866.

29. Reports from Sub-Officers, September-October, 1867, Records of the Assistant Commissioner, BRFAL Mississippi, RG 105, N.A.

30. Farrar to Biddle, February 19, 1868; George Hitchen to Charles Sumner, Natchez, January 23, January 24, 1868; Hitchen to BRFAL, Miss., February 18, 1868, Commissioner, Letters Received, BRFAL, RG 105, N.A.

31. New York *Tribune,* June 30, 1869; Joel Williamson, *After Slavery: The Negro in South Carolina During Reconstruction, 1861-1877* (Chapel Hill: University of North Carolina Press, 1965), p. 156; Carol K. Rothrock Bleser, *The Promised Land: The History of the South Carolina Land Commission, 1869-1890* (Columbia: University of South Carolina Press, 1969), pp. 17-19; J. W. Alvord, *Letters from the South Relating to the Condition of the Freedmen Addressed to Major General O. O. Howard* (Washington, 1870), pp. 9-10, 15; *New York Times,* August 17, 1873.

32. Hortense Powdermaker, *After Freedom* (New York: Viking Press, 1939), pp. 95-98.

33. H. E. Cobb, "The Negro as a Free Laborer in Alabama, 1865-1875," *The Midwest Journal* (Fall 1954), 35; *Condition of Affairs in Alabama, House Executive Documents,* No. 262, 43rd Cong., 2nd sess. (Washington, D.C.: U.S. Government Printing Office, 1875), pp. 1113-1117; *Exodus Testimony,* part 2, 46th Cong., 2nd sess., p. 401.

34. *Ku Klux Conspiracy,* Alabama, p. 1739.

35. Lawrence D. Rice, *The Negro in Texas 1874-1900* (Baton Rouge: Louisiana State University Press, 1971), pp. 179-180, 207.

36. Teodor Shanin, "Peasantry as a Political Factor," in T. Shanin, ed., *Peasants and Peasant Societies* (Middlesex, England, and Baltimore: Penguin Books, 1971), p. 256.

37. Sidney W. Mintz, *Caribbean Transformations,* chap. 9, "Houses and Yards Among Caribbean Peasantries," pp. 225-250.

38. Ibid.

39. Philip D. Curtin, *Two Jamaicas: The Role of Ideas in a Tropical Colony* (Cambridge, Mass.: Harvard University Press, 1955).

CHAPTER 8

1. William Ivy Hair, *Bourbonism and Agrarian Protest: Louisiana Politics, 1877-1900* (Baton Rouge: Louisiana State University Press, 1969); *New York Times,* October 16, 17, 19, 1878.

2. *Transactions of the Kansas State Historical Society*, IX (1905-1906), Topeka, 1906, p. 385; *Ku Klux Conspiracy*, Georgia, p. 739.

3. Nashville *Daily Press and Times*, August 11, 1866.

4. Ibid., September 28, 1869.

5. *Transactions of the Kansas State Historical Society*, p. 385; *Exodus Testimony*, part 3, p. 379.

6. *The Colored Patriot* (Topeka, Kansas), May 4, 1882, cited in Martin E. Dann, ed., *The Black Press, 1827-1890: The Quest for National Identity* (New York: G. P. Putnam's Sons, 1971), pp. 275-276; an early group of 280 emigrants in 1878 viewed Kansas as a land of milk and honey. They expected to receive twenty acres of land, a team of mules, a farm wagon, household goods, and food supplied by the government *(New York Times*, April 7, 1879).

7. *Congressional Record*, 46th Cong., 2nd sess. (June 14, 1880), p. 4526.

8. Wharton, *The Negro in Mississippi*, p. 113.

9. *Exodus Testimony*, part 3, p. 381.

10. George W. Williams, *History of the Negro Race in America*, 2 vols. (New York, 1883; Arno Press ed., 1968), vol. II, p. 539, citing Chicago *Daily InterOcean*, April 9 [1880].

11. Henry Adams's work, which will be discussed shortly, is derived from his testimony before the Senate investigating committee and recorded in *Exodus Testimony*, part 2, pp. 122 ff. and pp. 175-192.

12. Ibid, pp. 141-142.

13. Ibid., pp. 151-152.

14. Ibid, pp. 252-254; Rice, *The Negro in Texas*, pp. 201-207; Tindall, *The Negro in South Carolina*, pp. 170-172.

15. *Transactions of the Kansas State Historical Society*, p. 386.

16. Aptheker, *Documentary History*, pp. 724-726; Du Bois, *The Souls of Black Folk* (Greenwich, Conn.: Fawcett ed., 1961), p. 116. The Douglass-Greener debate occurred during the September 1879 meeting of the American Social Science Association. Greener was then a professor at Howard University. He had been a member of the faculty at the University of South Carolina. Douglass opposed the migration from the South. He insisted that black people should stay and demand better terms. "Exodus is medicine, not food," he said, conceding its utility only as a tactic but not as a strategy. Greener denied that the exodus was "the sole, proper or only permanent remedy for the aggravated relation of landlord and tenant at the South."

17. *Exodus Testimony*, part 2, p. 235.

18. Michael A. Gordon, "The Labor Boycott in New York City, 1880-1886," *Labor History*, 16 (Spring 1975), 184-229; James J. Green, "Amer-

ican Catholics and the Irish Land League, 1879-1882," *Catholic Historical Review*, 35 (April 1949), 19-42.

19. A valuable, detailed, and provocative study of the migration to Kansas appeared while this book was in galley-proof stage: Nell Irvin Painter, *Exodusters: Black Migration to Kansas after Reconstruction* (New York: Alfred A. Knopf, 1977). Painter finds great cleavages between "leading men" and lower classes among blacks on the Exodus, but she agrees that the movement originated in rural laborers' needs.

CHAPTER 9

1. James S. Fisher, "Negro Farm Ownership in the South," *Annals of the Association of American Geographers*, 63 (December 1973), 482; *New York Times*, December 7, 1972.

2. Fisher, "Negro Farm Ownership," p. 483.

3. W. E. B. Du Bois, "The Negro Landholder of Georgia," *Bulletin of the United States Department of Labor* No. 35, (Washington, D.C.: U.S. Government Printing Office, 1901), p. 665.

4. Tindall, *South Carolina Negroes*, p. 103; Du Bois, *Black Reconstruction in America*, p. 6; *Exodus Testimony*, part 1, p. 50; Wharton, *The Negro in Mississippi*, p. 61-62; Virginia Writers' Project, *The Negro in Virginia*, p. 223.

5. C. Vann Woodward, *Origins of the New South, 1877-1913* (Baton Rouge: Louisiana State University Press, 1951), p. 178; William S. Mc-Feely, "Unfinished Business: The Freedmen's Bureau and Federal Action in Race Relations," in Nathan I. Huggins, Martin Kilson, Daniel M. Fox, eds., *Key Issues in the Afro-American Experience* (New York: Harcourt Brace Jovanovich, 1971), vol. 2, pp. 5-25.

6. Abram Colby to A. G. Eberhart, March 1, 1866, BRFAL Georgia, Greensboro Letters Received, RG 105, N.A.; LaWanda Cox and John H. Cox, eds., *Reconstruction, the Negro, and the New South* (New York: Harper Torchbooks, 1973), p. 341.

7. McFeely, "Unfinished Business," p. 15; Records of the Assistant Commissioner, States of Georgia and Mississippi, 1865-1869, BRFAL, RG 105, N.A.; W. F. Eaton, Bureau Agent, St. Simon's Island, to BRFAL Savannah, August 24, 1865, RG 105; Williamson, *After Slavery*, p. 306.

8. Woodward, *Origins of the New South*, pp. 206-207; Cox and Cox, *Reconstruction, the Negro, and the New South*, p. 337.

9. Monthly Reports, Subdistricts: Philadelphia, Robert P. Gardner, Subassistant Commissioner, January 31, 1868; Grenada and Greenville, January 31, 1868; Corinth, January 31, 1868; De Kalb, January 31, 1868; Columbus, February 4, 1868. All in Narrative Reports from Subordinate

Officers, BRFAL Mississippi, January-June 1868 (Microcopy 826, Roll 32). RG 105, N.A.

10. Ibid., Grenada report, January 31, 1868.

11. Ibid., Natchez report, James Biddle, February 12, 1868; Yazoo City, January 31, 1868; Port Gibson, W. H. Eldridge, January 31, 1868.

12. Du Bois, "The Negro Landholder in Georgia," pp. 667, 674-675.

13. Herbert G. Gutman kindly provided these computations.

14. R. Sutch and R. Ransom, "The Ex-Slave in the Post-Bellum South: A Study of the Economic Impact of Racism in a Market Environment," *Journal of Economic History,* 33 (March 1973), 131-148; William E. Highsmith, "Louisiana Landholding During War and Reconstruction," *Louisiana Historical Quarterly* 38 (January 1955), 41-42.

15. Aptheker, *Documentary History,* pp. 635-636.

16. Ibid., pp. 684-685.

17. William L. Bittle and Gilbert E. Geis, "Racial Self-Fulfillment and the Rise of an All-Negro Community in Oklahoma," *Phylon,* 18 (Third Quarter, 1957), reprinted in August Meier and Elliott Rudwick, eds., *The Making of Black America* (New York: Atheneum, 1969), pp. 106-112. Boley was one of fourteen all-black towns in Oklahoma, in 1925, and one of seventy in the United States. R. Edgar Iles, "Boley—An Exclusively Negro Town in Oklahoma," *Opportunity* (August 1925), 232.

18. *The People's Advocate* (Washington, D.C.), February 23, 1884, cited in Dann, ed., *The Black Press,* p. 281.

19. Herbert G. Gutman, "The Negro and the United Mine Workers of America: The Career and Letters of Richard L. Davis and Something of Their Meaning: 1890-1910," in Julius Jacobson, ed., *The Negro and the American Labor Movement* (New York: Anchor Books, 1968), p. 115.

20. R. L. Smith, "Village Improvement Among the Negroes," *Outlook,* 64 (March 31, 1900), 735-736; Allen W. Jones, "The Role of Tuskegee Institute in the Education of Black Farmers," *The Journal of Negro History,* 60 (April 1975), 252-267.

21. Du Bois, *The Souls of Black Folk,* pp. 113-114.

22. *De Bow's* cited in Highsmith, "Louisiana Landholding," p. 44; *New York Times,* May 10, 1879.

23. John Lee Eighmy, "The Baptists and Slavery: An Examination of The Origins and Benefits of Segregation," in Norval D. Glenn and Charles M. Bonjean, *Blacks in the United States* (San Francisco: Chandler, 1969) p. 299.

24. B. A. Botkin, ed., *Lay My Burden Down: A Folk History of Slavery* (Chicago: University of Chicago Press, 1945), p. 78.

Appendixes

APPENDIX I

Abandoned Land Held by the Freedmen's Bureau, 1865

State	Amount of Property Now in Possession of Bureau of Refugees, Freedmen, and Abandoned Lands					Amount of Property Returned	
	Number of Acres of Land				Number of Pieces of Town Property	Number of Acres of Land	Number of Pieces of Town Property
	Cultivated	Uncultivated	Unclassified	Aggregate			
Georgia and South Carolina	9,364	50,799	374,837	435,000	398		384
Kentucky and Tennessee	10,177	29,072	25,880	65,129	414		
Missouri and Arkansas	18,736			18,736	72		
Alabama			2,116	2,116	13		
Virginia	2,625	49,110	23,918	75,653	34	26,730	310
North Carolina	4,868	9,207	22,267	36,342	112	50,029	287
Mississippi and Louisiana (part)	50,751	4	8,525	59,280	52	11,411	60
Louisiana	62,528			62,528	501		
Maryland and Virginia (part)	2,282	5,027	6,497	13,806			136
Total	161,331	143,219	464,040	768,590	1,596	88,170	1,177

SOURCE: *Autobiography of Oliver Otis Howard* (New York: The Baker & Taylor Company, 1908), vol. 2, p. 231.

APPENDIX II

Freedmen, Women, and Children in Contraband Camps, 1863-1864

The Sea Islands of South Carolina and Georgia	15,000
Newbern and Eastern North Carolina	20,000
Norfolk and Portsmouth, Va., and vicinity	20,000
Fortress Monroe, and vicinity	10,000
Yorktown, and vicinity	8,000
Alexandria, Va., and vicinity	10,000
Arlington, Va.	3,500
Washington, D.C.	7,500
Cairo	500
Columbus	801
Island No. 10	1,000
Fort Pillow	311
Memphis, including President's Island, etc.	5,682
Helena	1,925
Island No. 63	75
Mouth of White River	500
Little Rock, Ark.	700
Pine Bluff	1,500
Duvall's Bluff	200
Skipwith's Landing	500
Goodrich's Landing	1,600
Paw Paw Island	870
Milliken's Bend	625

A P P E N D I X II (continued)

Van Buren Hospital	575
Young's Point	3,000
Burnett's Plantation	1,425
Blake's Plantation	625
Palmyra Bend	1,325
Natchez (vicinity)	2,100
Vandalia	930
Port Adams	2,000
Port Hudson	3,000
Baton Rouge	2,000
New Orleans	6,000
City of Memphis	5,000
City of Vicksburg	2,000
City of Natchez	5,000
Since this estimate was made, there are reported	
to have arrived at Vicksburg	4,500
At New Orleans	3,000
Black refugees, who followed Gen. Sherman's army	
on its return from military expeditions to Merriden,	
Miss., and other parts of Tennessee, Northern	
Alabama, and Georgia—probably about	30,000
Total	183,000

SOURCE: *Freedmen's Advocate,* June 1864.

Strife Reflecting New Labor Relations,
August 1 to December 31, 1865: Report of Outrages to Adjutant General's Office

Number of Cases Reported by Assistant Commissioners	South Carolina	North Carolina (Jan. 9, 1866)	Department of Mississippi	Virginia (Jan. 27, 1866)	Alabama (Jan. 10, 1866)	Department of Tennessee (Jan. 8, 1866)	TOTALS
Assault and Battery							
White v. Black	60	56 7*	4 10*	30 21*	14 17*	53 9*	281
Black v. White	123	26	1 1*	4		4	159
Larceny							
White	90	29	2	1	1	2	125
Black	605	45		2		1	653
Disorderly Conduct							
White	25						25
Black	45						45
Drunkenness							
White	135						135
Black	55						55
Manslaughter							
White				1			1
Black							

Number of Cases Reported by Assistant Commissioners	South Carolina	North Carolina (Jan. 9, 1866)	Department of Mississippi	Virginia (Jan. 27, 1866)	Alabama (Jan. 10, 1866)	Department of Tennessee (Jan. 8, 1866)	TOTALS
Murder							
White		13	22	7	4	3	49
Black		1				2	3
Rape or Attempted Rape							
White		3					3
Black		5/1				1/2	6/3
Arson							
White			2	1		1	4
Black		7					7
Kidnapping of Black Children							
White		2	1				3
Attempt to Poison							
White							
Black				1			1

SOURCE: Report of Outrages, August 1 to December 31, 1865, in "Reports of Racial Violence in the South and the Consequent Actions Taken by Military Authorities, Apr. 1865-Jan. 1866," Letters Received by the Office of the Adjutant General, Main Series, 1861-1870 (Reel 505, Microcopy 619, Record Group 94) National Archives.

* With a drawn weapon.

APPENDIX IV

Freedmen's Complaints, June-December 1866:
A Sampling of Two Cotton-Producing Counties

Nature of the Complaints	Albemarle County, Virginia, June-August	Dallas County, Alabama, October-December	Totals
Employer refuses to pay or discharges freedmen without pay or share of crop	26	34	60
Employer drives off freedmen	2	3	5
Assault and battery on freed men/women	4	15	19
Freedmen v. freedmen (miscellaneous complaints)	17	2	19
Illegal arrests for "vagrancy" or "curfew violation"		18	18
Miscellaneous	5	11	16
Unlawfully holds freedmen's children	2	2	4

SOURCE: Freedmen's Complaint Books, BRFAL, Record group 105, National Archives.

APPENDIX V

Medway Church, Liberty county
Nov. 28th 1865

To Col. H. F. Sickles
Com^r Beauro of R. F. & A. L.
Dear Sir

We the People of *Liberty county, State* of *georgia,* Set Free from the op-
pression of Slavery, Desire through our *Delegates, Messrs. Toney Golden,
Gabriel Andrews, & Toney Axon* To appeal to you *asking aid* and *counsel*
in this our *Distressed condition,* We *Learned* from the Address of general
Howard that we were to *Return* to the *Plantation* and *Work for our For-
mer owners* at a *Reasonable contract as Freemen;* and find, a *Home* and
Labour, Provided We can agree But these owners of *Plantation* out here
Says they only will Hire or Take the *Prime Hands* and our *old* and *Infirm
Mothers* and *Fathers* and our *children Will not Be Provided for;* and this
you Will See Sir Put us in *confusion;* yet there are some that have *Become
free are upon Plantations, that Do not Know of their Freedom and we
Dare not Mention that they are free. We cannot Labour for the Land own-
ers and Know that our Infirm and children are Not Provided for,—and not
Allowed to educate* or *Learn more than they were permitted in Slavery,—*
our *School* that was established in the county are *Broken up and We are
Destitute of Religious Worship, having No Home or Place to Live when
We Leave the Plantations Returned* to *our Former owners,—We are A
Working Class of People* and We are *Willing* and are *Desirous* to Work
for A *Fair compensation,—*But to *return* to *work upon the Terms that
are at Present offered to us, Would Be We Think going Backe into the
State of Slavery that we have just to some extent Been Delivered from.*
    We *Appeal* to *you Sir and through you* to the *Rulers* of the *country*
in our *Distressed state, and Declare that we feel unsettled as Sheep Without A Shepard, and Beg your Advice* and *Assistance, and Believe Sir that
this is an Earnest Appeal from A Poor But Loyal Earnest People*
        Most Respectfully Submitted for your consideration In Be-
half of the People of Liberty county By

*William Toney Golden
Gabriel Andrews
Toney Axon*

APPENDIX VI

Petition

To Col C C Sibley Assistant Commissioner of the Freedmen's Bureau for the State of Georgia

We the colored labours of the city of Savannah pray that you will be pleased to protect us and your families, from *Starvation* and threated outrage of the Mayor of the said city under under [sic] a misconception of the word *Porter* in the city laws which we have had no voice in enacting; notwithstanding all just laws, derive their power from the consent of the governed. This city "Ordinance or regulation," is a violation of the first section of the Civil rights bill, "the same right to make and enforce contracts" on the docks "and to full and equal benefit of all laws and proceedings" which we have not.

And your humble Petitioners further says, that they are not Porters nor Stewarts, but Labors and the city Ordinance requires that all Porters shall have a Badge which does not in law apply to a common Labor. 10 Georg 4 Chapter 40th Section 14 and also law Dictionarys.

And your humble Petitioners comes, and call your attention to the 14th Section of Freedmen's bureau bill of June 11th 1866 in these words to wit "That in every State or district where the ordinary course of judicial proceedings has been interrupted by the rebellion, and until the same shall be duly represented in the Congress of the United States personal liberty, enjoyment and including the constitutional right to bear arms shall be secured, without respect to race or color or previous condition of Slavery. And the President shall through the Commissioner, and the Officers of the Bureau extend military protection, and have military jurisdiction over all cases & questions concerning the free enjoyment of such Immunities & rights." Sec. 14. Therefore we pray, that you may *"extend* military protection," to the Poor colored Labors of the city of Savannah that we may not be made paupers under the unconstitutional statutes and ordinance, regulations or custom not yet recognized by the Congress of the United States.

James Mackey of the Union League and 200 others

A Alpeora Bradley
Atty for
Petitioners

SOURCE: Records of the Assistant Commissioner for the State of Georgia, BRFAL, 1865-1869, Unbound Miscellaneous Papers. Record Group 105, National Archives

Bibliographical Note

An indispensable reference work is *A List of References for the History of Agriculture in the Southern United States, 1865-1900,* compiled and edited by Helen H. Edwards (Agricultural History Center, University of California, Davis, March 1971). Also valuable are the quarterly listings of recent periodical literature in *The Journal of American History* and the annual listings of *The Journal of Southern History* and *Civil War History.*

Manuscripts

The records of the Bureau of Refugees, Freedmen, and Abandoned Lands (better known as the Freedmen's Bureau) Record Group 105, National Archives, Washington, D.C., constituted the major manuscript source of this book. Only a fraction of the massive collection was used. As the Bureau maintained headquarters in Washington and subcommissioners in each of the former Confederate states, as well as in Maryland, Kentucky, and Tennessee (loyal slave states during the war), and as subassistant commissioners and local Bureau agents were located in hundreds of places, their correspondence and other papers, reports, and orders quite expectedly make a veritable paper mountain that the researcher must dig into. This could be an endless but possibly a gratifying pursuit. The Bureau papers for localities of Georgia, South Carolina, and Mississippi were especially selected for this book. However, local Bureau records of North Carolina, Virginia, Alabama, Florida, and Louisiana were also used. The papers of the Bureau's Land Division, responsible for the disposition of the abandoned lands, proved disappointingly slim. This is understandable because the division quickly lost its reason for existence when lands were restored to former owners. Registers and Letters Received by the Commissioner, 1865-1872, General Otis Oliver Howard, in Washington (on Microcopy No. 752), proved useful in locating letters that had been sent up from assistant commissioners. Two invaluable bibliographical aids to the Bureau's records are: (1) *Preliminary Inventory of the Records of the Field Offices of the Bureau of Refugees, Freedmen,*

and Abandoned Lands, parts 1 and 2, compiled by Elaine Everly and
Willna Pacheli (National Archives and Records Service, General Services
Administration, Washington, D.C., 1973); and (2) *National Archives
Microfilm Publications,* pamphlet accompanying Microcopy No. 752 and
other microcopies in RG 105.

Another important manuscript source for this study was the collection of papers and record of testimony taken by the American Freedmen's Inquiry Commission, 1863-1864, in Letters Received by the Office
of the Adjutant General, Main Series, 1861-1870, RG 94, N.A. Also useful in that record group were "Reports Relating to Freedmen and Destitute Whites in the Department of Virginia, 1864-1865" and "Reports of
Racial Violence in the South and of Consequent Action Taken by Military Authorities, April 1865 to January 1866." All of these are on microfilm rolls 199-201, 429, and 505, respectively (Microcopy M-619).

Record Group 94 also aided in identifying members of Mississippi's
black regiments; see Muster Rolls and Regimental Papers, the Muster Out
Rolls of the 6th U.S. Colored Heavy Artillery Regiment.

The American Freedmen's Inquiry Commission Papers at the Houghton Library, Harvard University, furnish an important complement to
the testimony taken in the field and deposited in RG 94.

Information that helped the study of freedmen communities came
from Record Group 101, National Archives. These contained various
records of the ill-fated Freedmen's Savings and Trust Company, 1865-
1874.

Considerable light was shed on the freedmen by U.S. Congress publications: *Senate Executive Documents,* No. 27, 39th Cong., 1st sess.,
(serial 1238), and *House Executive Documents,* No. 70, 39th Cong., 1st
sess., containing reports of the assistant commissioners of the Freedmen's
Bureau in late 1865 and early 1866 on the exodus of 1879-1880, *House
Executive Documents,* No. 262 (serial 1661), 1875, and *Senate Reports,*
Nos. 671 to 725, and especially No. 693, 46th Cong., 1st and 2nd sess.
(serials 1899 and 1900), 1880. *Testimony Taken by the Joint Select
Committee to Inquire into the Condition of Affairs in the Late Insurrectionary States,* 13 vols. (Washington, D.C.: U.S. Government Printing
Office, 1872), revealed much about local black leaders and their com-
munities. The notes to this volume cite additional congressional documents
that I used. Also consulted were the *Congressional Globe* and *Official
Records of the Rebellion.*

Several other manuscript collections in the National Archives were
also useful in tracing some Treasury Department agents' activities. One
of these was the collection of records of the Bureau of Internal Revenue,
U.S. Direct Tax Commissioners, Record Group 58, National Archives.

A small number of private manuscript collections helped to fill in some details of the freedmen's quest for land. Most useful were the William F. Allen Papers, State Historical Society of Wisconsin, Madison. Others consulted were the Alexander K. Farrar Papers, Louisiana State University Library, Baton Rouge, the Abishai Scofield Papers, Burton Historical Collection, Detroit Public Library, and some of the Mississippi teachers' reports and letters in the American Missionary Association Archives, microfilm copy at the library of the University of Maryland, College Park.

Occasional hints of what former slaves really experienced during Reconstruction came from Federal Writers' Project, *Slave Narratives: A Folk History of Slavery in the United States from Interviews with Former Slaves* (Washington, D.C.: Library of Congress, 1941). These have been published in nineteen volumes by Greenwood Press (Westport, Conn.), 1973.

Inasmuch as freedmen did not make systematic written records of their activities, I was forced to consult the reports of men close to them, the freedmen's or Negro Affairs officers. These were Thomas W. Conway, *Report on the Condition of the Freedmen of the Department of the Gulf,* Sept. 9, 1864 (New Orleans, 1864), *Final Report of the Bureau of Free Labor, Department of the Gulf* (New Orleans, 1865); John Eaton, *Report of the General Superintendent of Freedmen, Department of the Tennessee and State of Arkansas* (Memphis, Tenn., 1865); Reverend Horace James, *Annual Report of the Superintendent of Negro Affairs in North Carolina, 1864* (Boston, 1865); John W. Alvord, *Letters from the South Relative to the Condition of the Freedmen Addressed to Major General O. O. Howard* (Washington, D.C., 1870); Reverend Joseph Warren, *Extracts from the Reports of Superintendents of Freedmen Compiled from Records in the Office of Colonel John Eaton, Jr., General Superintendent of Freedmen, Department of the Tennessee and State of Arkansas* (Vicksburg, 1864).

Similarly useful as sympathetic surrogates of the freedmen were reports of the freedmen's aid societies. Outstanding among them are: *Second Annual Report, New England Freedmen's Aid Society* (Boston, 1864); *Statistics of the Operations of the Executive Board of the Friends Association of Philadelphia and its Vicinity, for the Relief of Colored Freedmen* (Philadelphia, 1864) and *Second Report of the Executive Board, Friends Association of Philadelphia for the Relief of Colored Freedmen* (Philadelphia, 1865).

NEWSPAPERS AND PERIODICALS

Expressions and news of Afro-Americans were found in the black newspapers, the Nashville *Colored Tennessean* and the Augusta, Georgia, *Loyal*

Georgian. Outstanding as a voice of the New Orleans black community was the New Orleans *Tribune.*

Among the mass-circulation newspapers of the 1860s and 1870s the useful ones were the New York *Tribune,* New York *Herald,* and *New York Times,* also the Nashville *Daily Press and Times,* and the *Savannah Republican.*

A rich source of information about freedmen came through the monthly newspapers and magazines published by various organizations in the freedmen's aid movement. A number of items from these publications were generously provided by Herbert G. Gutman, who researched them for his *The Black Family in Slavery and Freedom, 1750-1925* (New York: Pantheon Books, 1976). This book obviously is basic to my own studies of the Afro-American community. I consulted the *American Freedman, National Freedmen, American Missionary, Freedmen's Record for the Relief of Freedmen, Pennsylvania Freedmen's Bulletin, Freedmen's Advocate,* and William Lloyd Garrison's *The Liberator.*

A large number of secondary works went into the making of this book. They are cited in the notes to each of the chapters. Among the useful books the most enlightening on the general history of the freedmen were: James S. Allen, *Reconstruction: The Battle for Democracy* (New York: International Publishers, 1937); W. E. B. Du Bois, *Black Reconstruction* (New York, 1935; reprint ed., S. A. Russell, 1956); Willie Lee Rose, *Rehearsal for Reconstruction* (New York: Bobbs-Merrill, 1964).

Perceptive studies of freedmen in several Southern states are in: Francis Butler Simkins and Robert Hilliard Woody, *South Carolina During Reconstruction* (Chapel Hill, N.C.: University of North Carolina Press, 1932; reprinted Gloucester, Mass: Peter Smith, 1966); Peter Robert Kolchin, *First Freedom: The Response of Alabama's Blacks to Emancipation and Reconstruction* (Westport, Conn.: Greenwood Press, 1972); Joe M. Richardson, *The Negro in the Reconstruction of Florida* (Tallahassee, Florida State University, 1965); Alrutheus Ambush Taylor, *The Negro in South Carolina During Reconstruction* (Washington, D.C.: Association for the Study of Negro Life and History, 1924); Vernon Lane Wharton, *The Negro in Mississippi, 1865-1890* (New York: Harper & Row, 1965; reprint of original ed., Chapel Hill, 1947); Joel Williamson, *After Slavery: The Negro in South Carolina During Reconstruciton, 1861-1877* (Chapel Hill: University of North Carolina Press, 1965). In this connection, we still lack book-length studies of Arkansas, Georgia, and Texas freedmen for the Reconstruction era.

Chapters in three scholarly local histories aided this study: George C. Rogers, Jr., *The History of Georgetown County, South Carolina* (Columbia: University of South Carolina Press, 1970); William Warren Rogers, *Thomas County 1865-1900* (Tallahassee: Florida State University Press, 1973), and J. Carlyle Sitterson, *Sugar Country: The Sugar Industry in the South, 1753-1950* (Lexington: University of Kentucky Press, 1953). A combination of journalistic flair with scholarly skill made useful and enjoyable relevant chapters in the work of the Virginia WPA Writers Program, *The Negro in Virginia* (New York: Hastings House, 1940).

The Freedmen's Bureau and its commissioner, O. O. Howard, recently have received both sympathetic and critical treatments. The first approach is in John A. Carpenter, *Sword and Olive Branch: Oliver Otis Howard* (Pittsburgh: University of Pittsburgh Press, 1964), and the second approach is in William S. McFeely, *Yankee Stepfather: General O. O. Howard and the Freedmen* (New Haven, Conn.: Yale University Press, 1968; Norton Paperback, 1970). Careful studies of the Bureau in two states have been published and have proved helpful: Martin Abbott, *The Freedmen's Bureau in South Carolina, 1865-1872* (Chapel Hill: University of North Carolina Press, 1967), and Howard A. White, *The Freedmen's Bureau in Louisiana* (Baton Rouge: Louisiana State University Press, 1970).

A small book that makes a large contribution to our understanding of the land question is Carol K. Rothrock Bleser, *The Promised Land: The History of the South Carolina Land Commission, 1869-1890* (Columbia: University of South Carolina Press, 1969).

UNPUBLISHED DISSERTATIONS

Outstanding for its close study of local sources as well as Freedmen's Bureau records is Joseph C. Vance, "The Negro in the Reconstruction of Albemarle County" (Virginia), M.A. thesis, University of Virginia, 1953. Other valuable studies that provided details for a history of freedmen's self-reliance and assertiveness are Ethel Maude Christler, "Participation of Negroes in the Government of Georgia, 1867-1870," M.A. thesis, Atlanta University, 1933; Austin Marcus Drumm, "The Union Leagues in the Carolinas," Ph.D. dissertation, University of North Carolina, 1956; Clifton L. Ganus, "The Freedmen's Bureau in Mississippi," Ph.D. dissertation, Tulane University, 1953; Inabel Burns Lindsay, "The Participation of Negroes in the Establishment of Welfare Services, 1865-1900," Doctor of Social Work dissertation, University of Pittsburgh, 1952 (I consulted a copy in the library of the School of Social Work at the University of California, Berkeley); William G. Paul, "The Shadow of Equality: The Negro in Baltimore, 1864-1911," Ph.D. dissertation, University of Wisconsin, 1972; Robert E. Perdue, "The Negro in Savannah, 1865-1900," Ph.D. dissertation, University of Georgia, 1971.

Index